High Stakes

TESTING FOR TRACKING, PROMOTION, AND GRADUATION

Jay P. Heubert and Robert M. Hauser, *Editors*

Committee on Appropriate Test Use

Board on Testing and Assessment

Commission on Behavioral and Social Sciences and Education

National Research Council

NATIONAL ACADEMY PRESS
Washington, D.C. 1999

NATIONAL ACADEMY PRESS • 2101 Constitution Avenue, N.W. • Washington, D.C. 20418

NOTICE: The project that is the subject of this report was approved by the Governing Board of the National Research Council, whose members are drawn from the councils of the National Academy of Sciences, the National Academy of Engineering, and the Institute of Medicine. The members of the committee responsible for the report were chosen for their special competences and with regard for appropriate balance.

The study was supported by Contract/Grant No. ED-98-CO-0005 between the National Academy of Sciences and the U.S. Department of Education. Any opinions, findings, conclusions, or recommendations expressed in this publication are those of the author(s) and do not necessarily reflect the view of the organizations or agencies that provided support for this project.

Library of Congress Cataloging-in-Publication Data

High stakes : testing for tracking, promotion, and graduation / Jay P. Heubert and Robert M. Hauser, editors ; Committee on Appropriate Test Use.
    p. cm.
    Includes bibliographical references and index.
    ISBN 0-309-06280-2 (pbk.)
    1. Educational tests and measurements—United States. 2. Educational accountability—United States. 3. Education and state—United States. I. Heubert, Jay Philip. II. Hauser, Robert Mason. III. National Research Council (U.S.). Committee on Appropriate Test Use.
    LB3051 .H475 1999
    371.26′0973—dc21   98-40215

Additional copies of this report are available from National Academy Press, 2101 Constitution Avenue, N.W., Washington, D.C. 20418

Call (800) 624-6242 or (202) 334-3313 (in the Washington metropolitan area)

This report is also available on line at **http://www.nap.edu**

Printed in the United States of America

COMMITTEE ON APPROPRIATE TEST USE

BOARD ON TESTING AND ASSESSMENT

Foreword

President Clinton's 1997 proposal to create voluntary national tests in reading and mathematics catapulted testing to the top of the national education agenda. The proposal turned up the volume on what had already been a contentious debate and drew intense scrutiny from a wide range of educators, parents, policy makers, and social scientists. Recognizing the important role science could play in sorting through the passionate and often heated exchanges in the testing debate, Congress and the Clinton administration asked the National Research Council, through its Board on Testing and Assessment (BOTA), to conduct three fast-track studies over a 10-month period.

This report and its companions—*Uncommon Measures: Equivalence and Linkage Among Educational Tests* and *Evaluation of the Voluntary National Tests: Phase 1*—are the result of truly heroic efforts on the part of the BOTA members, the study committee chairs and members, two co-principal investigators, consultants, and staff, who all understood the urgency of the mission and rose to the challenge of a unique and daunting timeline. Michael Feuer, BOTA director, deserves the special thanks of the board for keeping the effort on track and shepherding the report through the review process. His dedicated effort, long hours, sage advice, and good humor were essential to the success of this effort. Robert Hauser deserves our deepest appreciation for his superb leadership of the committee that produced this report.

These reports are exemplars of the Research Council's commitment to scientific rigor in the public interest: they provide clear and compelling statements of the underlying issues, cogent answers to nettling questions, and highly readable findings and recommendations. These reports will help illuminate the toughest issues in the ongoing debate over the proposed voluntary national tests. But they will do much more as well. The issues addressed in this and the other two reports go well beyond the immediate national testing proposal: they have much to contribute to knowledge about the way tests—all tests—are planned, designed, implemented, reported, and used for a variety of education policy goals.

I know the whole board joins me in expressing our deepest gratitude to the many people who worked so hard on this project. These reports will advance the debate over the role of testing in American education, and I am honored to have participated in this effort.

Robert L. Linn, *Chair*
Board on Testing and Assessment

Dedication

In early October 1998, after the public release of this report but before its formal publication, we were saddened to learn of the death of our fellow committee member, Samuel Messick. Sam spent almost all of his career at the Educational Testing Service, and he made legendary contributions to the science and profession of educational measurement. Even had he not been a member of the committee, Sam would have guided the committee's deliberations through his earlier National Research Council work on the use of tests to make decisions about students with mental retardation—which provided the overarching framework of our report—and his creative reconstruction of the concept of test validity. As it was, Sam made even greater contributions to the project through his drafts of major sections of the text as well as his cordial, but ever crisp, incisive, and often wryly humorous contributions to our discussions. Sam was a wonderful scholar, intellect, and friend, and we dedicate this book to him.

Acknowledgments

The Committee on Appropriate Test Use wishes to thank the many people who helped make possible the preparation of this report on an accelerated schedule.

An important part of the committee's work was to gather data about testing research, policy, and practice in states and school districts. Many people gave generously of their time, at meetings and workshops of the committee, in interviews with committee staff, and by drafting short papers to assist the committee's thinking.

Lorrie A. Shepard, University of Colorado, Boulder, provided an excellent overview of educational issues in high-stakes testing of individual students. Floraline Stevens, of Los Angeles, provided insights into state and local high-stakes test policies. At a workshop on testing of English-language learners, Jamal Abedi, University of California, Los Angeles, shared his experimental findings on effects of question wording and format among English-language learners. Toni Marsnik, Language Acquisition and Bilingual Development Branch, Los Angeles Unified School District, and Lynn Winters, assistant superintendent for research, planning, and evaluation, Long Beach Unified School District, offered perspectives on practices for testing English-language learners in their districts and in California more generally.

At a committee workshop in Washington, D.C., six leading educational policymakers offered local, state, and national perspectives on the use of high-stakes tests for promotion or retention; the presenters included Arlene Ackerman, superintendent of schools, Washington, D.C.; Philip Hansen, chief accountability officer, Chicago Public Schools; Nancy Grasmick, superintendent of schools, State of Maryland; Jim Watts, vice president for state services, Southern Regional Education Board; Michael Cohen, special assistant to the president for educational policy; and Bella Rosenberg, assistant to the president, American Federation of Teachers.

The committee also commissioned short papers to assist in deliberations about alternate strategies for promoting appropriate test use. Those who prepared such papers include: Tyler Cowan, George Mason University; Ernest House, University of Colorado, Boulder; Don Kettl, University of Wisconsin, Madison; Henry Levin, Stanford University; Theodore Marmor, Yale University; and Anne Schneider, Arizona State University. We are grateful to David Klahr, Carnegie Mellon University, for his insights.

Jennifer C. Day, Population Division, U.S. Bureau of the Census, provided access to unpublished tabulations of school enrollment data from the October Current Population Survey. In addition, staff of several state education agencies provided valuable information about state retention rates: Alabama, Arizona, California, Delaware, District of Columbia, Florida, Georgia, Indiana, Kentucky, Louisiana, Maryland, Massachusetts, Michigan, Mississippi, New Mexico, New York, North Carolina, Ohio, South Carolina, Tennessee, Texas, Vermont, Virginia, West Virginia, and Wisconsin.

We are also grateful to those who served as consultants to the committee. Marguerite Clarke, research associate at Boston College, provided invaluable contributions during all phases of the study, especially on psychometric issues. Edward Miller joined the project midway as editor, and he skillfully, tirelessly pulled our bits, scraps, and—sometimes—avalanches of text into clear, concise prose. Diane August provided important advice and assistance on the testing of English-language learners and prepared early drafts of Chapter 9 of the report. Susan E. Phillips, Michigan State University, and William L. Taylor, a member of the Board on Testing and Assessment, provided valuable advice on legal issues in testing. Taissa S. Hauser volunteered to collect and assemble statistical data on school retention and age-grade retardation, and her good company and quiet advice were a source of support to all on the project staff.

We owe an important debt of gratitude to the scientific and professional staff of the Commission on Behavioral and Social Sciences and Education (CBASSE), without whose guidance, support, and hard work we could not conceivably have completed this report. Barbara B. Torrey, executive director of the commission, and Sandy Wigdor, director of the Division on Education, Labor, and Human Performance, have been enthusiastic supporters of the project and a timely source of gracious reminders that we keep our priorities in line. Michael J. Feuer, director of the Board on Testing and Assessment (BOTA), brought our research team together, created staff support and resources whenever we needed them, and was our most valuable guide, sounding board, and humorist as we pondered the complexities of educational policy analysis. Patricia Morison made major contributions to our work on students with disabilities and English-language learners and was a constant source of support and thoughtful ideas. Allison Black contributed to many phases of the project; she developed many of the background materials for the committee, and her structured interviews with school administrators were a key source of information about local testing policies and practices. Naomi Chudowsky took major responsibility for the investigation of high school graduation and also contributed to the presentation of psychometric concepts, and Robert Rothman made important contributions to the analysis of policy alternatives. During her summer internship, Yale University doctoral student Marilyn Dabady was a careful and critical in-house reader of our drafts. National Research Council (NRC) staff were always available to pitch in when expertise or energy were called for. They were key members of the study team, and it is hard to see how the study could have been completed without their expert help.

Kimberly Saldin served unflappably and flawlessly as the committee's senior project assistant. She dealt smoothly with the logistics of our four committee meetings in five months, with our voluminous collections and distributions of published and unpublished research materials, and with a seemingly endless stream of text files, e-mail file attachments, and file revisions in seemingly incompatible word-processing formats.

Other BOTA staff—Steve Baldwin, Alix Beatty, Meryl Bertenthal, Cadelle Hemphill, Lee Jones, Karen Mitchell—offered advice, help, and support at key stages of the process. Kimberly Saldin received support when she needed it from other wonderful project assistants to the board: Lisa Alston, Dorothy Majewski, Jane Phillips, and Holly Wells. Viola Horek, administrative associate to BOTA, was always there, instrumental in seeing that the entire project ran smoothly.

We are deeply grateful to Eugenia Grohman, associate director for reports of CBASSE. Genie has and shares enormous knowledge and experience in keeping a committee on track and putting a report together from beginning to end. We also appreciate the superb work of Christine McShane, to whom fell the responsibility for final editing of the full report. We are indebted, also, to the whole CBASSE staff for indulging our scheduling exigencies. Thanks also to Sally Stanfield and the whole Audubon team at the National Academy Press for their creative and speedy support.

Several members of the Board on Testing and Assessment were not members of the committee but attended our meetings ex officio and were constant sources of wisdom and encouragement: Robert L. Linn, University of Colorado at Boulder, chair of the Board on Testing and Assessment, and committee member ex officio; William L. Taylor, Attorney at Law; and Carl F. Kaestle, Brown University.

Individual committee members have made outstanding contributions to the study. Several of them drafted sections on particular topics, prepared background materials, or helped to organize workshops and committee discussions. Everyone contributed constructive, critical thinking, serious concern about the difficult and complex issues that we faced, and an open-mindedness that was essential to the success of the project.

A word of acknowledgment to the sponsors of this study. We have benefited from supportive and collegial relations with members of the various House and Senate committee staffs—on both sides of the aisle—for whom the results of our work have such important implications. We thank them all for understanding and respecting the process of the NRC. Our contracting officer's technical representative, Holly Spurlock, of the U.S. Department of Education, has been a most effective project officer; we thank her for her patience and guidance throughout. Many other officials in the department, the National Assessment Governing Board, and in numerous private and public organizations involved in testing also deserve our thanks and recognition for their cooperation in providing information.

This report has been reviewed by individuals chosen for their diverse perspectives and technical expertise, in accordance with procedures approved by the NRC's Report Review Committee. The purpose of this independent review is to provide candid and critical comments that will assist the authors and the NRC in making the published report as sound as possible and to ensure that the report meets institutional standards for objectivity, evidence, and responsiveness to the study charge. The content of the review comments and draft manuscript remain confidential to protect the integrity of the deliberative process.

We wish to thank the following individuals, who are neither officials nor employees of the NRC, for their participation in the review of this report: Lloyd Bond, School of Education, University of North Carolina, Greensboro; Wayne J. Camara, The College Board, New York, New York; John Fremer, Educational Testing Service, Princeton, New Jersey; Adam Gamoran, Wisconsin Center for Education Research, University of Wisconsin; Arthur S. Goldberger, Department of Economics, University of Wisconsin; Lyle V. Jones, L.L. Thurstone Psychometric Laboratory, University of North Carolina, Chapel Hill; Jeannie Oakes, Graduate School of Education and Information Studies, University of California, Los Angeles; Diana Pullin, School of Education, Boston College; Henry W. Riecken, Professor of Behavioral Sciences (emeritus), University of Pennsylvania School of Medicine.

Although the individuals listed above have provided many constructive comments and suggestions, responsibility for the final content of this report rests solely with the authoring committee and the NRC.

The two of us were unacquainted when we began the project, and—one a legal scholar and the other a demographer—we had little in common beyond our shared belief in the importance of our mandate. Each of us has benefited from the other's strengths, and working together has been an unalloyed pleasure.

Jay Heubert, *Study Director*
Robert M. Hauser, *Chair*
Committee on Appropriate Test Use

The National Academy of Sciences is a private, nonprofit, self-perpetuating society of distinguished scholars engaged in scientific and engineering research, dedicated to the furtherance of science and technology and to their use for the general welfare. Upon the authority of the charter granted to it by the Congress in 1863, the Academy has a mandate that requires it to advise the federal government on scientific and technical matters. Dr. Bruce M. Alberts is president of the National Academy of Sciences.

The National Academy of Engineering was established in 1964, under the charter of the National Academy of Sciences, as a parallel organization of outstanding engineers. It is autonomous in its administration and in the selection of its members, sharing with the National Academy of Sciences the responsibility for advising the federal government. The National Academy of Engineering also sponsors engineering programs aimed at meeting national needs, encourages education and research, and recognizes the superior achievements of engineers. Dr. William A. Wulf is president of the National Academy of Engineering.

The Institute of Medicine was established in 1970 by the National Academy of Sciences to secure the services of eminent members of appropriate professions in the examination of policy matters pertaining to the health of the public. The Institute acts under the responsibility given to the National Academy of Sciences by its congressional charter to be an adviser to the federal government and, upon its own initiative, to identify issues of medical care, research, and education. Dr. Kenneth I. Shine is president of the Institute of Medicine.

The National Research Council was organized by the National Academy of Sciences in 1916 to associate the broad community of science and technology with the Academy's purposes of furthering knowledge and advising the federal government. Functioning in accordance with general policies determined by the Academy, the Council has become the principal operating agency of both the National Academy of Sciences and the National Academy of Engineering in providing services to the government, the public, and the scientific and engineering communities. The Council is administered jointly by both Academies and the Institute of Medicine. Dr. Bruce M. Alberts and Dr. William A. Wulf are chairman and vice chairman, respectively, of the National Research Council.

Contents

PART III
ENSURING APPROPRIATE USES OF TESTS

High Stakes

Public Law 105-78, enacted November 13, 1997

SEC. 309. (a) STUDY—The National Academy of Sciences shall conduct a study and make written recommendations on appropriate methods, practices, and safeguards to ensure that—

(1) existing and new tests that are used to assess student performance are not used in a discriminatory manner or inappropriately for student promotion, tracking or graduation; and

(2) existing and new tests adequately assess student reading and mathematics comprehension in the form most likely to yield accurate information regarding student achievement of reading and mathematics skills.

(b) REPORT TO CONGRESS—The National Academy of Sciences shall submit a written report to the White House, the National Assessment Governing Board, the Committee on Education and the Workforce of the House of Representatives, the Committee on Labor and Human Resources of the Senate, and the Committees on Appropriations of the House and Senate not later than September 1, 1998.

Executive Summary

The use of large-scale achievement tests as instruments of educational policy is growing. In particular, states and school districts are using such tests in making high-stakes decisions with important consequences for individual students. Three such high-stakes decisions involve tracking (assigning students to schools, programs, or classes based on their achievement levels), whether a student will be promoted to the next grade, and whether a student will receive a high school diploma. These policies enjoy widespread public support and are increasingly seen as a means of raising academic standards, holding educators and students accountable for meeting those standards, and boosting public confidence in the schools.

Because the stakes are high, the Congress wants to ensure that tests are used properly and fairly, and it asked the National Academy of Sciences, through its National Research Council, to "conduct a study and make written recommendations on appropriate methods, practices and safeguards to ensure that—

A. existing and new tests that are used to assess student performance are not used in a discriminatory manner or inappropriately for student promotion, tracking or graduation; and

B. existing and new tests adequately assess student reading and mathematics comprehension in the form most likely to yield accurate information regarding student achievement of reading and mathematics skills."

This study focuses on tests with high stakes for individual students. The committee recognizes that accountability for students is related in important ways to accountability for educators, schools, and school districts. Indeed, the use of tests for accountability of educators, schools, and school districts has significant consequences for individual students, for example, by changing the quality of instruction or affecting school management and budgets. Such indirect effects of large-scale assessment are worth studying in their own right. By focusing on the congressional interest in high-stakes decisions about individual students, this report does not address accountability at those other levels, apart from the issue of participation of all students in large-scale assessments.

BASIC PRINCIPLES OF TEST USE

The use of tests in decisions about student tracking, promotion, and graduation is intended to serve educational policy goals, such as setting high standards for student learning, raising student achievement-levels, ensuring equal educational opportunity, fostering parental involvement in student learning, and increasing public support for the schools. The committee recognizes that test use may have negative consequences for individual students even while serving important social or educational policy purposes. The development of a comprehensive testing policy should therefore be sensitive to the balance among the individual and collective benefits and costs of various uses of tests.

Determining whether high-stakes testing of students produces better overall educational outcomes requires that its potential benefits be weighed against its potential unintended negative consequences. Thus, the value of tests should also be weighed against the use of other information in making high-stakes decisions about students. Tracking, promotion, and graduation decisions will be made with or without tests.

The committee adopted three principal criteria, developed from earlier work by the National Research Council, for determining whether a test use is appropriate:

(1) measurement validity—whether a test is valid for a particular purpose, and whether it accurately measures the test taker's knowledge in the content area being tested;

(2) attribution of cause—whether a student's performance on a test reflects knowledge and skill based on appropriate instruction or is attributable to poor instruction or to such factors as language barriers or disabilities unrelated to the skills being tested; and

(3) effectiveness of treatment—whether test scores lead to placements and other consequences that are educationally beneficial.

These criteria, based on established professional standards, lead to the following basic principles of appropriate test use for educational decisions:

- The important thing about a test is not its validity in general, but its validity when used for a specific purpose. Thus, tests that are valid for influencing classroom practice, "leading" the curriculum, or holding schools accountable are not appropriate for making high-stakes decisions about individual student mastery unless the curriculum, the teaching, and the test(s) are aligned.
- Tests are not perfect. Test questions are a sample of possible questions that could be asked in a given area. Moreover, a test score is not an exact measure of a student's knowledge or skills. A student's score can be expected to vary across different versions of a test—within a margin of error determined by the reliability of the test—as a function of the particular sample of questions asked and/or transitory factors, such as the student's health on the day of the test. Thus, no single test score can be considered a definitive measure of a student's knowledge.
- An educational decision that will have a major impact on a test taker should not be made solely or automatically on the basis of a single test score. Other relevant information about the student's knowledge and skills should also be taken into account.
- Neither a test score nor any other kind of information can justify a bad decision. Research shows that students are typically hurt by simple retention and repetition of a grade in school without remedial and other instructional support services. In the absence of effective services for low-performing students, better tests will not lead to better educational outcomes.

The committee has considered how these principles apply to the appropriate use of tests in decisions about tracking, promotion, and graduation, to increasing the participation of students with disabilities and English-language learners in large-scale assessments, and to possible uses of the proposed voluntary national tests in making high-stakes decisions about individual students. The committee has also examined existing and potential strategies for promoting appropriate test use.

USES AND MISUSES OF TESTS

Blanket criticisms of tests are not justified. When tests are used in ways that meet relevant psychometric, legal, and educational standards, students' scores provide important information that, combined with information from other sources, can lead to decisions that promote student learning and equality of opportunity. For example, tests can identify learning differences among students that the education system needs to address. Because decisions about tracking, promotion, and graduation will be made with or without testing, proposed alternatives to the use of test scores should be at least equally accurate, efficient, and fair.

It is also a mistake to accept observed test scores as either infallible or immutable. When test use is inappropriate, especially in making high-stakes decisions about individuals, it can undermine the quality of education and equality of opportunity. For example, the lower achievement test scores of racial and ethnic minorities and students from low-income families reflect persistent inequalities in American society and its schools, not inalterable realities about those groups of students. The improper use of test scores can reinforce these inequalities. This lends special urgency to the requirement that test use with high-stakes consequences for individual students be appropriate and fair.

Decisions about tracking, promotion, and graduation differ from one another in important ways. They differ most importantly in the role that mastery of past material and readiness for new material play. Thus, the committee has considered the role of large-scale high-stakes testing in relation to each type of decision separately in this report. But tracking, promotion, and graduation decisions also share common features that pertain both to appropriate test use and to their educational and social consequences.

Members of some minority groups, English-language learners, and students from low socioeconomic backgrounds are overrepresented in lower-track classes and among those denied promotion or graduation on the basis of test scores. Moreover, these same groups of students are underrepresented in high-track classes, "exam" schools, and "gifted and talented" programs. In some cases, such as courses for English-language learners, such disproportions are logical: one would not expect to find native English speakers in classes designed to teach English to English-language learners. In other circumstances, such disproportions raise serious questions. For example, grade retardation among children cumulates rapidly after age 6, and it occurs disproportionately among males and minority group members. These disproportions are especially disturbing in view of other evidence that, as typically practiced, grade retention and assignment to low tracks have little educational value. For example, assignment to low tracks is typically associated with an impoverished curriculum, poor teaching, and low expectations. It is also important to note that group differences in test performance do not necessarily indicate problems in a test, because test scores may reflect real differences in achievement. These, in turn, may be due to a lack of access to a high-quality curriculum and instruction. Thus, a finding of group differences calls for a careful effort to determine their cause.

RECOMMENDATIONS

The committee offers more detailed recommendations in Chapter 12 about the appropriate uses of tests. Those recommendations cover cross-cutting issues that affect testing generally; specific issues and problems pertaining to the uses of tests in tracking, promotion, and graduation; and the inclusion of students with disabilities and students who are English-language learners. The organization of the recommendations in Chapter 12 follows the logic of the chapters in this report. In this executive summary, we present overarching recommendations and discuss the possible use of the proposed voluntary national tests for high-stakes decisions about individual students.

• Accountability for educational outcomes should be a shared responsibility of states, school districts, public officials, educators, parents, and students. High standards cannot be established and maintained merely by imposing them on students. Moreover, if parents, educators, public officials, and others who share responsibility for educational outcomes are to discharge their responsibility effectively, they should have access to information about the nature and interpretation of tests and test scores. Such information should be freely available to the public and should be incorporated into teacher education and into educational programs for principals, administrators, public officials, and others.

• Tests should be used for high-stakes decisions about individual mastery only after implementing changes in teaching and curriculum that ensure that students have been taught the knowledge and skills on which they will be tested. Some school systems are already doing this by planning a gap of several years between the introduction of new tests and the attachment of high stakes to individual student performance, during which schools may achieve the necessary alignment among tests, curriculum, and instruction. But others may see attaching high stakes to individual student test scores as a way of leading curricular reform, not recognizing the danger that such uses of tests may lack the "instructional validity" required by law—that is, a close correspondence between test content and instructional content.

• The consequences of high-stakes testing for individual students are often posed as either-or propositions, but this need not be the case. For example, "social promotion" and repetition of a grade are really only two of many educational strategies available to educators when test scores and other information indicate that students are experiencing serious academic difficulty. But neither social promotion nor retention alone is an effective treatment for low achievement, and schools can use a number of other possible strategies to reduce the need for these either-or choices, for example, by coupling early identification of such students with effective remedial education.

• Some large-scale assessments are used to make high-stakes decisions about individual students, but most often in combination with other information, as recommended by the major professional and scientific organizations concerned with testing. For example, most school districts say they base promotion decisions on a combination of grades, achievement test scores, developmental factors, attendance, and teacher recommendations. As our study has shown, however, a number of jurisdictions have adopted policies that rely exclusively on achievement test scores to make high-stakes decisions. A test score, like other sources of information, is not exact. It is an estimate of the student's understanding or mastery at a particular time. Therefore, high-stakes educational decisions should not be made solely or automatically on the basis of a single test score but should also take other relevant information into account.

• The preparation of students plays a key role in appropriate test use. It is not proper to expose students ahead of time to items that will actually be used on their test or to give students the answers to those questions. Test results may also be invalidated by teaching so narrowly to the objectives of a particular test that scores are raised without actually improving the broader set of academic skills that the test is intended to measure. The desirability of "teaching to the test" is affected by test design. For example, it is entirely appropriate to prepare students by covering all the objectives of a test that represents the full range of the intended curriculum. We therefore recommend that test users respect the distinction between genuine remedial education and teaching narrowly to the specific content of a test. At the same time, all students should receive sufficient preparation for the specific test so their performance will not be adversely affected by unfamiliarity with its format or by ignorance of appropriate test-taking strategies.

- Accurate assessment of students with disabilities and English-language learners presents complex technical and policy challenges, in part because these students are particularly vulnerable to potential negative consequences when high-stakes decisions are based on tests. We recommend that policymakers pursue two key policy objectives in modifying tests and testing procedures in these special populations:

(1)   to increase such students' participation in large-scale assessments, in part so that school systems can be held accountable for their educational progress; and

(2)   to test each such student in a manner that provides appropriate accommodation for the effect of a disability or of limited English proficiency on the subject matter being tested, while maintaining the validity and comparability of test results among all students.

These objectives are sometimes in tension, and the goals of full participation and valid measurement thus present serious technical and operational challenges to test developers and users.

- The purpose of the proposed voluntary national tests (VNT) is to inform students (and their parents and teachers) about their performance in 4th grade reading and 8th grade mathematics relative to the standards of the National Assessment of Educational Progress and to performance in the Third International Mathematics and Science Study. The proposal does not suggest any direct use of VNT scores to make decisions about the tracking, promotion, or graduation of individual students, and thus it is not being developed to support those uses. However, states and school districts would be free to use scores on the voluntary national tests for these purposes. Given their design, the proposed voluntary national tests should not be used for decisions about the tracking, promotion, or graduation of individual students. The committee takes no position on whether the voluntary national tests are practical or appropriate for their primary stated purposes.

• The committee sees a strong need for better evidence on the intended benefits and unintended negative consequences of using high-stakes tests to make decisions about individuals. A key question is whether the consequences of a particular test use are educationally beneficial for students—for example, by increasing academic achievement or reducing dropout rates. It is also important to develop statistical reporting systems of key indicators that will track both intended effects (such as higher test scores) and other effects (such as changes in dropout or special education referral rates). Indicator systems could include measures such as retention rates, special education identification rates, rates of exclusion from assessment programs, number and type of accommodations, high school completion credentials, dropout rates, and indicators of access to high-quality curriculum and instruction.

PROMOTING APPROPRIATE TEST USE

At present, professional norms and legal action (through administrative enforcement or litigation) are the principal mechanisms available to enforce appropriate test use. These mechanisms are inadequate. Compliance with provisions of the Joint Standards for Educational and Psychological Testing and the Code of Fair Testing Practices in Education is largely voluntary, and enforcement is often weak. Legal action is typically adversarial, time-consuming, and expensive, and applicable law can vary by jurisdiction, making enforcement uneven.

New methods, practices, and safeguards could take any of several forms, but in general they would appear at various points on a continuum between professional norms and legal enforcement, some less coercive, some more so. Deliberative forums, an independent oversight body, labeling, and federal regulation represent a range of possible options that could supplement professional standards and litigation as means of promoting and enforcing appropriate test use.

The committee is not recommending adoption of any particular strategy or combination of strategies, nor does it suggest that these four approaches are the only possibilities. We do think, however, that ensuring proper test use will require multiple strategies. Given the inadequacy of current methods, practices, and safeguards, there should be further research on these and other policy options to illuminate their possible effects on test use. In particular, we would suggest empirical research on the effects of these strategies, individually and in combination, on testing products and practice, and an examination of the associated potential benefits and risks.

Large-scale assessments, used properly, can improve teaching, learning, and equality of educational opportunity. That tests are sometimes used improperly should not discourage policymakers, teachers, and parents. Rather, it should motivate action to ensure that educational tests are used fairly and effectively. This report is a contribution to that essential work.

Part I
Background and Context

Introduction

Most people seem to agree that America's public schools are in need of repair. How to fix them has become a favorite topic of policymakers, and for many the remedy includes increased reliance on the testing of students. The standards-based reform movement, for example, is premised on the idea of setting clear, high standards for what children are supposed to learn and then holding students—and often educators and schools—to those standards.

The logic seems clear: Unless we test students' knowledge, how will we know if they have met the standards? And the idea of accountability, which is also central to this theory of school reform, requires that the test results have direct and immediate consequences: a student who does not meet the standard should not be promoted, or awarded a high school diploma. This report is about the appropriate use of tests in making such high-stakes decisions about individual students.

In his 1997 State of the Union address, President Clinton challenged the nation to undertake "a national crusade for education standards—not federal government standards, but national standards, representing what all our students must know to succeed in the knowledge economy of the twenty-first century. . . . Every state should adopt high national standards, and by 1999, every state should test every fourth-grader in reading and every eighth-grader in math to make sure these standards are met. . . . Good tests will show us who needs help, what changes in teaching to make, and which schools need to improve. They can help us to end social promotion. For no child should move from grade school to junior high, or junior high to high school until he or she is ready."

Test-based reform strategies have enjoyed wide acceptance across the political spectrum—at least in theory—for two reasons. First, who could possibly be against "high standards"? Second, most Americans believe in the accuracy and fairness of judging students by what the president called "good tests." But what constitutes a good test? How do we know a test is good—that it really measures what it is supposed to measure? And, equally important, how do we know that the test and its results are being used properly by the teachers and administrators who have the power to make important decisions about individual children?

In fact, the use of tests in school reform raises difficult questions in relation to so-called high-stakes consequences for students—that is, when an individual student's score determines not just who needs help but whether a student is allowed to take a certain program or class, or will be promoted to the next grade, or will graduate from high school. Despite the appearance of mathematical exactness in a numerical score, standardized achievement tests do not yield exact measurements of what individuals know and can do. Tests and their applications are subject to both statistical and human error. Tests useful for some purposes are inappropriate for others. Can we be sure that the use of tests for high-stakes decisions will lead to better outcomes for all students, regardless of their special educational needs or their social, economic, racial, or ethnic backgrounds?

The very term "high stakes" embodies both the hopes and the fears these tests inspire. Only if the stakes are high, say their advocates on one hand—only if there is something valuable to be gained or lost—will teachers and students take the tests seriously and work hard to do their best, thus serving both their own interests and the public interest in higher achievement. Skeptics, on the other hand, worry that such policies may produce harmful consequences for individual students and perhaps for society as a whole.

The Clinton administration's proposal for new voluntary national tests (VNTs)—standardized, large-scale tests of 4th grade reading and 8th grade mathematics achievement—has aroused controversy, in part because of these questions of equity and fairness. But whether or not the VNTs are created, large-scale achievement testing is already a major feature of American education, and it appears to be getting more popular.

GROWING RELIANCE ON STANDARDIZED TESTS

For more than three decades, under Title I of the Elementary and Secondary Education Act of 1965, program evaluation through large-scale testing has been an integral part of federal support for the education of low-achieving children in poor neighborhoods. The minimum competency testing movement, beginning in the 1970s, gave large-scale, standardized achievement tests a visible and popular role in holding students (and sometimes schools) accountable. Such tests are widely used in decisions about promotion and graduation; their role in tracking—that is, assigning students to a course of study based on perceived achievement or skill level—is less clear. Tracking decisions are usually made at the school level, based on multiple sources of evidence.

By the mid-1980s, 33 states had mandated some form of minimum competency testing (Office of Technology Assessment, 1992). A decade later, 18 states had test-based requirements for high school graduation (Bond et al., 1996). In many states, both schools and students are held accountable for achievement-test performance. Almost all states administer standardized assessments in several core areas and report findings at the school level; in most states, these findings are supplemented by state-representative samples from the National Assessment of Educational Progress (NAEP). In almost half the states, students' test performance can have serious consequences for their schools, including funding gains or losses, loss of autonomy or accreditation, and even external takeover (Bond et al., 1996). In some places, like Chicago, the same achievement test is used both to hold schools accountable and to make individual student promotion decisions.

The political debate about voluntary national testing has focused on the inevitable tensions between uniform national standards and traditions of state and local school governance. But other important questions about the VNT proposal have been raised: Do we need new tests to hold American students to uniform high standards, or could the results of existing tests be reported in a common metric? The VNT proposal calls for public release of all test items soon after the administration of each test, but can new tests be developed each year that will meet high technical demands—for validity, reliability, fairness, and comparability? How should the VNT or similar tests be designed in order to measure achievement accurately and encourage higher academic performance by all students? How can potential misuses of the VNT or other tests be identified, remedied, and prevented?

These issues have been considered by the Congress in its deliberations on voluntary national testing, and it has called on the National
Academy of Sciences to carry out studies addressing several of them.[1]
This report addresses the set of questions bearing on the appropriate,
nondiscriminatory use of educational tests. Congress has asked the Academy, through its National Research Council, to "conduct a study and
make written recommendations on appropriate methods, practices and
safeguards to ensure that—

A. existing and new tests that are used to assess student performance
are not used in a discriminatory manner or inappropriately for student
promotion, tracking or graduation; and

B. existing and new tests adequately assess student reading and mathematics comprehension in the form most likely to yield accurate information regarding student achievement of reading and mathematics skills."

The questions the Congress has framed reflect concern about the
increasing reliance on tests that have a direct impact on students, including the impact of high-stakes testing on various minority communities
and on children with disabilities or whose native language is not English.
This study therefore focuses on tests that have high stakes for individual
students, although the committee recognizes that accountability for students is related in important ways to accountability for educators, schools,
and school systems. Indeed, the use of tests for accountability of educators, schools, and school districts has significant consequences for individual students, for example, by changing the quality of instruction or
affecting school management and budgets. Such indirect effects of large-
scale assessment are worth studying in their own right. This report is
intended to apply to all schools and school systems in which tests are used
for promotion, tracking, or graduation.

---

[1]Results of the study addressing questions related to the feasibility of a common reporting metric appear in *Uncommon Measures: Equivalence and Linkage Among Educational
Tests* (National Research Council, 1999b). A third study, *Evaluation of the Voluntary
National Tests: Phase 1* (National Research Council, 1999a), is an evaluation of the first
year of the VNT development process.

ENSURING APPROPRIATE USE OF TESTS

Large-scale cognitive testing has always been controversial. On one hand, standardized testing promises to hold all students to the same standards, appealing to widely held values of fairness and equity. It is also an efficient and highly visible way to assess the progress of students and schools—and to communicate what the public expects of them. As an administrative tool, testing offers a rare economy of scale in school management. On the other hand, tests can be used arbitrarily to sort students into winners and losers, and their validity has thus always been scrutinized and criticized in light of the benefits and costs to test takers and other interested parties. Tests have been used improperly to make decisions about which they provide little or no valid information. Occasionally, tests have provided a cover for arbitrary or discriminatory decisions made with little or no reference to test performance. As the Office of Technology Assessment noted in its 1992 report, "Everyone may agree that testing can be a wedge, but some see the wedge forcing open the gates of opportunity while others see it as the doorstop keeping the gates tightly shut (p. 8)."

Efforts to regulate test use have been based on two principal mechanisms: professional norms, including education and self-regulation, and legal action, including legislation, regulation, and litigation (Office of Technology Assessment, 1992). Through its *Mental Measurement Yearbooks*, the Buros Institute of Mental Measurement has sought to inform test users about appropriate practices for the past 60 years. Several scientific and professional organizations, acting separately and jointly, have issued standards for appropriate test use. These include the *Standards for Educational and Psychological Testing* (American Educational Research Association et al., 1985) and the *Code of Fair Testing Practices in Education* (Joint Committee on Testing Practices, 1988).

These standards have been addressed chiefly to those who develop and publish tests, but the mechanisms for enforcing them are inadequate. Moreover, those who actually use tests in states, school districts, and schools are often poorly informed about the standards. Teachers are usually the first-line administrators and users of tests, but they are often not technically prepared to interpret test findings, nor is the public adequately informed about the uses and limits of testing.

Legal action has played a significant but limited role in ensuring the appropriate use of tests. Before the 1960s, there was little litigation in this area. Since then, courts have occasionally limited the use of tests to make high-stakes decisions about individuals, but they have generally been reluctant to limit the professional judgment and discretion of educators (Office of Technology Assessment, 1992:72-74). Most major court interventions have dealt with specific uses of tests that sustained earlier patterns of racial discrimination in Southern schools.

Federal legislation has affected the testing of individual students in two major ways: first, by encouraging or requiring testing, for example, in the Goals 2000: Educate America Act of 1994 and, more significantly, in Title I of the Elementary and Secondary Education Act of 1965;[2] and, second, by regulating the use of educational tests and information based on them. An example of the latter is the Family Education Rights and Privacy Act of 1974, commonly known as the Buckley Amendment. It established the rights of parents to inspect school records and limited the release of those records (including test scores) to those with a legitimate educational need for the information.

Under the Rehabilitation Act of 1973, the Americans with Disabilities Act of 1990, and the Individuals with Disabilities Education Act of 1997, children with disabilities are entitled to several important protections when they are tested for placement. Among these are the right to be tested in the language spoken at home; the right to take a test that is not culturally biased; the right to accommodations or modifications based on special needs; and the right to be tested in several different ways, so that no special education placement decision is based on a single test score. These protections have not, however, been extended to other uses of educational tests, such as awarding or withholding a high school diploma.

USES AND MISUSES OF STANDARDIZED TESTS

Tests are used in a variety of ways. As elaborated in Chapter 2, they can provide feedback to individual students and their teachers about

---

[2]Title I of the Elementary and Secondary Education Act of 1965, also known as Title I, is the largest federal program in elementary and secondary education, with an annual budget of roughly $8 billion. It is intended to assist low-achieving, disadvantaged students. Title I exerts a powerful influence on schools across the country, particularly in the area of testing. Since the Congress revamped Title I in 1994, the law has required states to develop both challenging standards for student performance and assessments that measure student performance against those standards. The law also states that the standards and assessments should be the same for all students, regardless of whether they are eligible for Title I. This statute is discussed more fully in Chapters 3 and 11.

problems and progress in learning. They can inform administrators and the public about the overall state of learning or academic achievement. They can be used as management tools to make placement or certification decisions about individual students. In many cases it is inappropriate to use the same test for different purposes. Yet that is often what happens.

Consider, for example, how public perceptions about the performance of American schools are formed. They are based in part on personal experience and journalistic anecdotes: the counter clerk at the local store who cannot make change, the business leader's complaint that high school graduates lack basic job skills. But much of the information about academic achievement comes from students' performance on tests, and public opinion about the quality of schooling rises or falls with the latest results from NAEP and the Third International Mathematics and Science Study (TIMSS) (Forgione, 1998).

Test results, like those from NAEP, are based on large, scientifically chosen national samples, and they are repeated periodically. They are designed to provide an overview—a measure of the aggregate performance of a very large number of students. They do not measure the performance of individual students. In fact, the tests are designed so no single student is ever asked the full battery of test questions, and an individual student's results are never released.

This important use of achievement test questions to assess national progress began about 1970, although state and local testing programs date back to the 19th century. Before 1970, there were administrations of achievement tests in well-designed national samples, but these were one-time studies, and they were never extended to compare the performance of all students or of major population groups over time.

Large-scale standardized tests—such as the Scholastic Assessment Test (SAT) and the American College Test (ACT) for college admissions and the Armed Services Vocational Aptitude Battery (ASVAB) for military selection and placement—are valuable decision-making tools. They were not designed to provide information about overall levels of academic achievement for groups of students or changes in them over time. The number of students taking these tests may be very large, but the sample of test takers is far from representative. Public reports based on these tests are therefore often misleading (Hauser, 1998). The annual newspaper reports of average SAT scores, for example, comparing students across time or among states, are a prime example of inappropriate test use. Test-taking populations vary widely from year to year and from state to state in ways that render such comparisons almost meaningless. Wisconsin regularly tops the list of state average scores on the SAT, mainly because its state colleges and universities require a different test, the ACT, for admission; Wisconsin students who take the SAT are generally those applying to elite out-of-state colleges—thus the state's average score is inflated.

This kind of test misuse dates back at least to the mass ability testing of military recruits in World War I (the Army Alpha and Beta tests), which were used by some to disparage blacks and new immigrant groups. However large the scale of such tests, their main purpose is to make decisions about individuals, not to inform the public. They have never provided accurate assessments of scholastic achievement or aptitude in the general population (Hauser, 1998). Accurate descriptions of populations, based on valid tests and samples, are a valuable tool of public policy; inaccurate descriptions of populations are serious misuses of tests because of their possible social, political, and economic consequences.

Although the use of tests to describe populations is important, the committee, responding to the Congress's charge, has focused primarily on the use of tests to make high-stakes decisions about individual students. These decisions also have broad and long-lasting consequences for population groups. Tests may be used appropriately or inappropriately—either to create opportunities, or to deny them.

It is helpful to keep in mind that standardized tests have often been used historically to promote equal opportunity. In the early 1930s, the Wisconsin State Testing Service gave a standard test of academic ability to all graduating high school seniors and sent the names of high-scoring students to the state's colleges and universities, so they could identify academically promising recruits. In later years, the testing program was expanded to lower grades, to identify promising students who might need greater academic encouragement.

In some cases, test uses that might have created obstacles to attainment may have led to improved academic performance and enhanced opportunities. Minority advocates feared that the minimum academic requirements imposed by the National Collegiate Athletic Association on aspiring college athletes (known as Proposition 48) would reduce minority college opportunities, but Klein and Bell (1995) found that the higher standards actually had little effect on minority recruitment and led to higher graduation rates among minority athletes. Klein and Bell argue that student athletes apparently studied harder in school and took courses that would prepare them better for college. This is a potentially important positive exemplar of test use because the introduction of higher standards through testing parallels broader proposals for standards-based educational reform—including some of the hopes for VNTs.

History provides equally striking examples of the actual or potential misuse of standardized tests to make decisions about individuals. Unhappy with the increasing numbers of immigrants living in New York City, the president of Columbia University in 1917 embraced the use of the Thorndike Tests for Mental Alertness "to limit the number of Jewish students without a formal policy of restriction" (Crouse and Trusheim, 1988:20). In one well-known California case (*Larry P. v. Riles*, 1984), the court found that inadequately validated IQ tests had been used to discriminate against black schoolchildren, who were assigned disproportionately to classes for the educable mentally retarded, and that California's classes for such students were often an educational dead end. In a Florida case, the state was enjoined from using a high school graduation test because black students, forced to attend segregated, inferior schools, had not been taught the material covered in the test (*Debra P. v. Turlington*, 1981). And in Rockford, Illinois, testing was recently used to rationalize the assignment of some black high school students to lower tracks, even when their test scores were higher than the scores of some whites assigned to higher tracks (*People Who Care v. Rockford Board of Education*, 1997).

The case of *Debra P.* offers an especially clear illustration of a crucial distinction between appropriate and inappropriate test use. Is it ever appropriate to test students on material they have not been taught? Yes, if the test is used to find out whether the schools are doing their job. But if that same test is used to hold students "accountable" for the failure of the schools, most testing professionals would find such use inappropriate. It is not the test itself that is the culprit in the latter case; results from a test that is valid for one purpose can be used improperly for other purposes.

In the examples above, it seems easy with the advantage of hindsight to identify the appropriate and inappropriate uses of tests. In practice it is often not at all obvious, and the judgment may well depend on the position of the observer. Some population groups see their low scores on achievement tests as a stigmatizing and discriminatory obstacle to educational progress. Other groups, with high scores on the same tests, view their performance as a sign of merit that opens doors to learning and success. The judgments become harder when one cannot predict the behavioral effects of testing, as in the case of Proposition 48. How does one know whether a high-stakes test use is appropriate or not?

HOW THE COMMITTEE APPROACHED ITS TASK

The charge to the committee from the Congress was potentially massive in scope. The three high-stakes policies under scrutiny—tracking, promotion (and its opposite, retention in grade), and graduation (and its opposite, withholding of the diploma)—are themselves complex and controversial practices. Researchers and policymakers disagree about their effectiveness. Where the research evidence on specific practices is strong, our findings are based on that evidence. But in general, the committee has had neither the time nor the resources to investigate broader educational policy issues. Nevertheless, these issues remain critical. Our specific findings about the appropriate uses of tests should be read with the understanding that retention in grade, tracking, and the withholding of diplomas are decisions that have very significant effects on the lives of students and that those decisions will be made with or without the use of tests.

Public understanding of decisions about tracking, promotion, and graduation is poorly served when they are portrayed simplistically as either-or propositions. The simple alternative to social promotion, for example, is retention—making students repeat the grade with the same curriculum they have just failed. But the available evidence suggests that simple retention only compounds the problem: it produces lower achievement and an increased likelihood that the student will eventually drop out of school. Social promotion and simple retention are really only two of several strategies available to educators when tests and other information show that students are experiencing serious academic difficulty. Other strategies may be more successful in promoting learning and reducing the need for either-or choices. These include early identification of students who are not learning, coupled with the assistance these students need to meet standards for promotion. Therefore, the committee believes that this kind of high-stakes test use should always be part of a larger set of strategies aimed at identifying and addressing educational problems when they are most susceptible to intervention and before they lead to negative consequences for students. Test users should consider a wide range of interventions with students who perform poorly.

The committee organized the study by defining "appropriateness" and establishing three criteria for judging whether a test use meets the definition. In our deliberations, we have assumed that the use of tests in decisions about student promotion, tracking, and graduation is intended to serve educational policy goals, such as setting high standards for student learning, raising student achievement levels, ensuring equal educational opportunity, fostering parental involvement in student learning, and increasing public support for the schools.

The three criteria for judging the appropriateness of a particular test use correspond to three broad criteria identified in a previous National Research Council study of the use and misuse of tests (National Research Council, 1982):

A. **Measurement validity:** Is the test appropriate for a particular purpose? Is there evidence that the constructs to be measured are relevant in making a decision? Does the test measure those constructs? Is it confounded with other constructs that are not relevant to the decision? Is the test reliable and accurate?

B. **Attribution of cause:** Does a student's performance on a test reflect knowledge and skill based on appropriate instruction, or is it attributable to poor instruction? Or is it attributable to factors such as language barriers or disabilities that are irrelevant to the construct being measured?

C. **Effectiveness of treatment:** Does performance on the test lead to placements or other decisions that are educationally beneficial and well matched to the student's needs?

The committee has applied each of these standards to the uses of testing that we have examined. A full investigation of the third standard, as noted above, would require an effort that exceeds the committee's resources.

Determining whether the use of tests for promotion, tracking, and graduation produces better overall educational outcomes requires that the intended benefits of the policy be weighed against unintended negative consequences. These costs and benefits must also be balanced with those of making high-stakes decisions about students in other ways, without tests. Moreover, the committee recognizes that test policies may

have negative consequences for some students even while serving important social or educational policy purposes. Perhaps some would be willing
to accept, for example, that some students will be harmed, not helped, by
a strict rule linking promotion with getting a certain test score—if that
policy leads to increased public confidence and support for the schools.
The committee takes no position on the wisdom of such a trade-off; but it
is our view that policymakers should fully understand what is at stake and
who is most likely to be harmed.

The Congress also asked the National Academy of Sciences to consider whether "existing and new tests adequately assess student reading
and mathematics comprehension in the form most likely to yield accurate
information regarding student achievement of reading and mathematics
skills." This could refer to a wide range of issues, including, for example,
the balance of multiple-choice and constructed-response items, the use of
student portfolios, the length and timing of the test, the availability of
calculators or manipulatives, and the language of administration. However, in considering test form, the committee has chosen to focus on the
needs of English-language learners and students with disabilities, in part
because these students may be particularly vulnerable to the negative
consequences of large-scale assessments. (In the literature, English-language learners have been known as "limited-English-proficient students."
We adopt the current nomenclature in referring to this group.) We
consider, for these students, in what form and manner a test is most likely
to measure accurately a student's achievement of reading and mathematics skills.

Two policy objectives are key for these special populations: one is to
increase their participation in large-scale assessments, so that school systems can be held accountable for their educational progress. The other is
to test each such student in a manner that accommodates for a disability
or limited English proficiency to the extent that either is unrelated to the
subject matter being tested, while still maintaining the validity and comparability of test results among all students. These objectives are in
tension, and thus present serious technical and operational challenges to
test developers and users.

ORGANIZATION AND LIMITS OF THE REPORT

The remainder of Part I provides a broad review of the background
and context of large-scale standardized achievement testing with high
stakes for individual students. Chapter 2 reviews the policy context and

frameworks of testing, including the history of test use, the several purposes of testing, the place of testing in current public policy debates, and the perceptions of testing by the public. Chapter 3 summarizes the legal issues in test use, reviewing litigation in which testing was alleged to have been used in a discriminatory fashion or in violation of due process and discussing the legal requirements for curriculum and assessment created by the 1994 reauthorization of Title I of the Elementary and Secondary Education Act. Chapter 4 reviews key concepts in testing as a process of psychological measurement, including validity, reliability, and fairness.

Part II examines the uses of tests for making high-stakes decisions about individual students. Three chapters focus on specific practices: tracking and placement (Chapter 5), promotion and retention (Chapter 6), and awarding or withholding high school diplomas (Chapter 7). In each of these chapters, the committee has investigated the ways in which tests have been used to make decisions about students. It has considered the purposes of each policy and the conditions under which tests can appropriately be used to further those purposes. It has reviewed evidence about the use of tests to make each kind of decision and about the educational consequences of those decisions. It has also looked for examples of test-based decision making that improve on the traditional options in each type of decision.

In the next two chapters, the committee focuses on special groups of students: those with disabilities (Chapter 8) and English-language learners (Chapter 9). In the committee's judgement, however, the issues affecting these students cannot be separated from the larger questions of test use for tracking, promotion, and graduation. In Chapter 10, the committee considers whether it would be appropriate to make tracking, promotion, or graduation decisions about individual students based on their VNT scores.

Part III turns to methods of ensuring the appropriate use of tests for making high-stakes decisions about individuals. Chapter 11 reviews the history of professional norms and legal action in the social control of test use and offers several options for improving test use. Chapter 12 presents the committee's findings and recommendations.

Throughout its work, the committee has observed that statements about the benefits or harms of achievement testing often go beyond what the evidence will support. On one hand, blanket criticisms of standardized testing are mistaken. When tests are used in ways that meet technical, legal, and educational standards, students' scores provide important information that, combined with information from other sources, can promote both learning and equal opportunity. On the other hand, tests can reinforce and legitimize biases and inequalities that persist in American society and its schools. Used improperly, tests can have serious negative consequences—for individuals, particular groups, and society as a whole. Test developers and test users therefore bear a heavy responsibility to ensure that tests are used appropriately and without discrimination.

The committee has used many sources of information to prepare this report. Initially, we looked for evidence in the scientific and professional literature of testing and of educational practice and in reports of major test publishers and of federal statistical agencies. We have relied on reports of public and professional groups and on the existing and draft standards for appropriate test use of the major educational and psychological organizations. We also analyzed data, in particular pertaining to student promotion and retention. We have interviewed educational administrators in several large school districts, and we have solicited information from state education agencies. Finally, we held a workshop in which committee members were able to discuss the uses of large-scale assessments with educators in national, regional, state, and local agencies and jurisdictions.

The appropriate use of tests is a complex and multifaceted issue. It raises many problems, and they have many solutions. In its short life, the committee has attempted to identify key issues in high-stakes testing, to review and assess current uses of testing in key educational decisions about individual students, and to suggest ways of improving the use of tests to ensure better outcomes. We have necessarily had to limit the scope of our inquiry and, in particular, we have identified the consequences of certain kinds of decisions as a critical arena for educational policy. When educators and parents make decisions about tracking, promotion, and graduation, in many parts of the nation the current range of options may not be those that best serve the interests of students. In the committee's view, new policy options should be explored and their consequences for educational outcomes should be evaluated.

REFERENCES

American Educational Research Association, American Psychological Association, and National Council on Measurement in Education
    1985   *Standards for Educational and Psychological Testing.* Washington, DC: American Psychological Association.

Bond, L.A., D. Braskamp, and E.D. Roeber
    1996   *The Status of State Student Assessment Programs in the United States.* Oak Brook, IL: North Central Regional Educational Laboratory and Council of Chief State School Officers.

Crouse, James, and Dale Trusheim
    1988   *The Case Against the SAT.* Chicago, IL: University of Chicago Press.

Forgione, P.D., Jr.
    1998   *Achievement in the United States: Progress Since A Nation at Risk?* Washington, D.C.: Center for Education Reform and Empower America.

Hauser, R.M.
    1998   Trends in black-white test score differences: I. Uses and misuses of NAEP/SAT data. Pp. 219-249 in *The Rising Curve: Long-Term Gains in IQ and Related Measures,* Ulric Neisser, ed. Washington, DC: American Psychological Association.

Joint Committee on Testing Practices
    1988   *Code of Fair Testing Practices in Education.* Washington, DC: National Council on Measurement in Education.

Klein, S.P., and R.M. Bell
    1995   How will the NCAA's new standards affect minority student-athletes? Reprinted from *Chance* Summer 8(3):18-21.

National Research Council
    1982   *Placing Children in Special Education: A Strategy for Equity,* K.A. Heller, W.H. Holtzman, and S. Messick, eds. Committee on Child Development Research and Public Policy. Washington, DC: National Academy Press.
    1999a   *Evaluation of the Voluntary National Tests: Phase 1,* L.L. Wise, R.M. Hauser, K.J. Mitchell, and M.J. Feuer, eds. Board on Testing and Assessment. Washington, DC: National Academy Press.
    1999b   *Uncommon Measures: Equivalence and Linkage Among Educational Tests,* M.J. Feuer, P.W. Holland, B.F. Green, M.W. Bertenthal, and F.C. Hemphill, eds. Committee on Equivalency and Linkage of Educational Tests, Board on Testing and Assessment. Washington, DC: National Academy Press.

Office of Technology Assessment
    1992   *Testing in American Schools: Asking the Right Questions.* OTA-SET-519. Washington, DC: U.S. Government Printing Office.

LEGAL REFERENCES

Debra P. v. Turlington, 474 F. Supp. 244 (M.D. Fla. 1979); *aff'd in part and rev'd in part,* 644 F.2d 397 (5th Cir. 1981); *rem'd,* 564 F. Supp. 177 (M.D. Fla. 1983); *aff'd,* 730 F.2d 1405 (11th Cir. 1984).

Family Education Rights and Privacy Act of 1974, 20 U.S.C. §1232(g).

Goals 2000: Educate America Act, 20 U.S.C. sections 5801 *et seq.*

Individuals with Disabilities Education Act, 20 U.S.C. section 1401 *et seq.*

Larry P. v. Riles, 495 F. Supp. 926 (N.D. Cal. 1979); *aff'd*, 793 F.2d 969 (9th Cir. 1984).

People Who Care v. Rockford Board of Education, 111 F.3d 528 (7th Cir. 1997).

Section 504 of the Rehabilitation Act of 1973, 29 U.S.C. sections 794 *et seq.*

Title I, Elementary and Secondary Education Act, 20 U.S.C. sections 6301 *et seq.*

Title II, Americans with Disabilities Act of 1990, 42 U.S.C. sections 12131 *et seq.*

2

Assessment Policy and Politics

Current concerns about proper test use represent only the latest round in a continuing debate over the use of standardized assessments to advance education policy goals.[1] Beginning with the introduction in the mid-19th century of written examinations given to large numbers of students, standardized tests have served as an instrument for accomplishing a variety of policy purposes, including determining the types of instruction individual students receive, shaping the content and format of that instruction, and holding schools and students accountable for their performance.

Standardized tests are believed to be one of the most powerful levers that elected officials and other policymakers have for influencing what happens in local schools and classrooms. A growing body of research suggests that tests often do in fact change school and classroom practices (Corbett and Wilson, 1991; Madaus, 1988; Herman and Golan, 1993; Smith and Rottenberg, 1991), although such changes may or may not

---

[1]It is important to note that "standardized" is not synonymous with multiple-choice or any other test format or scoring system, but refers rather to uniform conditions under which many different students take similar tests—regardless of their format. For example, even a written examination, one that is scored by teachers or other human judges and not by machine, is considered standardized if all students respond to the same (or nearly the same) questions and take the examination under similar conditions. See, e.g., Office of Technology Assessment (1992) for more detail.

improve student learning (Mehrens, 1998). Furthermore, compared with other interventions, standardized tests are inexpensive. Now required by all three levels of government, tests have become a central feature of American public schooling.

At the same time, some testing experts and others concerned about the effects of inappropriate test use caution against using tests to promote broader policy goals. They warn that, if test scores are used to bestow rewards or impose sanctions, there are several risks: widening the gap in educational opportunities between haves and have-nots, narrowing the curriculum, centralizing educational decision making, and deprofessionalizing teachers (Haertel, 1989; Airasian, 1987).

TWO PERSISTENT DILEMMAS

The tension between the enthusiasm of policymakers and the caution of experts is symptomatic of two fundamental dilemmas posed by standardized tests when they are used as policy strategies. First, policy and public expectations of testing generally exceed the technical capacity of the tests themselves. One of the most common reasons for this gap is that policymakers, under constituent pressure to improve schools, often decide to use existing tests for purposes for which they were neither intended nor adequately validated. So, for example, tests designed to produce valid measures of performance only at the aggregate level—for schools or classrooms—are used to report on and make decisions about individual students. In such instances, serious consequences (such as retention in grade) may be unfairly imposed on individual students. That injustice is further compounded if the skills being tested do not reflect or validly measure what students have been taught.

Policymakers sometimes acknowledge these problems and the need for more research. Nevertheless, they often choose to rely on an available test because they see only a fleeting opportunity for action, or because they believe that, even with imperfect tests, more good than harm will be done. From this perspective, technical constraints are problems that should be remedied to the extent possible, but in an iterative fashion simultaneous with the implementation of the test-based policy (McDonnell, 1994).

In one recent case in point, Paul G. Vallas, the chief executive officer of the Chicago Public Schools, decided to continue use of the nationally norm-referenced Iowa Test of Basic Skills (ITBS) to identify low-performing schools and students, even though it has not been validated for that purpose. He agrees with researchers who argue that the ITBS should be replaced with a test directly linked to the city's academic standards. Vallas noted, however, that developing such a test would take three years; in the meantime, the ITBS will continue to be used for accountability (Olson, 1998).

Moreover, Philip Hansen, chief accountability officer for the Chicago Public Schools, told the committee that "we are committed to use the Iowa forever and ever." He went on to explain that, if the district were to drop the ITBS, it would lose credibility with the media and the public, who would view with suspicion any change to a new test. The new assessments, he said, would probably be used as course midterms and finals and be factored in as one component of a student's course grade.

The second dilemma stems from tensions between two motives for testing: the desire for more fairness and efficiency and the impulse to sort and classify students. Achievement testing first became a fixture of American public schools during the huge growth in mass education between 1870 and 1900, when enrollments more than doubled as waves of immigrants created a newly diverse student population. Demand grew for more efficient school management, including "the objective and efficient classification, or grading of pupils" (Tyack, 1974:44). Relying on tests was seen as fairer and more efficient than the prevailing system, in which children of varying ages and levels shared classrooms, and essay exams received widely varying grades from different teachers (Office of Technology Assessment, 1992; Haney, 1984).

The introduction of widespread intelligence testing during World War I allowed schools to begin measuring what testers believed to be students' aptitude for future learning, the IQ, in addition to using achievement tests to measure their past learning.[2] As the technology of intelli-

---

[2]In her history of the IQ test, Fass (1980) notes that the historical record shows a complete absence of agreement on a precise definition of intelligence and little concern among experts about the practical consequences of that absence. Intelligence came to be defined in practice as whatever a particular intelligence test measured. Consequently, according to Fass, "the significance of intelligence testing lies not in some intellectual formulation with a specific content, but in a methodology with instrumental results. In the course of creating, elaborating, and refining a method to evaluate the undefined, those who worked in the field of testing, those who used the tests in the schools, and the public, which welcomed the answers it provided, fashioned an instrument which would henceforth define what intelligence was. They had translated the culture's perceptions, and its needs, into a method for ordering, selecting, and directing its own evolution" (p. 452).

gence or IQ tests developed, they were quickly adopted by schools na-
tionwide and became an entrenched component of educational administration. Fass (1980:446) explains their appeal:

> The IQ grew out of the many issues and concerns facing American society in
> the early century. It was almost inevitable that it be adopted by the schools,
> which were the arena in which these problems were played out and which were
> also expected to solve them. The IQ established a meritocratic standard which
> seemed to sever ability from the confusions of a changing time and an increas-
> ingly diverse population, provided a means for the individual to continue to
> earn his place in society by his personal qualities, and answered the needs of a
> sorely strained school system to educate the mass while locating social talent.

As well-intentioned as some motivations for the IQ and other tests
may have been, they were not actually measures of innate ability, and
their use sometimes caused harm. In their worst manifestations, the uses
were racist and xenophobic. In the early part of the century, prominent
scientists argued on the basis of test results that blacks and immigrants
from Southern and Eastern Europe were mentally inferior, with these
pronouncements contributing to laws restricting immigration from countries assumed to be sources of inferior mental stock (Haney, 1984). Later,
tests were used by Southern schools resisting desegregation, as a way to
resegregate black students into lower tracks (Office of Technology Assessment, 1992).

The misuse of test data in policy debates continues today. The publication of The Bell Curve, arguing that social and economic inequality
among racial and ethnic groups can be explained by differences in intelligence as measured by tests, is a recent example (Hernnstein and Murray,
1994). Despite detailed critiques of the authors' statistical analysis, their
conception and measurement of intelligence, and their explanations of
the causes of inequality (Fischer et al., 1996), the book fueled a highly
charged, racialized debate. No policy actions can be attributed directly to
inferences that the authors drew from their analysis of test data. Nevertheless, Hernnstein's and Murray's argument that the sources of inequality are largely immutable has served as a rationale for those seeking to
limit education and social welfare policies aimed at reducing inequalities.

Neither the gap between expectations and capacity nor past misuses
of tests mean that we should give up on testing as an education policy
strategy. As Fischer and his colleagues (1996) note, the history of testing
shows that, although it has been used for discriminatory purposes, testing
has also been a tool for equalizing educational opportunities. Wisconsin's

use of standardized aptitude tests to encourage students to apply to college was mentioned in the preceding chapter. Similarly, many of the country's leading state university systems admit all students with a minimum grade-point average, but they also enable those with averages below the cutoff to apply based on their standardized admissions test scores. This type of "second pathway" is quite commonplace. As Donald Stewart, the president of the College Board, argued in a recent letter to the *New York Times*, "More than 50 million college applicants have taken the SAT since 1926, and most have arrived on campus, including millions of disadvantaged students who had often been excluded in the past" (May 8, 1998).

Furthermore, policymakers, who have few instruments at their disposal to affect schools directly, are unlikely to abandon a tool potentially as powerful as tests simply because people sometimes use them badly. The challenge for the policy community, then, is to make decisions about test use that allow them to pursue their broader objectives within a constrained political environment, staying mindful of both the limitations of any given test and its capacity to influence classroom behavior and students' educational opportunities. In the remainder of this chapter, we survey the range of assessment policies and describe the political context in which contemporary debates over appropriate test use are occurring.

TESTING AS A POLICY INSTRUMENT

Current federal, state, and local policies use student assessments for seven distinct purposes, with the same test often serving multiple functions.[3] The first is aiding in instructional decisions about individual students. For example, teachers may use test results in grouping students or in identifying areas in which particular students need additional or different instruction. But some form of standardized diagnostic test is typically used as one basis for deciding whether students are eligible for services provided by a variety of programs, including those related to the Individuals with Disabilities Education Act and state programs for students with disabilities, state and federal bilingual education programs for English-language learners, and the federal and state compensatory education programs for poor, underachieving students. Testing is thus used to

---

[3]Although we have cast this discussion in terms of seven distinct purposes, we do not mean to imply that this is the only way of looking at the question.

allocate an educational benefit and to decide what form that benefit should take in a student's program.

The second purpose is providing information about the status of the education system. One such test is the National Assessment of Educational Progress (NAEP). Since its inception in 1969, NAEP has served as "the nation's report card," periodically assessing a nationally representative sample of students, ages 9, 13, and 17, in several core academic subjects, with additional subjects being tested on a rotating basis. NAEP reports on achievement trends over time and across different subgroups. Over the past decade, NAEP has also included representative samples for 44 states, so that these states can compare their students' performance to the national sample. To provide a context for interpreting information about student achievement, NAEP also surveys students, their teachers, and school administrators about their backgrounds and the teaching in their schools.[4] Similarly, 46 states administer standardized assessments in three to five core subjects and publicly report the results, usually disaggregated to the school building level. The purpose of these assessments is to inform the public about how well the schools and students in their communities are performing over time and compared with those in other places.

Closely linked to assessments documenting the status of the educational system is a third function: tests as motivation for change. In a study of policymakers' expectations about the effects of student assessments, federal and state officials said they hoped test results would "shake people up." One respondent spoke of state policymakers who see assessments as a way to "embarrass people into change." Still others felt that, if assessments were tied to specific performance standards, even parents in affluent communities would be surprised to find that their children were not learning as much as they had assumed (McDonnell, 1994:9). But when policymakers in this study talked about the motivational purpose of assessments, they typically had parents, not students, in mind. Assessment results were seen as a way to influence parents to take action to improve the quality of local schools.[5]

---

[4]The federal government also periodically sponsors international assessments that provide data on how well U.S. students are performing compared with their counterparts in other countries. The most recent was the Third International Mathematics and Science Study (TIMSS), which, in addition to reporting test results, also provided information on how different countries organize their mathematics and science instruction.

[5]Among these policymakers, the kinds of assessments that they expected would moti-

Standardized tests play a fourth policy role in program evaluations. Because many educational interventions are intended to produce improved achievement, the results of standardized tests, administered to participants before and after the intervention, constitute a critical indicator of program effectiveness. The most widespread use of standardized testing in program evaluation is in the federal Title I program, first enacted as part of the Elementary and Secondary Education Act. For over 20 years, the law has required that local districts test Title I students yearly and report the results. Local districts are expected to use these data in making their programs more effective, and trend data aggregated across states and districts inform congressional deliberations each time the program is reauthorized. The evaluation requirements in Title I and other federal and state programs are a major factor in explaining the growth of local testing systems.

A fifth function of assessment is to hold schools, as public institutions, and educators accountable for student performance. Standardized tests are an integral part of this process. Providing information to the public about school performance is one aspect of accountability. But 23 states now attach consequences at the school level to assessment results, such as funding gains and losses, warnings, assistance from outside experts, loss of accreditation, and, in a few places, the eventual state takeover of schools (Bond et al., 1996).

These five purposes offer examples of low- and high-stakes tests that represent two fundamentally different ways of using testing in the service of policy goals. A low-stakes test has no significant, tangible, or direct consequences attached to the results, with information alone assumed to be a sufficient incentive for people to act. The theory behind this policy is that a standardized test can reliably and validly measure student achievement; that politicians, educators, parents, and the public will then act on the information generated by the test; and that actions based on test results will improve educational quality and student achievement. In contrast, high-stakes policies assume that information alone is insufficient to motivate educators to teach well and students to perform to high standards. Hence, it is assumed, the promise of rewards or the threat of sanctions is needed to ensure change. Rewards in the form of financial

---

vate students are ones used to certify that students have attained particular levels of mastery and that have personal consequences attached. We discuss this type of testing as a final policy purpose of assessment.

bonuses may be allocated to schools or teachers; sanctions may be imposed through external oversight or takeover by higher-level authorities.

In a sixth policy use, testing acts as a lever to change classroom instruction and may be implemented with either a high- or a low-stakes assessment. Although standardized tests have long been used as an education reform strategy for changing classroom instruction, this use has become more central with the advent of the standards-based reforms now promoted by states and the federal government. This movement seeks to improve educational quality by setting high content standards that define the knowledge and skills that teachers should teach and students should learn, and by holding educators and teachers accountable for meeting performance standards that set the expectations for proficiency. It assumes that educators and the public can agree on a set of curricular values; that those values can be translated into a set of standards; and that assessments can measure how well students perform on the standards (National Research Council, 1997).

About half the states have revamped their assessment systems over the past decade to align them more closely with specific content and performance standards, and most of the rest are in the alignment process or planning to begin it. In an effort to increase the authenticity of tasks on assessments, many states have also diversified their testing format beyond a sole reliance on multiple-choice items; 34 now require writing samples of tested students, and 10 include constructed, open-response items (Bond et al., 1996).

Most standards-based assessments have only recently been implemented or are still being developed. Consequently, it is too early to determine whether they will produce the intended effects on classroom instruction. A recent review of the available research evidence by Mehrens (1998) reaches several interim conclusions. Drawing on eight studies that used teacher surveys, classroom observations, or analysis of teachers' classroom assignments to examine the implementation of new assessments in six states, he found that, if stakes are high enough and if teachers deem the content appropriate, curriculum and instruction are likely to change to reflect more closely the content sampled by the test. If the stakes are low, if teachers believe that the test is measuring developmentally inappropriate content, or if teaching consistent with the assessment would reduce the amount of time teachers could spend on what they consider to be more important content, then the assessment apparently has less impact on teaching and curriculum.

The effects of standards-based assessments on practice depend not only on teachers' willingness to teach what is being tested but also on their capacity to do so. The curriculum standards now being adopted by many states, however, expect teachers to teach very different material in ways that are fundamentally different from their accustomed practice. In most cases, teachers have not been adequately prepared for the reforms. Therefore, even those who are willing to change may lack a sufficient understanding of what the reforms require and may filter their teaching innovations through traditional approaches to instruction (Cohen and Peterson, 1990). As a result, tests are likely to produce only modest effects as incentives for curricular change without a considerable investment in teacher training.

The seventh policy use for standardized tests is certifying individual students as having attained specified levels of achievement or mastery. These are high-stakes uses with rewards to individual students: special diplomas, graduation from high school, or promotion to the next grade. Sanctions typically consist of the withholding of those rewards or benefits. Currently, 18 states require that students pass an exit examination before they graduate from high school, and 4 offer honors diplomas on the basis of examination results (Bond et al., 1996). The requirement that students pass a test as a condition for high school graduation is typically imposed by states, but some local districts use tests to decide whether students should be promoted to the next grade. Although there are no national data summarizing how local districts use standardized tests in certifying students, we do know that several of the largest school systems have begun to use test scores in determining grade-to-grade promotion (Chicago) or are considering doing so (New York City, Boston). In addition, in a survey of 85 of the largest school systems, the American Federation of Teachers (AFT) found that, at the elementary level, 39 percent of the districts use standardized test scores, usually in combination with other information, in deciding whether to retain a student in grade. But both teacher-assigned grades and teacher recommendations were reportedly used at the elementary level in a higher proportion of districts: 48 percent. These other factors become even more significant in the higher grades, so that in high school, teacher-assigned grades are used in 65 percent of the districts and standardized tests in only 24 percent (American Federation of Teachers, 1997). With only a few notable exceptions, such as Chicago, districts typically use multiple indicators in making promotion decisions.

Current testing of students for high-stakes decisions is the latest version of a policy strategy that began with the state minimum competency tests implemented between 1975 and 1985. These tests were a response to public concerns about students leaving school without basic reading and mathematics skills, combined with a widespread perception that educational quality had declined (Office of Technology Assessment, 1992). Minimum competency tests, which coincided with the "back to basics" movement of the 1970s, typically tested students on basic literacy and numeracy skills considered essential in life. The tests were often calibrated to measure the skills expected of an 8th grader, and they required that students attain a specific score to pass.

Many of the legal challenges to testing that have arisen over the past 20 years were prompted by the minimum competency movement. These tests raise due process and equal protection issues when they serve a gatekeeping function, such as determining whether students can graduate from high school. One of the most important cases posing these questions grew out of a challenge to Florida's minimum competency test. In the case of *Debra P. v. Turlington* (1981), a U.S. court of appeals ruled that if a high school graduation test covers material not taught to the students, then it is unfair and violates the Fourteenth Amendment to the U.S. Constitution. These and other legal issues related to the use of standardized tests are discussed in Chapters 3, 8, and 9.

Research has found the effects of minimum competency tests to be mixed (Chapter 7). Newer assessments aligned with more rigorous content standards are in part a response to the shortcomings of these earlier tests. States can now usually point to test score gains, particularly in the proportion of students passing high school graduation tests between the time they are first tested in grade 8 or 9 and when they must finally pass the test in grade 12. Scholars (e.g., Koretz et al., 1991) have questioned these gains, however, observing that score increases could be due in part to "teaching to the test," whereby students are drilled on questions that mirror those on the actual test (Mehrens, 1998).

Much has been written about the narrowing effect of minimum competency tests on the curriculum and on the drill-and-practice instruction that it encourages. These outcomes result from a combination of the low-level skills tested and the policy assumption that a student's failure on the test is the school's responsibility to remedy (Office of Technology Assessment, 1992). In states in which policymakers believe that schools should certify student mastery of required skills and that tests can adequately gauge such mastery, the response to the shortcomings of minimum competency tests has been to design tests that measure higher-order analytical skills. Although most high school exit exams still measure basic skills, the trend is toward more difficult and sophisticated tests. Some states, including Maryland and New York, are now implementing high school graduation assessments tied to demanding state standards and requiring greater mastery of more complex skills. A few other states, including North Carolina, are moving toward requiring high school students to pass standardized, statewide end-of-course exams in all the subjects—algebra, English, U.S. history, and so on—needed for high school graduation, rather than passing a single exit exam. Some states have postponed implementation of tests carrying high stakes for students until they have put in place systems of accountability for schools and educators.

The close links between education policy and testing are clear. Although standardized tests are merely measurement tools to obtain information about student and school performance, they have come to function also as symbols. So, for example, assessments are often portrayed as synonymous with accountability policies or with high school graduation requirements, even though the imposition of rewards and sanctions constitutes the core of these policies, and the test results merely inform decisions about their allocation.

Precisely because of the tight connection between testing and policy, standards for proper test use are essential. All seven policy uses require that assessments measure student performance consistently across tasks (reliability), that the scores are meaningful and reflect the domains being measured (validity), and that the meaning of the test scores does not differ across individuals, groups, or settings (fairness). These standards are explored in Chapters 4 through 9.

Meeting these standards is both more important and more problematic when a test is used for high-stakes purposes, particularly if it involves consequences for individuals rather than institutions. If students are not afforded the opportunity to learn the content on which they are tested (a growing possibility as curriculum and performance standards are raised), or if tests are not interpreted consistently from one locale to another (as is often the case in decisions about special education placement), then testing can create new inequalities or exacerbate existing ones.

Avoiding this outcome may be difficult, however. Politicians are elected to solve problems, and often that means acting with the tools available under severe time pressures and fiscal and political constraints.

The result is that tests are used for purposes for which they were not intended. In such cases, the outcome for individuals may be unfair. Moreover, the tests themselves may be corrupted as valid and reliable measuring devices (Linn, 1998).

CURRENT POLICY LANDSCAPE

As student assessment becomes a more prominent part of education reform strategies, several trends stand out as having significant implications. One is the goal of including most, if not all, students in assessment systems. A variety of recent policy initiatives aims to test even those students who were previously exempted from common assessments or who were tested with alternative instruments. If all students are included in the same assessment system, it is assumed, system accountability will be greater, particularly for students who have often been shortchanged in their schooling. Including more students in large-scale assessments, however, does not necessarily mean that all students will be subject to the high stakes that some states and school districts attach to scores on such tests.

At the federal level, Title I of the Elementary and Secondary Education Act and the Individuals with Disabilities Education Act of 1997 are being used as levers to ensure that students participating in these programs take tests that incorporate the same content and performance standards that apply to other students. They are also to be included in state assessment systems, and the states are to determine whether local districts and schools are helping these students make adequate yearly progress toward meeting the common standards. This strategy, in effect, combines several policy purposes of assessment: program evaluation, school-level accountability, and changing classroom instruction. Federal law does not, however, require that all students be subject to high-stakes test requirements.

Policy discussions have focused mainly on whether a standards-based strategy will work for all students, what testing accommodations are needed, and how test scores should be reported. The question of how tests are used is likely to become especially salient in this context, because many of the students who will be included in expanded assessment systems are English-language learners or students with disabilities. For these students, it is important to ensure that the tests truly measure their achievement and are not corrupted by language barriers or lack of appropriate modifications. Appropriate test use for these students, as for all students, requires that their scores not lead to decisions or placements that are educationally detrimental.

The connection between assessment as a reform strategy and appropriate test use has been joined in the debate over voluntary national tests (VNTs). The Clinton administration, in proposing the development of national assessments to test 4th graders in reading and 8th graders in mathematics, argued that by testing students in two critical subjects at two critical grades, using national standards, parents would know how their own children were doing, and policymakers, educators, and the public would know how well their schools were performing. The underlying assumption was that those concerned about education could act more effectively to raise standards and improve instruction if better information were available.

Critics of the VNTs have charged, among other things, that national testing is unnecessary, that it will lead to more centralized control of education, and that it will usurp the prerogatives of states and local communities. But the criticism most relevant to our charge comes from civil rights groups: that implementing national tests could harm poor students and minority students if test scores are linked to high-stakes consequences for individual students, unless there are protections to ensure that all students receive access to high-quality curriculum and instruction. From this perspective, the VNTs are surely problematic: under the proposed arrangement, in which the test would be licensed to private test publishers, the federal government would be unable to regulate how states and local districts would use the test results.[6]

The education policy landscape is also dominated at present by efforts to end social promotion, in part through testing. In his 1998 State of the Union speech, President Clinton asserted that "when we promote a child from grade to grade who hasn't mastered the work, we don't do that child any favors. It is time to end social promotion in America's schools." The president thus joined a host of other political leaders, from the Democratic mayor of Chicago to the Republican governor of Texas, all calling for an end to the promotion of students whose achievement does not meet expectations for that grade level.

---

[6]It is perhaps worth noting that increasing the stringency of test-use standards for the VNT could discourage states and school districts from using the new tests and encourage them to continue using tests for which more relaxed requirements apply. The potential consequences of such behavior should be considered by policymakers.

Advocates have argued that ending social promotion does not necessarily mean retaining students in grade. They maintain, in fact, that one can be equally opposed both to social promotion and to retention in grade. Indeed, Michael Cohen, the president's special assistant for education, told the committee that social promotion versus retention was a "false choice" because "we know that [retention] doesn't do them a lot of good either." The answer, he said, was "to find a sort of a middle ground, where you're actually starting early to provide kids who need it with extra help, putting effective practices in place, giving them extended opportunities, and in [the] process assuming that all kids you're dealing with can meet standards if you give them the right opportunities."

The Clinton administration recommends that schools use specific grade-by-grade standards and a challenging curriculum aligned with those standards, smaller classes, well-prepared teachers, and after-school and summer-school programs for those students who need them (Clinton, 1998). Similarly, in its report on district promotion policies and practices, the AFT (1997:21) notes:

> Policy alternatives must ensure that students learn what they need to know to be successful in the next grade, and ultimately, in life. Ignoring the problem of failure (social promotion) and doing again what failed to work the first time (simple retention) is not the answer. Policy changes must address the underlying problem of why children do not achieve and what changes in school organization, curriculum, instruction, and educational programs are necessary if children are to succeed.

Despite these assurances and suggested alternatives to retaining students in grade, a number of researchers and advocacy groups have argued that, even though districts may rely on a variety of interventions for ending social promotion, many will also retain students in the same grade for an additional year. Yet most research on retention shows that retained students are generally worse off than their promoted counterparts on both personal adjustment and academic outcomes (Shepard and Smith, 1989).

Chicago has become a focal point for the social promotion debate. It was the first large district to announce its intention to end the practice, basing promotion decisions solely on a test that its developers maintain was not designed for that purpose. In other districts that are moving to end social promotion, debate has focused more on the merits of the policy, because test scores are only one criterion for decisions. For example, under a proposal now being considered in New York City, 4th and 7th graders' readiness to advance to the next grade would be measured by a new state reading test as well as by a comprehensive evaluation of their course work and a review of their attendance records (Steinberg, 1998).

In short, testing policy has become a focal point for political debates over schooling. Its role as an electoral campaign issue, the position of major interest groups on assessment questions, and public attitudes toward testing all shape the context in which policymakers decide what constitutes appropriate test use.

POLITICS OF ASSESSMENT

With the growth of testing as a policy strategy, discussions about its use have moved more and more from the technical realm to the political world of electoral campaigns, interest groups, and public opinion. It is now quite common for those running for public office to call for greater test-based accountability, to take stands on which tests should be used for which students, and to support the use of testing for specific purposes, such as ending social promotion. Although the extent to which politicians are leading public opinion or following it is unclear, their focus on testing has certainly tapped a strong vein of support among the American public.

In a variety of national and state public opinion polls, large majorities of respondents favor using tests to identify student and teacher weaknesses, to decide who is promoted, and to rank schools. For example, requiring students to pass tests for grade-to-grade promotion (70 percent) and for high school graduation (80 percent) was strongly supported in a 1994 Public Agenda survey (Johnson and Immerwahr, 1994). In the 1995 Phi Delta Kappan/Gallup poll, 65 percent of the respondents supported requiring students in their local communities to pass standardized tests for promotion from one grade to another, a proportion that has remained constant over the four times since 1978 that the question has been asked (Hochschild and Scott, 1998). In the same poll, 60 percent reported believing that raising standards would encourage students from low-income backgrounds to do better in school (with no statistically significant differences by race of respondent).

The public also seems willing to accept some of the negative consequences associated with this kind of high-stakes testing: 65 percent of those queried in the 1995 poll favored stricter requirements for high school graduation even if fewer students graduate, again with no differences by race (Elam and Rose, 1995). In a March 1997 NBC/*Wall Street*

Journal poll, 70 percent of the respondents reported that requiring students to pass standardized tests in order to move on to the next grade would represent a "big improvement" (Ferguson, 1997).

Recent state polls show similar results. In a 1997 poll of Massachusetts residents (Mass Insight, 1997), 61 percent of the respondents supported passing a 10th grade competency test as a condition of high school graduation. About half of those with an opinion thought that no more than 10 percent of the students in their own communities would fail the exam, and 25 percent thought more than 20 percent would fail. But 61 percent of the respondents said that, even if 25 percent of their hometown students failed the exam, they would still require students to pass it. In the same poll, about the same proportion (65 percent) approved of students not being promoted to the next grade until they pass a required test.

Similarly, a 1998 PACE/Field Institute poll of Californians found that 62 percent favored setting uniform student promotion requirements "based on students passing an achievement test, rather than leaving this up to teachers" (Fuller et al., 1998). Likewise, 82 percent of the general public and 67 percent of teachers surveyed in South Carolina in 1997 felt that standards for promotion from elementary to middle school should be raised and that students should be allowed to move ahead only if they pass a test showing that they have reached those standards (Immerwahr, 1997).

Poll data present a consistent picture of strong public support for the use of tests for high-stakes decisions about individual students.[7] Despite some evidence that the public would accept some of the potential trade-offs, it seems reasonable to assume that most people are unaware of the full range of negative consequences related to this kind of high-stakes test use. Moreover, it seems certain that few people are aware of limits on the information that tests can provide. No survey questions, for example, have asked how much measurement error is acceptable when tests are used to make high-stakes decisions about individual students. The sup-

---

[7]At the same time, these data, like most surveys about public education, are hard to interpret because there is virtually no research on public attitudes toward the schools. We know little about how parents and the public form their attitudes; what role expert information plays compared with other influences, such as friends, neighbors, and elites; how attitudes are related to each other; and how attitudes change or remain stable over time. There has been no in-depth survey that asked more nuanced questions about standardized tests and their use.

port for testing expressed in polls might decline if the public understood these things. Nevertheless, public opinion continues to play an important legitimating function in support of these high-stakes uses of tests.

Interest groups with a direct stake in the educational enterprise express a wider range of views than the public's broad support of high-stakes testing. We learned, for example, that the AFT supports the high-stakes use of tests for making promotion and graduation decisions, arguing that, unless there are consequences, the rigorous content standards it espouses will not be real to students. The organization also sees high school exit exams, based on high standards, as a way to avoid the costly remediation now being undertaken by postsecondary institutions and business. At the same time, it believes that decisions about promotion or graduation should not be based solely on a single test score and that students who do not meet the standards should receive remedial education that would enable them to do so.

Although the National Education Association (NEA) takes no official position on the desirability of using tests for high-stakes decisions about individual students, it opposes their use "as a single criterion for high-stakes decision making," or when "they do not match the developmental levels or language proficiency of the student" (NEA 1997 Resolutions—B-55, Standardized Testing of Students). The national Parent-Teachers Association (PTA), which opposes federal legislation or regulations that mandate standardized testing or that would lead to such testing, takes a similar position on test use: "valid assessment does not consist of only a single test score, and . . . at no time should a single test be considered the sole determinant of a student's academic or work future, e.g., high school graduation, scholarship aid, honors programs, or college admissions" (PTA position statement, 1996).

Several civil rights organizations strongly oppose the high-stakes use of standardized tests, at least when test scores are the sole factor used in making high-stakes decisions for students or when students do not have equal access to high-quality instruction. For more than 20 years, the National Association for the Advancement of Colored People (NAACP) has called the use of testing as a sole criterion for the nonpromotion of students and the use of competency testing for high school graduation "another way of blaming the student victim." Rhonda Boozer, the NAACP education coordinator, reports that the organization is on record as opposing "the use of testing results in an adverse fashion and any movement geared to [the] use of scores on a national test as [a] prerequisite for high school graduation" (personal communication).

The Mexican American Legal Defense and Educational Fund has filed suit against the state of Texas for its use of the Texas Assessment of Academic Skills as an exit test for high school graduation. It argues that the test denies diplomas to students without sufficient proof that the policy will enhance students' education or life opportunities, and that the test does not correspond to what is actually taught in schools in many minority communities. The National Association for Bilingual Education has more specific concerns about the nature of standardized tests: students should be assessed with appropriate, performance-based tests, and English-language learners should not be assessed with tests that are inappropriate at their level of language competency.[8]

The contrast between strong public support for high-stakes testing of individual students and the more qualified positions of major education interest groups suggests a significant disjuncture between these organizations and their constituencies.[9] Whether this gap reflects incomplete information on the public's part or true differences between organizational policymakers and the public is unknown. In either case, test use will surely continue to be a highly politicized issue. If elected officials decide to pursue high-stakes strategies, they will be able to draw on latent public support, but they may also face considerable opposition from some quarters.

CONCLUSION

In a policy memo prepared for the committee, University of Wisconsin political scientist Donald Kettl argued that "performance measures and educational tests are not really about measurement. They are about political communication." Although he may have overstated the case, Kettl makes a telling point. Whether tests are used for high- or low-stakes purposes, the information they provide will feed public debate

---

[8]Patricia Loera, associate director for legislative and public affairs, National Association for Bilingual Education, personal communication.

[9]Other groups with an interest in education have not taken specific positions on testing. The National Business Roundtable strongly supports the VNT and wants to see high standards verified through rigorous testing. But it has not taken a position on any form of high-stakes testing, says its director of education initiatives. The National Urban League has no position on test use. The National Council of Teachers of Mathematics has taken no position, although it is encouraging a discussion of high-stakes testing among its members.

about educational goals and curricula and about whether schools are accomplishing their mission.

When serious personal consequences are attached to test results, test use enters the political realm in yet another way. Fundamental questions about what constitutes equal treatment and who should receive valued societal benefits come to the forefront. Moreover, high-stakes test uses force us to confront trade-offs between potential societal benefits, such as a better-trained workforce and a more informed citizenry, and potential costs to individuals who do not meet the common performance standards as measured by an assessment.

The technical standards for appropriate test use outlined in Chapter 4 should inform the search for answers to those questions. In the end, however, decisions about how we choose to use tests rest largely with political institutions—with legislatures, courts, and school boards. The resulting policies will be interpreted and implemented by technical experts and professional educators, but their underlying intent will be the result of political choices.

REFERENCES

Airasian, P.W.
    1987   State mandated testing and educational reform: Context and consequences. *American Journal of Education* 95(3):393-412.
American Federation of Teachers
    1997   *Passing on Failure: District Promotion Policies and Practices.* Washington, DC: American Federation of Teachers.
Bond, L.A., D. Braskamp, and E. Roeber
    1996   *The Status Report of the Assessment Programs in the United States.* Washington, DC: The Council of Chief State School Officers and Oak Brook, IL: North Central Regional Educational Laboratory.
Clinton, W.J.
    1998   *Public Papers of the Presidents of the United States.* Washington, DC: Government Printing Office.
Cohen, D.K., and P.L. Peterson
    1990   Special issue of *Educational Evaluation and Policy Analysis* 12(3):233-353.
Corbett, H.D., and B.L. Wilson
    1991   *Testing, Reform, and Rebellion.* Norwood, NJ: Ablex Publishing.
Elam, S.M., and L.C. Rose
    1995   The 27th annual Phi Delta Kappan/Gallup Poll of the public's attitudes toward the public schools. *Phi Delta Kappan* 77(1):41-56.
Fass, P.S.
    1980   The IQ: A cultural and historical framework. *American Journal of Education* 88(4):431-458.

Ferguson, G.A.
   1997   Searching for consensus in education reform. *The Public Perspective* 8(4):49-52.
Fischer, C.S., M. Hout, M.S. Jankowski, S.R. Lucas, A, Swidler, and K. Voss
   1996   *Inequality by Design: Cracking the Bell Curve Myth.* Princeton, NJ: Princeton University Press.
Fuller, B., G. Hayward, and M. Kirst
   1998   *Californians Speak on Education and Reform Options.* PACE/Field Institute School Reform Poll. Berkeley, CA: Policy Analysis for California Education.
Haertel, E.
   1989   Student achievement tests as tools of educational policy: Practices and consequences. Pp. 25-50 in *Test Policy and Test Performance: Education, Language and Culture*, B.R. Gifford, ed. Boston: Kluwer Academic Publishers.
Haney, W.
   1984   Testing reasoning and reasoning about testing. *Review of Educational Research* 54(4):597-654.
Herman, J.L., and S. Golan
   1993   The effects of standardized testing on teaching and schools. *Educational Measurement, Issues and Practice* 12(4):20-25, 41-42.
Hernnstein, R.J., and C. Murray
   1994   *The Bell Curve: Intelligence and Class Structure in American Life.* New York: Free Press.
Hochschild, J., and B. Scott
   1998   Trends: Governance and reform of public education in the United States. *Public Opinion Quarterly* 62(1):79-120.
Immerwahr, J.
   1997   *What Our Children Need: South Carolinians Look at Education.* New York: Public Agenda.
Johnson, J., and J. Immerwahr
   1994   *First Things First: What Americans Expect from the Public Schools.* New York: Public Agenda.
Kettl, D.F.
   1998   Uses of Educational Tests. Memorandum to the Board on Testing and Assessment.
Koretz, D.M., R.L. Linn, S.B. Dunbar, and L.A. Shepard
   1991   The Effects of High-Stakes Testing on Achievement: Preliminary Findings About Generalization Across Tests. Paper presented at the annual meeting of the American Educational Research Association and the National Council on Measurement in Education, Chicago, IL.
Linn, R.L.
   1998   Assessments and Accountability. Paper presented at the annual meeting, American Educational Research Association, San Diego, CA.
Madaus, G.F.
   1988   The influence of testing on the curriculum. Pp. 83-121 in *Critical Issues in Curriculum*, Eighty-Seventh Yearbook of the National Society for the Study of Education, L.N. Tanner, ed. Chicago: University of Chicago Press.

Mass Insight
1997   *The Public's View of Standards and Tests: Executive Summary.* Cambridge, MA: Mass Insight.
McDonnell, L.M.
1994   *Policymakers' Views of Student Assessment.* Santa Monica, CA: RAND.
Mehrens, W.A.
1998   Consequences of Assessment: What Is the Evidence? Vice Presidential Address for Division D, annual meeting of the American Educational Research Association, San Diego.
National Research Council
1997   *Educating One and All: Students with Disabilities and Standards-Based Reform,* L.M. McDonnell, M.L. McLaughlin, and P. Morison, eds. Board on Testing and Assessment. Washington, DC: National Academy Press.
Office of Technology Assessment
1992   *Testing in American Schools: Asking the Right Questions.* OTA-SET-519. Washington, DC: U.S. Government Printing Office.
Olson, L.
1998   Study warns against reliance on testing data. *Education Week* (March 25):10.
Shepard, L.A., and Smith, M.L.
1989   *Flunking Grades: Research and Policies on Retention.* Philadelphia: Falmer Press.
Smith, M.L., and Claire Rottenberg
1991   Unintended consequences of external testing in elementary schools. *Educational Measurement, Issues and Practice* 10(4):7-11.
Steinberg, J.
1998   New York's chancellor vows to end routine promotions to the next grade. *New York Times* April 21:A23.
Tyack, D.B.
1974   *The One Best System.* Cambridge: Harvard University Press.

LEGAL REFERENCES

Debra P. v. Turlington, 644 F.2d 397 (5th Cir. 1981)
Individuals with Disabilities Education Act, 20 U.S.C. section 1401 *et seq.*
Title I, Elementary and Secondary Education Act, 20 U.S.C. sections 6301 *et seq.*

3

Legal Frameworks

Law plays a dual role as far as educational tests are concerned. First, law is typically the means by which policymakers define test policy. In Chapter 2 we discussed the principal objectives of federal, state, and local test policy, mentioning some of the statutes that aim to advance these objectives. This chapter looks at the second role that law can play with regard to testing: as a source of rules that define the circumstances in which test use may be discriminatory or otherwise inappropriate. Many of these rules are rooted in the U.S. Constitution, federal civil rights statutes, and judicial decisions. And although a comprehensive treatment of state law is beyond the scope of this report, many of the issues discussed are affected in significant ways by state law.

In terms of the committee's congressional mandate, the law constitutes one set of norms relevant to whether existing or new tests are used in a discriminatory manner or inappropriately for student promotion, tracking, or graduation. Legal considerations also play a part in discussions of how best to measure the reading and mathematics achievement of English-language learners and students with disabilities and whether to include them in large-scale assessments.

This chapter describes the legal frameworks that apply generally when tests have high-stakes consequences for students and considers how courts have applied these principles to situations involving student tracking, promotion, and graduation.[1] The first section considers issues of discrimination on the basis of race, national origin, or sex; it includes discussion of English-language learners. The second section explores other circumstances in which courts have invalidated tests having high stakes for students, either because students have received insufficient notice of test requirements or because the test measures knowledge and skills that students have not been taught. The third section describes testing requirements under the Improving America's Schools Act of 1994, which amends Title I. Chapter 8 considers the legal rights of students with disabilities under federal law.

Several general points are worth noting from the outset. First, the standards of testing professionals—who practice the science of psychometrics (see Chapter 4)—are often invoked in legal challenges to high-stakes testing, and testing programs are more likely to withstand legal challenges if professional standards have been met. Indeed, legal standards and psychometric standards reflect many common concerns, including those of appropriate measurement, proper attribution of cause, and, in some contexts, the educational consequences of test use (National Research Council, 1982).

Second, just as different test *uses* may raise particular legal concerns, so may the use of different *kinds* of assessments. Performance assessments, for example, may raise certain legal questions that traditional multiple-choice instruments do not (Phillips, 1996b).

Finally, there is often no single legal view on what constitutes nondiscriminatory or appropriate test use. The U.S. Supreme Court has settled certain questions, but legal rules, like psychometric norms and notions of sound educational policy and practice, are constantly evolving. If the Supreme Court has not resolved an issue, then courts in different jurisdictions may face similar disputes but reach different conclusions, or they may reach similar conclusions but on different grounds. The decision of a lower court is binding only in that court's jurisdiction, although it may influence judges, policymakers, and practitioners elsewhere.

---

[1]Such high-stakes tests are likelier than low-stakes tests to raise legal concerns—if only because, by definition, these high-stakes tests can lead to adverse consequences for individuals. Thus, to the extent that the objectives of a testing program can be achieved through low-stakes test uses, legal problems become less likely.

DEFINING DISCRIMINATION IN THE CONTEXT OF HIGH-STAKES TESTING

The legal literature reveals several distinct arguments that courts have considered in determining whether the use of a test to make high-stakes decisions about individual students is illegally discriminatory. The outcomes of some cases depend on whether the decision to administer a high-stakes test is based on a present intent to discriminate. Other cases depend on whether a test carries forward or preserves the effects of prior illegal discrimination. A third claim, grounded in federal civil rights statutes and accompanying regulations, employs an "effects test" that considers whether a high-stakes test has a disproportionate, adverse impact; whether the use of a test having such an impact can be adequately justified on educational grounds; and whether there are equally feasible alternative tests that have less disproportionate impact. These legal claims bear directly on whether tests are used in a discriminatory manner for tracking, promotion, or graduation. Each type of claim is therefore considered separately below.

Claims of Intentional Discrimination

The equal protection clause of the Fourteenth Amendment forbids public employees and entities—including state and local school officials—from engaging in acts of intentional discrimination on the basis of race, color, national origin, or sex (*United States v. Fordice*, 1992; *Personnel Administrator v. Feeney*, 1979). Findings of current intentional discrimination have been rare, especially in recent decades; the applicable legal standard is a stringent one, and few courts have been prepared to find that educators are acting out of invidious motives. The plaintiffs' burden cannot be met merely by showing that a policy or practice has a disproportionate, adverse impact on some group, or even by demonstrating that the disproportionate impact was foreseeable or actually foreseen (*Washington v. Davis*, 1976). Thus, for example, lower courts have refused to find intentional discrimination solely on the basis of evidence showing that high-stakes graduation tests had a disproportionate, adverse impact by race or national origin (*Debra P. v. Turlington*, 1979; *Anderson v. Banks*, 1981).

According to the Supreme Court, those who allege intentional discrimination must show not only foreseeable, disproportionate adverse impact but also that "the decisionmaker selected or reaffirmed a particular course of action *at least in part 'because of,'* not merely 'in spite of,' its adverse effects" on the group disproportionately affected (*Personnel Administrator v. Feeney*, 1979:279) (emphasis added).[2]

Where high-stakes testing programs are concerned, courts have almost uniformly dismissed claims of intentional discrimination. Most often courts have found that there are legitimate, nondiscriminatory educational reasons for adopting such programs. In sustaining high-stakes graduation tests, for example, lower courts have found "no present intent to discriminate" (Phillips, 1991:178), accepting the defendants' view that such tests can help to improve students' educational performance, to identify students who need remedial assistance, and to evaluate the attainment of state educational objectives (*Debra P. v. Turlington*, 1979; *Anderson v. Banks*, 1981). This is true even when decisions to deny high school diplomas have been made automatically on the basis of one or more test scores. Similarly, despite legal challenges to tracking, whether based on tests or on other information, there are only a few reported decisions in which courts found that tracking, or student classification more generally, constituted intentional racial segregation (Welner and Oakes, 1996:455). One of these is an older case (*Hobson v. Hansen*, 1967),[3] and one is a decision that an appellate court later reversed in pertinent part (*People Who Care v. Rockford Board of Education*, 1997).

A third such case is *Larry P. v. Riles* (1984). It involved a challenge to the use of an IQ test as a basis for assigning California public school students to classes for the educable mentally retarded (EMR). Use of the

---

[2]Recognizing that each situation "demands a sensitive inquiry into such circumstantial and direct evidence of intent as may be available," the Supreme Court has identified criteria to aid courts in determining whether a decision maker has acted "because of" the disproportionate adverse effects its policy or practice will have (*Village of Arlington Heights v. Metropolitan Housing Development Corp.*, 1977:266-270). As applied in the testing context, these criteria include (1) whether the test produces a disproportionate, adverse impact on the group that alleges discrimination; (2) whether the test's disproportionate impact was reasonably foreseeable or actually foreseen; (3) whether adoption or administration of the test can be explained on grounds other than an intent to discriminate; (4) whether the historical background of the decision supports a claim of intentional discrimination; (5) whether adoption or use of the test represents a departure from the decision maker's normal policies or procedures; and (6) whether there is direct evidence of intent to discriminate, such as statements evincing discriminatory intent.

[3]Current standards for proving intentional discrimination evolved nearly a decade after *Hobson v. Hansen*, beginning with *Washington v. Davis* (1976) and other Supreme Court decisions noted above.

test resulted in the disproportionately high assignment of black students to such classes. A federal district court, affirmed by the U.S. court of appeals, found California's use of the IQ test for EMR placements to be intentionally discriminatory, based on a number of factors.

First, state department of education officials had foreseen that the test would have a significant disproportionate impact by race. Second, they had failed "to ascertain or attempt to ascertain the validity of the tests for minority children." Third, "the adoption of [a] mandatory IQ testing requirement was riddled with procedural and substantive irregularities, in which no outside sources were consulted . . . and . . . the person who oversaw [test] selection was not an expert in IQ testing." Fourth, the state had failed to use alternative tests that were "less discriminatory than the IQ-centered standard." Fifth, "the [state department of education's] actions revealed a complacent acceptance of [racial differences in intelligence] that was built on easy assumptions about the incidence of retardation or at least low intelligence among black children" (*Larry P. v. Riles*, 1984:974-976). Sixth, the court regarded EMR classes "as 'dead-end' classes . . . . [A] misplacement in E.M.R. causes a stigma and irreparable injury to the student" (*Larry P. v. Riles*, 1984:973).

A similar case, brought in California on behalf of Hispanic children and involving allegations of linguistic discrimination, was resolved through a settlement entered by a federal district court on June 18, 1973 (*Diana v. Board of Education*, 1973).[4]

An Illinois district court, however, reached opposite conclusions when faced with facts similar in many respects to those in *Larry P.* That court accepted the defendants' contentions (1) that the tests typically used to measure IQ were not racially biased,[5] (2) that IQ test scores were only one of several factors used to determine placements, (3) that erroneous placements of black children in EMR classes occurred infrequently and for reasons other than intentional discrimination, (4) that the referral and placement process in Chicago was not carried out hastily, and (5) that EMR classes, rather than being dead ends, were beneficial place-

---

[4]In *Larry P.* itself, an injunction issued in 1986 prevented California from using IQ tests as *any* part of the special education process. This injunction was later vacated, leaving in place the prohibition against using IQ tests as a basis for placing black children in EMR classes (*Crawford v. Honig*, 1994).

[5]The court, which examined the IQ tests for item bias and found very little, faulted the *Larry P.* court for not having examined more thoroughly whether the tests were, in fact, biased.

ments to which students had a federal and state legal entitlement (*Parents in Action on Special Education (PASE) v. Hannon*, 1980:150-164).

Although they reach different conclusions, these decisions are consistent in several important respects. First, even under a stringent intent standard, liability findings may turn in part on the extent to which courts believe that educators have complied with generally accepted standards and procedures governing proper test use. In *Larry P.* and *PASE*, for example, the outcomes depended in part on such measurement issues as test validity, item bias, and whether educators were relying on single test scores in making student placement decisions. The outcome in *Larry P.* also turned on an issue of proper attribution of cause, with the court questioning the defendants' claim that black students' IQ scores were an accurate reflection of mental retardation among blacks. Third, the decisions in *Larry P.* and *PASE* both rest partly on the courts' views of whether the resulting placements were beneficial or dead ends; both courts were interested in the educational consequences of test use for students (see National Research Council, 1982). More generally, the courts' concern with tracking, remediation, and special education is plainly focused on whether or not students will receive enhanced and effective educational opportunities as a result of the educational intervention. Furthermore, complying with relevant professional testing standards reduces the risk of legal liability for high-stakes assessments.[6]

Claims That Tests Preserve the Effects of Prior Discrimination

The Supreme Court has long held that the Constitution forbids practices that, although seemingly neutral, serve to preserve, or carry forward, the effects of prior illegal school segregation. This suggests that it would be unlawful for school officials to use tests to track minority students, deny them high school diplomas, or retain them in grade if those students' low test scores are traceable to their having attended illegally segregated schools.

---

[6]Based on an analysis of relevant law, Phillips advises state and local education agencies involved in high-stakes testing to "[f]ollow professional standards in all technical matters, including, but not limited to, item development, item selection, validity, reliability, item bias review, equating, scaling, setting passing standards, test security, accommodations, test administration, scoring, and score reporting" (Phillips, 1993a:xxi).

Such claims were more common in the 1970s and 1980s than they are today. Since there are relatively few school districts that still enroll students who attended illegally segregated schools, this legal claim will be available in relatively few situations.[7]

The leading court decision on competency testing illustrates a "pre-serve the effects" approach. In the mid-1970s, Florida had adopted a minimum competency test that students needed to pass in order to receive high school diplomas. The failure rate among black students, 20 percent, was 10 times that for white students. Black high school juniors who had attended illegally segregated schools for the first five grades argued that the test results reflected the discrimination they had suffered and claimed that the diploma sanction served to preserve the effects of the prior illegal segregation. The appeals court agreed, ruling that Florida could begin to withhold diplomas from black students only four years later, when the students taking the test would not have attended illegally segregated schools (*Debra P. v. Turlington*, 1981; see also *Anderson v. Banks*, 1981). Courts in several judicial circuits have applied the same principle to many cases involving tracking,[8] particularly in the years after initial school desegregation.

If a state or school district has had a recent history of segregation or intentional discrimination, judges will scrutinize more closely test-use policies that produce disproportionate adverse impact. Even in formerly

---

[7]It is, however, one legal ground on which Mexican-American students in Texas are currently challenging the use of a state test as the basis for granting or withholding high school diplomas (*G.I. Forum v. Texas Education Agency*, 1997).

[8]In one leading case, an appeals court reviewed the use by a recently desegregated school district of an arrangement under which students were assigned to classes within schools on the basis of teacher evaluations. This produced racially identifiable classrooms at every grade level in virtually every school. The court held that even a neutral student classification system could not be used if "children who have been the victims of educational discrimination in the dual systems of the past . . . find themselves resegregated in any school . . . solely because they still wear a badge of their old deprivation—under-achievement" (*McNeal v. Tate County School District*, 1975). Courts have reached similar results with other student assignment procedures that preserve the effects of past discrimination. Examples include assignment to schools within a previously segregated system on the basis of standardized tests (*Singleton v. Jackson Municipal Separate School District*, 1970) (*en banc*), *rev'd per curiam on other grounds sub nom. Carter v. West Feliciana Parish School Board*, 1970); assignments to classes based on test scores and teacher recom-mendations (*United States v. Gadsden County School District*, 1978); and assignments to classes for students with mental retardation on the basis of IQ tests (*Hobson v. Hansen*, 1967; *aff'd sub nom. Smuck v. Hansen*, 1969) (*en banc*).

segregated school districts, however, there are several arguments that educators may invoke to defend the use of high-stakes tests that have racially disproportionate impact (*McNeal v. Tate County School District*, 1975). First, it is permissible to use such a test if the state or school district can demonstrate that enough time has passed that the racially disproportionate impact no longer results from prior illegal segregation. Such an argument succeeded in *Georgia State Conference of Branches of NAACP v. Georgia*, 1985, in which a circuit court allowed racially identifiable within-school student grouping because the black children in low-track classes had begun attending school only after the start of court-ordered desegregation.

Second, lower courts have ruled that it is permissible to use a classification mechanism that has disproportionate impact if the classes that are disproportionately minority provide bona fide remedial instruction—that is, if the consequences of tracking decisions are beneficial rather than adverse. Thus the *Debra P.* court approved remedial education programs for students who had failed Florida's competency test, even though most of the students needing remedial help were black, because it believed that the programs would help remedy the effects of prior illegal segregation. Although the court did not ask whether remedial classes constituted the most effective available placements, it mattered to the *Debra P.* court whether tracking decisions produced beneficial educational consequences for the students placed.

As noted from the outset, claims of this nature are increasingly rare, if only because there are fewer children each year who can show that they themselves attended illegally segregated schools. Nonetheless, recent court decisions, such as *Simmons on Behalf of Simmons v. Hooks* (1994),[9] and the fact that school desegregation cases remain active in many other jurisdictions, suggest that such claims remain viable in some communities.

Claims of Disparate Impact

Several federal civil rights statutes prohibit recipients of federal funds, including state education agencies and public school districts, from dis-

---

[9]In *Simmons*, the district court rejected the arguments of school officials who claimed that low-track placements were educationally beneficial for black children. The court also found no educational justification for grouping classes of children for all subjects (*Simmons on Behalf of Simons v. Hooks*, 1994).

criminating against students. Title VI of the Civil Rights Act of 1964 prohibits discrimination on the basis of race, color, or national origin, including limited English proficiency (*Lau v. Nichols*, 1974). Title IX of the Education Amendments of 1972 forbids sex discrimination, and two federal civil rights statutes[10] (discussed in Chapter 8) prohibit discrimination against students with disabilities.

These statutes forbid intentional discrimination against students, as does the Constitution's equal protection clause, but federal regulations go further: they provide that a federal fund recipient may not "utilize criteria or methods of administration which have the *effect* of subjecting individuals to discrimination."[11] In interpreting this Title VI regulation and similar regulations under Title IX, courts have drawn on interpretations of a federal employment discrimination statute, Title VII.[12]

This method of proving a legal violation is known as a disparate impact claim, and lower courts in many jurisdictions have recognized a three-part legal test for judging such claims (*Debra P. v. Turlington*, 1981; *Larry P. v. Riles*, 1984; *American Association of Mexican-American Educators v. California*, 1996).

First, plaintiffs must show by a preponderance of the evidence that some policy or practice, such as the use of a test, has disproportionate adverse impact on a protected group. Whether a test's impact is disproportionate is not always easy to determine;[13] generally, it depends on a comparison of the entire pool of test takers with those the test identifies

---

[10]Section 504 of the Rehabilitation Act of 1973, and Title II of the Americans with Disabilities Act of 1990.

[11]34 C.F.R. section 100.3(b)(2) [emphasis added].

[12] 42 U.S.C. 2000(e) *et seq.* Courts have generally applied the standards applicable to disparate impact cases under Title VII to disparate impact cases arising under Title VI: *Larry P. v. Riles*, 1984; *accord, New York Urban League, Inc. v. New York*, 1995; *Elston v. Talladega County Board of Education*, 1993; *Groves v. Alabama State Board of Education*, 1991; *Georgia State Conference of Branches of NAACP v. Georgia*, 1985.

[13]In some cases, the relevant question is whether the mean score for one group was lower than that for another group, or whether members of one group were *misclassified* at a significantly higher rate than members of another group (*Georgia State Conference of Branches of NAACP v. Georgia*, 1985). In other cases, courts have had to decide how to account for individuals who were discouraged from taking a test that they alleged was discriminatory: *Groves v. Alabama State Board of Education*, 1991. If it is impossible to determine the pool precisely, courts typically make informed estimates.

for some educational placement or treatment.[14] If statistical analysis shows that the success rate for members of a protected class is significantly lower (or the failure rate is significantly higher) than what would be expected from a random distribution, then the test has disproportionate *adverse* impact.[15]

Even if the plaintiffs can establish disparate impact, the case is not over; rather, the burden of proof shifts to the defendant to justify its policy or practice; according to the Supreme Court, the legal standard of justification is one of educational necessity (*Board of Education of New York v. Harris*, 1979:151).[16] Federal regulations do not define the term "educational necessity"; some lower courts interpret it to mean that defendants must show "a substantial legitimate justification" for the challenged policy or practice (*New York Urban League, Inc. v. New York*, 1995; *American Association of Mexican-American Educators v. California*, 1996), whereas others require proof of a "manifest relationship" between the policy or practice and the defendants' educational objectives (*Larry P. v. Riles*, 1984; *Sharif v. New York State Education Department*, 1989).

In the testing context, defendants can usually meet their burden of proof by showing that the test in question meets professional standards that apply given the purpose for which the test is being used. Thus, psychometric standards—those that apply generally and those that apply to particular test uses (see American Educational Research Association et al., 1985, 1998; Joint Committee on Testing Practices, 1988)—are also relevant in the legal context.

Courts have invoked such standards in upholding or invalidating

---

[14]In *American Association of Mexican-American Educators v. California* (1996), the plaintiffs argued that the appropriate pool was first-time test takers, whereas the defendants argued that cumulative, rather than first-time, pass rates should be used in determining whether the test had disproportionate adverse impact. The court ruled for the plaintiffs on this issue (*American Association of Mexican-American Educators v. California*, 1996:31, 38).

[15]Another common rule of thumb for assessing disparate impact is set forth in guidelines of the Equal Employment Opportunity Commission (1978); disparate impact is generally found if the success rate of a protected group is less than four-fifths, or 80 percent, of the rate at which the most highly selected group (usually whites or males) is selected (29 C.F.R. section 1607.4(D)). This standard was used in *American Association of Mexican-American Educators v. California* (1996), which involved a teacher certification test.

[16]This requirement is analogous to the "business necessity" requirement under Title VII that employers must show when tests for hiring or promotion have adverse impact.

particular test uses having disproportionate adverse impact. In a Title IX sex discrimination case, for example, a court invalidated New York's use of the Scholastic Assessment Test (SAT) as a measure of high school achievement, finding that "the SAT was not designed to measure achievement in high school and has never been validated for that purpose" (*Sharif v. New York State Education Department*, 1989:362). Similarly, a California court upheld the use of a test as part of the teacher certification process once it concluded that the test in question was a "valid, job-related test for the teaching and non-teaching positions in the public schools for which it is a requirement" and that cutoffs or cutscores had been set properly despite the disproportionate impact they produced (*American Association of Mexican-American Educators v. California*, 1996:1403).[17] Applying similar standards in a different context, a court struck down Alabama's use of a fixed cutoff score on the American College Test (ACT) for admission to undergraduate teacher education programs. The court found both that the ACT was not valid for the purpose for which it was being used and that cutscores had been set arbitrarily rather than on the basis of professionally accepted norms (*Groves v. Alabama State Board of Education*, 1991).[18]

Thus, under a disparate impact standard, legal liability may depend in part on whether the test raises problems of measurement, which may be the case if the test has not been validated for the particular purpose for which it is being used or has not been validated for all parts of the test-taking population (American Educational Research Association et al., 1998:12;[19] *Larry P. v. Riles*, 1984). It may also depend in part on whether

---

[17]This was based in part on the court's finding that the defendants (1) had reviewed with teacher educators and content experts items to be included on the test; (2) had conducted several content validation studies and job analysis surveys, revising the test to eliminate items that were found not to be job-related; and (3) had set cutoff scores using acceptable standards and procedures (*American Association of Mexican-American Educators v. California*, 1996: 1416-1417, 1420-21).

[18]"There is no rational basis, let alone any professional research or study . . . from which to infer that [students] scoring at or above this level will be competent to teach . . . while those failing to achieve a 16 will not . . ." *Groves v. Alabama State Board of Education*, 1991:1531).

[19]Standard 7.1 of the draft standards states that "[w]hen previous research has established a substantial prior probability that test scores may differ in meaning across examinee subgroups, then to the extent feasible, the same forms of validity evidence collected for the examinee population as a whole should also be collected for each relevant sub-

test users make high-stakes decisions about students based on one test score or on multiple factors; in *United States v. Fordice*, for example, the Supreme Court rejected Mississippi's exclusive reliance on ACT composite scores in making college admissions decisions because the *ACT User's Manual* called instead for admissions standards based on ACT subtest scores, self-reported high school grades, and other factors (*United States v. Fordice*, 1992; see also American Educational Research Association et al., 1985:Standard 8.12; 1998:Draft Standard 13.6).

Similarly, whether a particular test use is proper depends in part on making attributions of cause: "It is imperative to account for various 'plausible rival interpretations of low test performance [such as] anxiety, inattention, low motivation, fatigue, limited English proficiency, or certain sensory handicaps' other than low ability" (National Research Council, 1996a:4, quoting Messick, 1989; American Educational Research Association et al., 1998:Draft Standard 16).[20] Thus, for example, "if students with limited English proficiency are tested in English—in areas other than language arts—and then classified on the basis of their test scores . . . [t]his constitutes discrimination under Title VI" (National Research Council, 1996a:4, citing *Diana v. State Board of Education*, 1970).

Finally, the likelihood of an adverse court ruling increases if the consequence of test use is a low-quality program or placement rather than one that is "educationally necessary." For example, using a Title VI disparate impact analysis in *Larry P.*, the district court ruled that, although tests having predictive validity may be the basis for denying a job, "if tests suggest that a young child is probably going to be a poor student,

---

group . . . ." Draft Standard 7.2 states that "[w]hen the evidence indicates that the test does not measure the intended construct with equal fidelity across subgroups of test takers, the test should only be used for those subgroups for which the intended construct is reasonably well measured."

[20]Draft Standard 7.10 states that "[w]hen the use of a test results in outcomes that affect the life chances or educational opportunities of examinees, evidence of mean test score differences betweeen relevant subgroups of examinees should be examined. Where mean differences are found an investigation should be undertaken to determine that such differences are not attributable to a source of construct-underrepresentation or construct-irrelevant variance. In educational settings, potential differences in opportunity to learn should be investigated as a source of mean differences." See Chapters 4 to 7 for discussion of how these standards can be met in practice.

the school cannot on that basis alone deny the child the ability to improve and develop the academic skills necessary to success in our society"
(*Larry P. v. Riles*, 1979:969). Whether a particular educational placement or treatment is beneficial or harmful depends on empirical evidence
about that program and, in court, on a judge's interpretation of that
evidence.

Even if a state or school district can establish that its use of a test is
educationally necessary, plaintiffs may nonetheless prevail by showing
that there exists "an equally effective alternative that would result in less
disproportionality" (*Georgia State Conference of Branches of NAACP v.
Georgia*, 1985:1403). In the testing context, such showings have been
infrequent.[21]

English-Language Learners

Title VI covers situations in which educational tests have a disproportionate adverse effect on English-language learners (*Lau v. Nichols*,
1974). Therefore the general legal principles discussed above apply to
them as well. There are complexities, however, and Chapter 9 describes
many issues of test validity that can arise when English-language tests are
used to assess students whose native language is not English.[22] These
include norming bias, content bias, linguistic and cultural biases, and the
great difficulty of determining what bilingual students know in their native languages. The challenges involved in validating high-stakes tests
for English-language learners raise special concerns about compliance
with Title VI.

Such difficulties may also raise questions of compliance with two
other federal statutes. One is the Improving America's Schools Act of

---

[21]In the Georgia case, the court rejected the argument that heterogeneous grouping
was an equally effective alternative to tracking that would result in less disproportionality.
The court relied on testimony to the effect (1) that heterogenous grouping would be
harmful to higher-achieving students and (2) that "intraclass grouping is not as beneficial as interclass grouping" (*Georgia State Conference of Branches of NAACP v. Georgia*,
1985:1420). In *Sharif v. New York State Education Department* (1989), however, the court
declared that New York's exclusive reliance on SAT scores in awarding scholarships for
high school achievement was illegal, partly because a combination of students' grades
and scores had less disparate impact on the basis of sex.

[22]See also American Educational Research Association et al. (1998:Draft Standards,
section 9).

1994, which, as discussed more fully below, amends Title I of the Elementary and Secondary Education Act of 1965. A second federal statute that may be relevant is the Equal Educational Opportunities Act of 1974, which provides, in part, that

> No State shall deny equal educational opportunity to an individual on account of his or her race, color, sex, or national origin by . . .
>
> (f) the failure by an educational agency to take appropriate steps to overcome language barriers that impede equal participation by its students in its instructional programs.

There is no reported decision in which a court has invalidated a high-stakes test use under this statute. Nonetheless, given the difficulties involved in assessing English-language learners, such a claim could be available if tests of questionable validity were used as the basis for making placement or promotion decisions for such students, or if the resulting educational settings were of questionable educational value.

Chapter 9 discusses more fully both (1) the challenges of assessing English-language learners validly, particularly when tests have high-stakes consequences for students and (2) what is known about accommodations that may increase the validity of such tests.

DUE PROCESS CHALLENGES TO HIGH-STAKES TESTS

High-stakes tests may be illegal even if they are not discriminatory. For example, high school graduation tests have been challenged successfully under the due process provisions of the U.S. Constitution (Fifth and Fourteenth Amendments). Such claims usually hinge either on whether students have received sufficient advance notice of high-stakes test requirements or on whether they have been taught the knowledge and skills that a high-stakes test measures. These claims rest on the proposition that students have a constitutionally protected property interest in receiving diplomas (*Debra P. v. Turlington*, 1981).

Adequate Notice

One concern, first raised in the context of high-stakes graduation tests, is that school officials must ensure fairness by giving students prior notice of a new high-stakes assessment requirement. In *Debra P. v. Turlington* (1981), the court found that four years constituted sufficient notice; courts in Georgia and New York have found that two years did *not* constitute adequate notice (Phillips, 1996a). As to the content of such notice (p. 6):

> [I]t is probably not necessary to communicate specific passing scores ahead of time, [but] students and school personnel should be provided with clear indications of the specific content . . . and performance for which they will be held accountable. General scoring guidelines and examples that demonstrate attainment of the standards should also be disseminated. Curricular frameworks, assessment specifications, sample tasks, and model answers may also be helpful in communicating expectations.

And although the issue has not been litigated to date, similar notice may be called for when states or school districts are adopting new high-stakes tests for promotion.

Curricular Validity

A second due process requirement concerns what the *Debra P.* court referred to as "curricular validity": "a state may condition the receipt of a public school diploma on the passing of a test so long as it is a fair test of that which was taught" (*Debra P. v. Turlington*, 1981:406).[23]

There have been disagreements over how educational entities can demonstrate that a test measures what students have been taught. Some argue that it is sufficient for a state or school district to show that the formal written curriculum mentions the knowledge and skills that the test is designed to measure. Others assert that what matters most is not the formal written curriculum but the actual curriculum and instruction in each classroom (Madaus, 1983)—that instructional rather than curricular validity is required. The *Debra P.* court accepted something in between: evidence that the test measured skills included in the official curriculum coupled with a showing that most teachers considered the skills to be ones they should teach (*Debra P.*, 1983:186). Similar evidence may be called for when a high-stakes test for promotion is involved.

The matter of curricular or instructional validity has several important implications for high-stakes testing of individual students. First, to the extent that new assessments designed to induce changes in curriculum and instruction are used for high-stakes purposes, there is a danger

---

[23]Conceptually, a claim that students have not been taught what the test measures is similar to a claim that students have been denied a fair opportunity to learn.

that the new instruments will lack the curricular or instructional validity that the Constitution requires. This is an important point, of which educators and policymakers must be aware as they design and implement new assessments. Use of the proposed voluntary national test for high-stakes purposes, although not recommended by the U.S. Department of Education, would almost certainly raise questions of this kind, if only because it would take time for states and school districts to align their curricula and their teaching with the requirements of a national test.

Policymakers who wish to use tests for high-stakes purposes must therefore allow enough time for such alignment to occur. The time needed, probably several years, would in practice depend on several factors, including the extent of the initial discrepancy and the availability of resources needed to bring curriculum and instruction into alignment with the new standards.

A second concern, potentially at odds with the first, is that administrators and teachers, wishing to ensure curricular and instructional validity, may teach students the very material that is on the test. "[I]f test exercises are used in instruction, the usefulness of the test as an instrument for measuring student achievement is destroyed . . . [and if] there is too close a match between the instructional materials and the test, 'the capacity to measure such important constructs as the understanding of a topic may be lost'" (Linn, 1983:127).

According to Linn, "the challenge [is] to convince the courts that knowledge was taught—without precluding the possibility of measuring it" (Linn, 1983:129). The fine line between what is required and what is impermissible—coupled with the existence of incentives to boost student scores by "teaching to the test"—suggests the need for careful policy-making, teacher training, and test security measures.

REQUIREMENTS OF THE IMPROVING AMERICA'S SCHOOLS ACT

The Improving America's Schools Act of 1994 made major changes in Title I, which serves millions of low-achieving students, chiefly though not entirely at the elementary level. Among the most important modifications are new requirements relating to testing and accountability. "[S]tates will need to develop their own assessments for Title I and ensure that they are aligned with challenging state standards for content and performance linked to state reforms affecting all students" (National Research Council, 1996b:vii). The stated purpose of the change in federal law is "to enable schools to provide opportunities for children served to acquire the knowledge and skills contained in the challenging content standards and to meet challenging state performance standards for all children (Improving America's Schools Act, 20 U.S.C. section 6301(d), 1994)." It requires that Title I students receive "accelerated," "enriched," and "high-quality" curricula, "effective instructional strategies," "highly qualified instructional staff," and "high-quality" staff development[24] (Weckstein, in press).

Under the new law, states had until the 1997-1998 school year to set content and performance standards, and they still have until the 2000-2001 school year to adopt new systems of assessment. There is wide recognition that "creating a new Title I testing system is one of the most demanding aspects of the new law" (National Research Council, 1996b: vii). The assessments (p. 1-2):

> must be administered at some time during grades 3 through 5, 6 through 9, and 10 through 12 . . . . Moreover, such assessments must also (1) be used only for purposes for which they are valid and reliable; (2) be consistent with nationally recognized professional and technical standards; (3) to the extent practicable, assess limited-English proficient children in the language and form most likely to yield accurate and reliable information on what such students know and can do; [and] (4) make reasonable adaptations for students with diverse learning needs.

Moreover, states will have to define what constitutes acceptable yearly progress for Title I students and work with school districts to take corrective action regarding schools and teachers (not students) when progress is insufficient.

It remains to be seen how states will satisfy the many objectives of Title I testing. The tests used to assess Title I students may become the subject of legal challenges if they do not meet the requirements of the Improving America's Schools Act. Questions have arisen, for example, about whether the proposed voluntary national tests will satisfy requirements governing assessment of Title I students who are English-language learners or students with disabilities (Hoff, 1997).

---

[24]Improving America's Schools Act, 20 U.S.C. sections 6314(b)(1),(a), 6315(c)(1), 6320 (a)(1), 1994.

CONCLUSION AND IMPLICATIONS

In reviewing the circumstances under which the law may define certain high-stakes test uses as discriminatory or inappropriate, we have relied in part on psychometric definitions of appropriate test use. Subsequent chapters of this report discuss more fully what constitutes psychometrically appropriate use of tests for student tracking, promotion, and graduation.

Because psychometric issues can play an important role in the determination of test legality under federal civil rights law, it is appropriate to consider here the advice that the National Research Council's Board on Testing and Assessment (BOTA), through a letter report, has offered the U.S. Department of Education's Office for Civil Rights as it drafts its own standards on fairness in testing.

The letter report notes that "establishing the validity of test scores as a basis for classifying students and placing them in different educational programs poses [a] . . . formidable challenge" (National Research Council, 1996a:3). It goes on to point out that "[t]he inferences regarding specific test uses are validated, not the test itself . . . . Because of the importance of linking test design to specific test uses, validation must be designed to provide evidence that test results provide a sound basis for inferences and action. Test validation is often costly, but it is a critical undertaking" (National Research Council, 1996a:5, citing Office of Technology Assessment, 1992).

More generally, the letter report states that, in reviewing the use of tests with disparate impact to classify students, the Office for Civil Rights "should make a determination not only about the test itself but about whether the entire process for classifying students is fair and nondiscriminatory and whether students are being provided an equal opportunity to learn" (National Research Council, 1996a:3).[25]

In the committee's view, although litigation over test use has not been common, the increasing reliance on high-stakes tests as an instrument of school reform could lead to new legal challenges by individuals and groups who are adversely affected by test outcomes. Given the need to establish the validity of these high-stakes uses, including the need to

---

[25]This is consistent with Draft Standard 7.10 (1998:16), which states that "[i]n educational settings, potential differences in opportunity to learn should be investigated as a source of mean differences."

show that such tests are a fair measure of what has been taught, it is essential that educators and policymakers alike be aware of both the letter of the laws and their implications for test takers and test users.

REFERENCES

American Educational Research Association, American Psychological Association, and National Council on Measurement in Education
  1985   *Standards for Educational and Psychological Testing.* Washington, DC: American Psychological Association.
  1998   *Draft Standards for Educational and Psychological Testing.* Washington, DC: American Psychological Association.
Hoff, D.
  1997   National tests, Title I at odds on language: Some experts see mismatch in policy. *Education Week*, October 22, 1997:1,15.
Joint Committee on Testing Practices
  1988   *Code of Fair Testing Practices in Education.* Washington, DC: National Council on Measurement in Education.
Linn, R.L.
  1983   Curricular validity: Convincing the court that it was taught without precluding the possibility of measuring it. Pp. 115-132 in *The Courts, Validity, and Minimum Competency Testing*, G. Madaus, ed. Boston: Kluwer-Nijhoff Publishing.
Madaus, G., ed.
  1983   *The Courts, Validity, and Minimum Competency Testing.* Boston: Kluwer-Nijhoff Publishing.
Messick, S.
  1989   Validity. Pp. 13-102 in *Educational Measurement*, 3rd Edition, R.L. Linn, ed. New York: American Council on Education and Macmillan Publishing Company.
National Research Council
  1982   *Placing Children in Special Education: A Strategy for Equity*, K.A. Heller, W.H. Holtzman, and S. Messick, eds. Committee on Child Development Research and Public Policy, National Research Council. Washington, DC: National Academy Press.
  1996a   *Letter Report from Richard Shavelson, Chair, Board on Testing and Assessment, to Norma Cantu, Assistant Secretary of Education for Civil Rights* (June 10, 1996). Washington, DC: National Academy of Sciences.
  1996b   *Title I Testing and Assessment: Challenging Standards for Disadvantaged Children*, J. Kober and M. Feuer, eds. Board on Testing and Assessment. Washington, DC: National Academy Press.
Office of Technology Assessment
  1992   *Testing in American Schools: Asking the Right Questions.* OTA-SET-519. Washington, DC: U.S. Government Printing Office.

Phillips, S.E.
　1991　Diploma sanction tests revisited: New problems from old solutions. *Journal of Law and Education* 20(2):175-199.
　1993a　*Legal Implications of High-Stakes Assessment: What States Should Know.* Oak Brook, IL: North Central Regional Educational Laboratory.
　1993b　Legal issues in performance assessment. *Education Law Reporter* 79: 709-738.
　1996a　Legal defensibility of standards: Issues and policy perspectives. *Educational Measurement and Practice 5*, Summer 1996:5-14.
　1996b　Legal defensibility of standards: Issues and policy perspectives. *Proceedings of the Joint Conference on Standard Setting for Large-Scale Assessments*, September 1996:379-398.
Weckstein, P.
　in press　School reform and enforceable rights to an adequate education. In *Law and School Reform: Six Strategies for Promoting Educational Equity*, J. Heubert, ed. New Haven: Yale University Press.
Welner, K., and J. Oakes
　1996　(Li)Ability grouping: The new susceptibility of school tracking systems to legal challenges. *Harvard Educational Review* 66(3):451-470.

LEGAL REFERENCES

American Association of Mexican-American Educators v. California, 937 F. Supp. 1397 (N.D. Cal. 1996).

Anderson v. Banks, 540 F. Supp. 472 (S.D. Ga. 1981).

Board of Education of New York v. Harris, 444 U.S. 130 (1979).

Crawford v. Honig, 37 F.3d 485 (9th Cir. 1994).

Debra P. v. Turlington, 474 F. Supp. 244 (M.D. Fla. 1979); *aff'd in part and rev'd in part*, 644 F.2d 397 (5th Cir. 1981); *rem'd*, 564 F. Supp. 177 (M.D. Fla. 1983); *aff'd*, 730 F.2d 1405 (11th Cir. 1984).

Diana v. State Board of Education, No. C-70-37 RFP, Consent Decree (N.D. Cal. June 18, 1973).

Equal Educational Opportunities Act of 1974, 20 U.S.C. sections 1703 *et seq.*

Equal Employment Opportunity Commission, Uniform Guidelines on Employment Selection Procedures, 29 C.F.R. sections 1607 *et seq.* (1978).

Elston v. Talladega County Board of Education, 997 F.2d 1394 (11th Cir. 1993).

Georgia State Conference of Branches of NAACP v. Georgia, 775 F.2d 1403 (11th Cir. 1985).

G.I. Forum v. Texas Education Agency, C.A. No. SA97CA1278, Complaint (W.D. Tex. October 14, 1997).

Groves v. Alabama State Board of Education, 776 F. Supp. 1518 (M.D. Ala. 1991).

Hobson v. Hansen, 269 F. Supp. 401 (D.D.C. 1967), *aff'd sub nom. Smuck v. Hansen*, 408 F.2d 175 (D.C. Cir. 1969) (*en banc*).

Improving America's Schools Act of 1994.

Individuals with Disabilities Education Act, 20 U.S.C. section 1401 *et seq.*

Larry P. v. Riles, 495 F. Supp. 926 (N.D. Cal. 1979); *aff'd*, 793 F.2d 969 (9th Cir. 1984).

Lau v. Nichols, 414 U.S. 563 (1974).

McNeal v. Tate County School District, 508 F.2d 1017 (5th Cir. 1975).
New York Urban League, Inc. v. New York, 71 F.3d 1031 (2d Cir. 1995).
Parents in Action on Special Education (PASE) v. Hannon, 506 F. Supp. 831 (N.D. Ill. 1980).
People Who Care v. Rockford Board of Education, 111 F.3d 528 (7th Cir. 1997).
Personnel Administrator v. Feeney, 442 U.S. 256 (1979).
Quarles v. Oxford Municipal Separate School Dist., 868 F.2d 750 (5th Cir. 1989).
Section 504 of the Rehabilitation Act of 1973, 29 U.S.C. sections 794 *et seq.*
Sharif v. New York State Education Department, 709 F. Supp. 345 (S.D.N.Y. 1989).
Simmons on Behalf of Simmons v. Hooks, 843 F. Supp. 1296 (E.D. Ark. 1994)
Singleton v. Jackson Municipal Separate School District, 419 F.2d 1211 (5th Cir.) (en banc), rev'd per curiam on other grounds sub nom. *Carter v. West Feliciana Parish School Board*, 396 U.S. 290 (1970).
Title I, Elementary and Secondary Education Act, 20 U.S.C. sections 6301 *et seq.*
Title II, Americans with Disabilities Act of 1990, 42 U.S.C. sections 12131 *et seq.*
Title VI, Civil Rights Act of 1964, 42 U.S.C. sections 2000(d) *et seq.*
Title VI Regulations, 34 C.F.R. sections 100 *et seq.*
Title VII, Civil Rights Act of 1964, 42 U.S.C. sections 2000(e) *et seq.*
Title IX, Education Amendments of 1972, 20 U.S.C. sections 1681 *et seq.*
U.S. Constitution, Amendments V and XIV.
United States v. Fordice, 505 U.S. 717 (1992).
United States v. Gadsden County School District, 572 F.2d 1049 (5th Cir. 1978).
Village of Arlington Heights v. Metropolitan Housing Development Corp., 429 U.S. 252 (1977).
Washington v. Davis, 426 U.S. 229 (1976).

4

Tests as Measurements

The high-stakes decisions for individual students on which this report focuses—tracking, promotion and retention, and graduation or denial of high school diplomas—have profound implications for the development and future life chances of young people. Tests used for such high-stakes purposes must therefore meet professional standards of *reliability*, *validity*, and *fairness*.

In this chapter, we examine these key concepts of testing to provide a basis for the discussion in the rest of the report of the psychometrics of particular high-stakes uses of tests. In addition, the principles of reliability, validity, and fairness in testing have been codified in various forms by professional organizations, and these codes are also addressed in this chapter. Although reliability and fairness are in fact aspects of the overarching concept of validity, the three concepts are addressed in turn to highlight their distinctive features.

In the simplest terms, *reliability* refers to the stability or reproducibility of a test's results. A test is highly reliable if a student taking it on two different occasions will get two very similar if not identical scores. The key issue of reliability, then, is to establish that *something* is being measured with a certain degree of consistency.

The key issue of *validity* is to determine the nature of that something—specifically, whether the test measures what it purports to measure and what meaning can be drawn from the results—and whether the conclusions and inferences drawn from the test results are appropriate.

Fairness incorporates not just technical issues of reliability and validity but also social values of equity and justice—for example, whether a test systematically underestimates the knowledge or skill of members of a particular group.

RELIABILITY OF MEASUREMENT

Reliability is typically estimated in one of three ways. One is to estimate the consistency of a test's results on different occasions, as explained above. A second way is to examine consistency across parallel forms of a test, which are developed to be equivalent in content and technical characteristics. That is, to what extent does performance on one form of the test correlate with performance on a parallel form? A third way is to determine how consistently examinees perform across similar items or subsets of items, intended to measure the same knowledge or skill, within a single test form. This concept of reliability is called internal consistency.

For judgmentally scored tests, such as essays, another widely used index is the coefficient of scorer reliability, which addresses consistency across different observers, raters, or scorers. That is, do the scores assigned by one judge using a set of designated rating criteria agree with those given by another judge using the same criteria?

How reliable must a test be? That depends on the nature of the *construct*—that is, the abstract skill, attribute, or domain of knowledge—being measured. For a very homogeneous, narrow construct, such as adding two-digit numbers, internal-consistency reliability should be extremely high. We would expect somewhat less high reliability for a more heterogeneous, broad construct, such as algebra, given the same length test. Measures of certain constructs, such as mood or anxiety (that is, states as opposed to traits), are generally less stable; thus high reliability would not be expected.

For most purposes, a more useful index than reliability is the *standard error of measurement*, which is related to the *un*reliability of a test. This index defines a range of likely variation, or uncertainty, around the test score—similar to when public opinion polls report a margin of error of plus or minus x points. The standard error thus quantifies and makes explicit the uncertainty involved in interpreting a student's level of performance; for example, "We can be 95 percent confident that this student's true score falls between x and y." This degree of uncertainty is particularly important to take into account when test scores are used to make high-stakes decisions about individual students.

VALIDITY OF TEST INTERPRETATION AND USE

Validity asks what a test is measuring, and what meaning can be drawn from the results. Hence, what is to be validated is not the test per se but rather the inferences derived from the test scores and the actions that follow (Cronbach, 1971).

On one hand, for example, the validity of a proficiency test can be subverted by inappropriate test preparation, such as having students practice on the actual test items or teaching students testwise strategies that might increase test scores without actually improving the skills the test is intended to measure. On the other hand, test preparation that familiarizes students with the test format and reduces anxiety may actually improve validity: scores that formerly were invalidly low because of anxiety might now become validly higher (Messick, 1982).

In essence, then, test validation is an empirical evaluation of test meaning and use. It is both a scientific and a rhetorical process, requiring both evidence and argument. Because the meaning of a test score is a *construction* based on an understanding of the performance underlying the score, as well as the pattern of relationships with other variables, the literature of psychometrics views the fundamental issue as *construct validity*.

The major threats to construct validity are *construct underrepresentation* (the test does not capture important aspects of the construct) and *construct irrelevance* (the test measures more than its intended construct). Test validation seeks evidence and arguments to discount these two threats and to evaluate the actions that are taken as a result of the scores.

Six Aspects of Construct Validity

Evaluating the validity of a test requires attention to a number of interrelated and persistent questions, such as:

- Are the right things being measured in the right balance?

- Is the scoring system consistent with the structure of the domain about which inferences or predictions are being made?
- Are the scores reliable and consistent across the different contexts for which they are used, as well as across different population groups?
- Are the scores applied fairly for the proposed purposes—that is, consistently and equitably across individuals and groups?
- What are the short- and long-term consequences of score interpretation and use?
- Are the consequences supportive of the general purposes for giving the test in the first place?

Validity is now widely viewed as an integral or unified concept (American Educational Research Association et al., 1985). Therefore, establishing validity requires the collection and integration of multiple complementary forms of evidence to answer an interdependent set of questions, such as those above. Nevertheless, differentiating validity into its several distinct aspects can clarify issues and nuances that might otherwise be downplayed or overlooked.

One useful way of looking at validity is to distinguish aspects of construct validity: *content, substantive, structural, generalizable, external,* and *consequential.* In effect, these six aspects function as general validity criteria or standards for all educational and psychological measurement (Messick, 1989, 1995). Taken together, these aspects of construct validity incorporate the three standards for test use named in Chapter 1—that is, appropriate measurement, appropriate attribution of cause, and appropriate treatment. In subsequent chapters, examples of the types of evidence that might be collected to address each of the six are provided in the context of using test scores for tracking, promotion, and graduation decisions.

The *content* aspect of construct validity (Lennon, 1956; Messick, 1989) refers to the extent to which test content represents an appropriate sample of the skills and knowledge that are the goals of instruction. Key issues here are specifying the boundaries of the content domain to be assessed and selecting tasks that are representative, so that all important parts of the domain are covered. Experts usually make these judgments. Also of concern here is the technical quality of the test items—for example, is the reading level appropriate and is the phrasing unambiguous?

The *substantive* aspect refers to the cognitive processes that underlie student performance and correlations across items. This aspect of validity calls for models of the cognitive processes required by the tasks

(Embretson, 1983), as well as empirical evidence that test takers are in fact using those processes. Note these two important points: the need for tests to assess *processes* in addition to the traditional coverage of *content* and the need to move beyond traditional professional judgment of content to accrue empirical evidence that the assumed processes are actually at work (Embretson, 1983; Loevinger, 1957; Messick, 1989). For instance, it would be desirable to have evidence that a test item intended to measure problem solving does in fact tap those skills and not just elicit a memorized solution. One way to collect such evidence during test development might be to observe a sample of students and ask them to think aloud as they work the test items.

The *structural* aspect (Loevinger, 1957; Messick, 1989) appraises the degree to which the score scales are consistent with the structure of the domain being measured. The theory of the construct domain should guide not only the creation of assessment tasks but also the development of scoring criteria. For example, on a test of American history and government, an item dealing with the functions of the judiciary might be weighted more heavily than an item asking the date of the Gadsden purchase.

The *generalizable* aspect examines the extent to which scores and interpretations are consistent across assessment tasks, populations, and settings (Cook and Campbell, 1979; Feldt and Brennan, 1989; Shulman, 1970). An assessment should provide representative coverage of the content and processes of the domain being tested, so that the score is a valid measure of the student's knowledge of the broader construct, not just the particular sample of items on the test. For instance, a test might require students to write short essays on several topics, each with a particular purpose and audience in mind. The degree to which one can generalize about a student's writing skill from such a test depends on the strength of the correlations between the tasks focusing on different topics and genres.

In one sense, this aspect of validity intersects with reliability: it refers to the consistency of performance across the tasks, occasions, and raters of a particular assessment (Feldt and Brennan, 1989). But in a second sense, generalizable validity refers to *transfer*, that is, the consistency of performance across tasks that are representative of the broader construct domain. Transfer refers to the range of tasks that performance on the tested tasks facilitates the learning of—or, more generally, is predictive of (Ferguson, 1956).

The issue of generalizable validity is particularly relevant to so-called performance assessments, which are designed to measure higher-order thinking skills in real-world contexts. Examples of performance assessments include writing an essay, conducting an experiment, and solving an open-ended mathematical problem and explaining one's reasoning. Performance assessments tend to involve a small number of tasks, each of which takes a lot of time. Thus, there is a conflict in performance assessment between time-intensive depth of examination on any one task and the number of tasks needed for broad domain coverage. This problem must be carefully negotiated in designing performance assessments (Wiggins, 1993).

The *external* aspect of construct validity refers to the extent to which performance on a test is related to external variables. These correlations may be either high or low; they are predicted by the theory underlying the construct being assessed (Campbell and Fiske, 1959; Cronbach and Gleser, 1965). *Convergent evidence* shows that the test measure in question is in fact related to other variables that it should, theoretically, relate to. For example, a test of math computation would be expected to correlate highly with whether a person can make correct change in a cashier's job. *Discriminant evidence* shows that the measure is not unduly related to other measures. Other things being equal (e.g. testing conditions, reliability of the measures), a computation test should not correlate as highly with a reading test as with another computation test.

It is especially important to examine the external relationships between test scores and criterion measures (that is, the desired behaviors that the test is intended to indicate or predict) when using test scores for selection, placement, certification of competence, program evaluation, and other kinds of accountability. So, for instance, before a college admissions officer uses a test to make decisions, she must have evidence that there is indeed a relationship between scores on that test and performance in college course work.

The *consequential* aspect—which corresponds most directly to the third of the three standards for test use named in Chapter 1, appropriate treatment—includes evidence and rationales for evaluating the intended and unintended consequences of score interpretation and use in both the short and long terms. Ideally, there should be no adverse consequences associated with bias in scoring and interpretation, with unfairness in test use, or with negative effects on teaching and learning (Messick, 1980, 1989). Test makers view it as their responsibility to minimize negative impact on individuals or groups due to any source of test invalidity, such as construct underrepresentation or construct-irrelevant variance (Messick, 1989). That is, validity is compromised when the assessment is missing something relevant to the focal construct that, if present, would have permitted the affected examinees to display their competence. Similarly, scores may be invalidly low because the measurement contains something irrelevant that interferes with the examinees' demonstration of competence.

In contrast, adverse consequences associated with the accurate measure of an individual's knowledge or skills—such as low scores resulting from poor teaching or limited opportunity to learn—are not the test makers' responsibility but that of the test users. Adverse consequences that result from such test scores represent problems not of measurement but of something else, such as teaching or social policy.

It is important that a strong set of validity evidence be collected when there are high individual stakes attached to test use. It should be clear that test validity cannot rely on any single one of these complementary forms of evidence. Neither does overall validity require a high level of every form, if there is good evidence supporting score meaning. What is required is a compelling argument that the available evidence justifies the test interpretation and use, even though some pertinent evidence may be lacking.

Validity as Integrative Summary

The six aspects of construct validity explained above apply to all educational and psychological measurement, including performance and other alternative assessments. Taken together, they provide a way of addressing the multiple and interrelated validity questions that need to be answered in justifying score interpretation and use. This is what is meant by validity as a unified concept.

One can set priorities about the forms of evidence needed to justify the inferences drawn from test scores (Kane, 1992; Shepard, 1993). The key point is that the six aspects of construct validity provide a means of checking that the rationale or argument that supports a particular test use touches the important bases. If not, an argument should be provided that explains why such omissions are defensible.

It should be clear that what needs to be validated is not the test in general or in the abstract, but rather each inference that is made from the test scores and each specific use to which the test is put. Although there is a natural tendency to use existing tests for new and different purposes, each new purpose must be validated in its own right.

FAIRNESS IN TESTING

There remains one overarching issue related to the validity of test use: fairness. Fairness, like validity, is not just a psychometric issue. It is also a social value, and there are alternative views about its essential features. In regard to test use, the core meaning of fairness we are concerned with here is *comparable validity:* a fair test is one that yields comparably valid scores from person to person, group to group, and setting to setting (Willingham, 1998). So, for example, if an assessment results in scores that substantially underestimate or overestimate the knowledge or skills of members of a particular group, then the test would be considered unfair. If an assessment claims to measure a single construct across groups, but in fact measures different constructs in different groups, it would also be unfair.

Alternative Views of Fairness

There are alternative views of fairness, but most relate to the central idea of comparable validity. For instance, the 1998 revision, *Draft Standards for Educational and Psychological Testing* (American Educational Research Association et al., 1998) cites four alternative views of fairness found in the technical and popular literature. Two of these views characterize fairness, respectively, as the absence of bias and as equitable treatment of all examinees in the testing process.

Bias is said to arise when deficiencies in the test itself result in different meanings for scores earned by members of different identifiable subgroups. For example, a test intended to measure verbal reasoning should include words in general use, not words and expressions associated with, for example, particular cultures or locations, as this might unfairly advantage test takers from these cultural or geographical groups. If these words or expressions are not removed from the test, then the unfair advantage could result in a lack of comparable score meaning across groups of test takers.

Fairness as equitable treatment of all examinees in the testing process requires that examinees be given a comparable opportunity to demonstrate their understanding of the construct(s) the assessment is intended to measure. Fair treatment includes such factors as appropriate testing conditions, opportunity to become familiar with the test format, and access to practice materials. There is broad consensus that tests should be free from bias and that all examinees should be treated fairly in the testing process itself.

The third view found in the literature characterizes fairness in terms of opportunity to learn. Opportunity to learn is an important issue to consider when evaluating the comparability of score meaning across groups. For example, if two classes of students are given the same test, and students from class A have been previously taught the material whereas students from class B have not, then the resulting scores would have different meanings for the two groups. Opportunity to learn is especially relevant in the context of high-stakes assessments of what a test taker knows or can do as a result of formal instruction. If some test takers have not had the opportunity to learn the material covered by the test, they are more likely to get low scores. These scores may accurately reflect their knowledge, but only because they have not had the opportunity to learn the material tested. In this instance, using these test scores as a basis for a high-stakes decision, such as withholding a high school diploma, would be viewed as unfair. The issue of opportunity to learn is discussed further in Chapters 6 and 7.

The fourth view of fairness involves equality of testing outcomes. But the idea that fairness requires overall passing rates to be equal across groups is not generally accepted in the professional literature. This is because unequal test outcomes among groups do not in themselves signify test unfairness: tests may validly document group differences that are real and may be reflective in part of unequal opportunity to learn (as discussed above). There is consensus, however, that a test should not systematically underpredict the performance of any group.

One final point needs to be made here. In discussing fairness, it is important to distinguish between *equality* (the state of being the same) and *equity* (justness or fairness) and to recognize that not all inequalities are inequities. Indeed, in education as in medicine, the watchword should not be equal treatment, but rather treatment appropriate to the characteristic and sufficient to the need (Gordon, 1998). This brings us to the issue of allowing room for accommodations to the different needs of students.

Equity and Accommodations in the Testing Process

The issue of equity and the need for testing accommodations goes directly to the heart of comparable construct validity and the fairness of the testing process. It is important to distinguish two kinds of comparability. One, called *score comparability*, means that the properties of scores, such as reliabilities, internal patterns of relationships between items, and external relationships with other variables, are comparable across groups and settings. Score comparability is important in justifying uniform score interpretation and use for different groups and in different circumstances.

The other kind, called *task comparability*, means that the tested task elicits the same cognitive processes across different groups and different circumstances. Within task comparability, two types of processes may be distinguished: those that are relevant to the construct measured and those that are ancillary to the construct but nonetheless involved in task performance. Comparability of construct-relevant processes is necessary to sustain common score meaning across groups and contexts.

Ancillary processes may be modified without jeopardizing score meaning. This provides a fair and legitimate basis for accommodating tests to the needs of students with disabilities and those who are English-language learners (Willingham et al., 1988). For example, a fair accommodation might be to read a mathematics test aloud to a student with certain disabilities, because reading is ancillary to the construct being measured (mathematics), whereas it would not be fair to read a reading test aloud. The availability of multimedia test presentation and response modes on computers promises an accommodation to serve the needs of certain students with disabilities, such as visually impaired and hearing-impaired students (Bennett, 1998).

Thus, comparable validity—and test fairness—do not require identical task conditions, but rather common construct-relevant processes, with ignorable construct-irrelevant or ancillary processes that may be different across individuals and groups. Such accommodations, of course, have to be justified with evidence that score meaning and properties have not been unduly eroded in the process.

Fairness Issues Throughout the Testing Process

Fairness, like validity, cannot be properly addressed as an afterthought once the test has been developed, administered, and used. It must be confronted throughout the interconnected phases of the testing process, from test design and development to administration, scoring, interpretation, and use. Indeed, one of the most critical fairness issues occurs at the design stage: the choice of constructs to measure. For example, consider the possible test requirements for awarding high school diplomas. If the test emphasizes reading and writing rather than science and mathematics, then graduation rates for males and females, as well as for language-minority students, will be quite different (Willingham and Cole, 1997). Any finite number of subjects covered by the test are likely to yield different graduation rates for different groups because they underrepresent the broad construct of school learning and because students have different opportunities to learn. Some alternatives are to assess school learning more comprehensively, to use more than one assessment mode (high school grades as well as test scores), and to justify any limited choice of subjects in terms of the social values of the school and the community.

There are other fairness considerations in test design, such as the format of the items (short-answer versus multiple-choice) and the contexts in which items are cast, which may be more familiar to some examinees than to others. Bias in test questions is usually addressed empirically by examining whether individuals having the same knowledge level (as defined by their overall score on the test) but from different groups have different probabilities of getting a particular question correct.

Fairness issues arise in the administration of tests because of non-standard testing conditions, such as those related to the environment (lighting, space, temperature) and the directions given to students, that may disadvantage some examinees. Fairness is also an issue whenever scoring is not completely objective, as with the hand-scoring of constructed-response items, or when raters are influenced by group-related characteristics of an examinee that are irrelevant to the construct and purpose of the test.

There is an inherent conflict of interest when teachers administer high-stakes tests to their own students or score their own students' exams. On one hand, teachers want valid information about how well their students are performing. On the other hand, there is often substantial external pressure on teachers (as well as principals and other school personnel) for their students to earn high scores. This external pressure may lead some teachers to provide inappropriate assistance to their students before and during the test administration or to mis-score exams.

Fairness issues related to test use include relying unduly on a single score and basing decisions on an underrepresented view of the relevant construct (Willingham, 1998). In contexts in which tests are used to make predictions of subsequent performance (e.g., grades), fairness also requires comparability of predictions for different groups. The latter concern is particularly important in the case of tests used for placement, such as tracking and some types of promotion decisions. For such uses, there should be evidence that the relationships between scores on the test and subsequent performance in certain tracks or at a certain grade level are comparable from group to group.[1]

In conclusion, what needs to be comparable across groups and settings for fair test use is score meaning and the actions that follow. That is, test fairness derives from comparable construct validity (which may draw on all six aspects of validity discussed earlier). These issues of fairness surrounding test use are explored in greater detail in Chapters 5, 6, and 7.

CODIFIED STANDARDS

The issue of testing standards is not new, and there have been a number of useful documents over the years attempting to codify the principles of good practice. The most recent efforts bearing on the educational uses of tests include the *Standards for Educational and Psychological Testing* of the American Educational Research Association, the American Psychological Association, and the National Council on Measurement in Education (1985), currently under revision; the *Code of Fair Testing Practices in Education* (Joint Committee on Testing Practices, 1988); *Responsibilities of Users of Standardized Tests* (Association for Mea-

---

[1]Considerable attention has been given to developing fair selection models in the context of college admissions and job entry. These models put a heavy emphasis on predictive validity (the extent to which test scores predict some desired future performance) but at the expense of other aspects of construct validity. In one way or another, all of the fair selection models address the possibility of differences in the predictor-criterion relationship for different groups (Cleary, 1968; Cole, 1973; Linn, 1973; Thorndike, 1971). With the recognition that fundamental value differences are at issue in fair selection, several utility models were developed that go beyond these selection models in that they require specific value positions to be articulated (Cronbach, 1976; Gross and Su, 1975; Petersen and Novick, 1976; Sawyer et al., 1976). In this way, social values are incorporated explicitly into the measurement technology involved in selection models. The need to make values explicit does not, however, determine or make easier the hard choices among them.

surement and Evaluation in Counseling and Development, 1992); *Responsible Test Use: Case Studies for Assessing Human Behavior* (Eyde et al., 1993); and the *Code of Professional Responsibilities in Educational Measurement* (National Council on Measurement in Education, 1995). These official statements of professional societies offer helpful guidelines; this report attempts both to build on and to go beyond them.

The existing codes alert practitioners to important issues that deserve attention, but they do so in general terms. In this volume, we attempt to inform professional judgment specifically, with respect to the use of tests for student tracking, for grade promotion or retention, and for awarding or withholding diplomas.

One of the limitations of existing testing guidelines is that compliance is essentially voluntary. There are no monitoring or enforcement mechanisms in place to ensure that producers and users of tests will understand and follow the guidelines. Chapter 11 considers some potential methods, practices, and safeguards that might be put in place in the future to better ensure proper test use.

REFERENCES

American Educational Research Association, American Psychological Association, and National Council on Measurement in Education
1985   *Standards for Educational and Psychological Testing.* Washington, DC: American Psychological Association.
1998   *Draft Standards for Educational and Psychological Testing.* Washington, DC: American Psychological Association.
Association for Measurement and Evaluation in Counseling and Development
1992   *Responsibilities of Users of Standardized Tests.* Alexandria, VA: American Association for Counseling and Development.
Bennett, R.E.
1998   Computer-based testing for examinees with disabilities: On the road to generalized accommodation. In S. Messick, ed., *Assessment in Higher Education.* Mahwah, NJ: Erlbaum.
Campbell, D.T., and D.W. Fiske
1959   Convergent and discriminant validation by the multitrait-multimethod matrix. *Psychological Bulletin* 56:81-105.
Cleary, T.A.
1968   Test bias: Prediction of grades of Negro and white students in integrated colleges. *Journal of Educational Measurement* 5(2):115-124.
Cole, N.S.
1973   Bias in selection. *Journal of Educational Measurement* 10(4):237-255.

Cook, T.D., and D.T. Campbell
  1979   *Quasi-Experimentation: Design and Analysis Issues for Field Settings.* Chicago,
          IL: Rand McNally.
Cronbach, L.J.
  1971   Test validation. Pp. 443-507 in *Educational Measurement,* 2nd Edition, R.L.
          Thorndike, ed. Washington, DC: American Council on Education.
  1976   Equity in selection: Where psychometrics and political philosophy meet.
          Journal of Educational Measurement 13(1):31-41.
Cronbach, L.J., and G.C. Gleser
  1965   *Psychological Tests and Personnel Decisions,* 2nd Edition. Urbana: University
          of Illinois Press.
Embretson (Whitely), S.
  1983   Construct validity: Construct representation versus nomothetic span. *Psy-
          chological Bulletin* 93:179-197.
Eyde, L.D., G.J. Robertson, S.E. Krug, K.L. Moreland, A.G. Robertson, C.M. Shewan,
P.L. Harrison, B.E. Porch, A.L. Hammer, and E.S. Primoff
  1993   *Responsible Test Use: Case Studies for Assessing Human Behavior.* Washing-
          ton, DC: American Psychological Association.
Feldt, L.S., and R.L. Brennan
  1989   Reliability. Pp. 105-146 in *Educational Measurement,* 3rd Edition, R.L. Linn,
          ed. New York: American Council on Education and Macmillan Publishing
          Co.
Ferguson, G.A.
  1956   On transfer and the abilities of man. *Canadian Journal of Psychology* 10:121-
          131.
Gordon, E.
  1998   Human diversity and equitable assessment. In *Assessment in Higher Education,*
          S. Messick, ed. Mahwah, NJ: Erlbaum.
Gross A.L., and W. Su
  1975   Defining a "fair" and "unbiased" selection model: A question of utilities.
          Journal of Applied Psychology 60:345-351.
Joint Committee on Testing Practices
  1988   *Code of Fair Testing Practices in Education.* Washington, DC: National Coun-
          cil on Measurement in Education.
Kane, M.T.
  1992   An argument-based approach to validity. *Psychological Bulletin* 112(Nov):527-
          535.
Lennon, R.T.
  1956   Assumptions underlying the use of content validity. *Educational and Psycho-
          logical Measurement* 16:294-304.
Linn, R.L.
  1973   Fair test use in selection. *Review of Educational Research* 43:139-161.
Loevinger, J.
  1957   Objective tests as instruments of psychological theory. *Psychological Reports*
          3:635-694 (Monograph Supplement 9).

Messick, S.
  1980   Test validity and the ethics of assessment. *American Psychologist* 35(11):1012-
          1027.
  1982   Issues of effectiveness and equity in the coaching controversy: Implications
          for educational and testing policy. *Educational Psychologist* 17(2):67-91.
  1989   Validity. Pp 13-103 in *Educational Measurement*, 3rd Edition., R.L. Linn, ed.
          New York: Macmillan.
  1995   Validity of psychological assessment: Validation of inferences from persons'
          responses and performances as scientific inquiry into score meaning. *Ameri-
          can Psychologist* 50(9):741-749.
National Council on Measurement in Education, Ad Hoc Committee on the Development of a Code of Ethics
  1995   *Code of Professional Responsibilities in Educational Measurement.* Washington,
          DC: National Council on Measurement in Education.
Petersen, N.S., and M.R. Novick
  1976   An evaluation of some models for culture-fair selection. *Journal of Educa-
          tional Measurement* 13(1):3-29.
Sawyer, R.L., N.S. Cole, and J.W.L. Cole
  1976   Utilities and the issue of fairness in a decision theoretic model for selection.
          Journal of Educational Measurement 13(1):59-76.
Shepard, L.A.
  1993   Evaluating test validity. *Review of Research in Education* 19:405-450.
Shulman, L.S.
  1970   Reconstruction of educational research. *Review of Educational Research*
          40:371-396.
Thorndike, R.L.
  1971   Concepts of culture fairness. *Journal of Educational Measurement* 8(2):63-70.
Wiggins, G.
  1993   Assessment: Authenticity, context, and validity. *Phi Delta Kappan* 75(3):200-
          214.
Willingham, W.W.
  1998   A systemic view of test validity. In *Assessment in Higher Education*, S. Messick,
          ed. Mahwah, NJ: Erlbaum.
Willingham, W.W., and N.S. Cole
  1997   *Gender Bias and Fair Assessment.* Hillsdale, NJ: Erlbaum.
Willingham, W.W., M. Ragosta, R.E. Bennett, H. Braun, D.A. Rock, and D.E. Powers,
eds.
  1988   *Testing Handicapped People.* Boston: Allyn and Bacon.

Part II

Uses of Tests to Make High-Stakes Decisions About Individuals

5

Tracking

In a typical American elementary or secondary school, the curriculum serves two purposes that often exist in tension with each other. One is to have all students master a common core of knowledge, an objective reflected in the current emphasis on "high standards for all." The other is to provide curricular differentiation—differentiated instruction suited to students' varied needs, interests, and achievement levels (Gamoran and Weinstein, 1998). This second purpose is pursued in many schools through practices variously known as "tracking," "ability grouping," and "homogeneous grouping." Put differently, educators "organize school systems so that students who appear to vary in their educational needs and abilities can be taught separately, either in specialized schools or in the same school in distinct programs, classes, or instructional groups within classrooms" (Oakes et al., 1992:570).

The literature on tracking is voluminous, and the effects of tracking have often been debated in recent years.[1] Tracking policies and practices vary from state to state, district to district, and school to school. A comprehensive survey of these practices and their effects on students would have been beyond the committee's resources. We have therefore tried to focus our work on matters directly within our charge.

---

[1]For a comprehensive survey of the literature, see Oakes et al. (1992).

LIMITATIONS OF TERMINOLOGY

Although many terms are used to describe practices of curricular differentiation, each has its limitations.

Tracking, the term used by the Congress in defining the committee's mandate, suggests the classic, rigid form of curricular differentiation in which a student's program or "track"—academic, general, or vocational— determines virtually every course that the student will take and at what level of difficulty. In recent decades, formal grouping systems this rigid have become less common in schools (Lucas, in press).

Ability grouping, a term used widely by scholars and practitioners, implies—incorrectly, in our view—that students are being grouped on the basis of "ability," a quality that some view as innate and immutable. As we will see, schools that group students usually do so on the basis of classroom performance and other measures of achievement that reflect acquired knowledge—something that can and does change over time— rather than ability. It is therefore misleading to use the term "ability grouping." Moreover, given the degree of racial and socioeconomic stratification that is often associated with grouping, it may reinforce false stereotypes to imply incorrectly that students in different groups are distinguished by ability. We find it more accurate to say that schools that group students typically try to do so by "skill level" or "achievement level" (Mosteller et al., 1996).

Homogeneous grouping is also a misnomer, based on studies of actual practice. The term "homogeneous" suggests that all the students in a given group are alike, or at least similar, in their achievement levels. Empirical studies cast doubt on this assumption, however. "Grouping's effect on reducing even cognitive diversity may be very small," report Oakes et al. in their comprehensive survey (1992:594). "Other studies document considerable overlap of students' skills and abilities among groups . . . . Thus the degree to which tracking reduces heterogeneity may be far less than we typically assume." For reasons discussed below, it appears that factors other than student achievement—scheduling constraints, parental interventions, and student choice, in particular—often help to determine who takes which classes. Although these other factors may be entirely legitimate, they often produce groupings that are not very homogeneous. In some circumstances, "it is unclear whether it is possible to organize classes that contain a narrow range of student ability" (Gamoran and Weinstein, 1998:387). At the same time, there is evidence of considerable homogeneity in secondary mathematics classes (Linn, 1998a).

The committee has decided to use in this report the term that the Congress chose—tracking—while recognizing that neither it nor any of the common alternatives is entirely satisfactory as a description of actual practice in most schools. The committee defines tracking as forms of placement whereby individual students are assigned, usually on the basis of perceived achievement or skill level, to separate schools or programs, classes within grade levels, groups within classes (at the elementary level), and courses within subject areas (at the secondary level).

NATURE AND EXTENT OF TRACKING

Tracking takes many forms in American schools. Among them are "exam" schools and "gifted and talented" programs or classes, to which only certain students are admitted usually on the basis of their perceived achievement levels or talents. [2] Some scholars and practitioners also see programs for students with mild mental disabilities (mild mental retardation, learning disabilities, and emotional problems) as a form of tracking (Lipsky and Gartner, 1989) because students are often referred for possible placement in such programs on the basis of their perceived abilities or achievement levels. When this is the case, the committee considers such referrals a potential form of tracking, even though actual placement depends on individualized assessments conducted with parental consent.

Although almost all elementary schoolchildren study the same core subjects, "in the United States, differentiation begins early, with most elementary schools employing between-class . . . grouping for the entire day, between-class grouping for specific subjects, and/or within-class grouping for specific subjects" (Oakes et al., 1992:571). In the last decade, however, there has been an increase in heterogeneous grouping within elementary schools, and new techniques, such as cooperative learning, offer promising ways of grouping children heterogeneously within classrooms (Slavin et al., 1989, 1996).

Tracking also remains typical in American secondary schools (Oakes

---

[2] An exam school is a public school to which students apply and are accepted based on exemplary test performance and academic record. A gifted and talented class or program provides an accelerated curriculum and requires students to demonstrate advanced achievement and/or test performance to participate.

et al., 1992:571), despite opposition from many middle school educators (Lynn and Wheelock, 1997) and despite the demise of formal tracking, under which a student's program of study (college preparatory, general, or vocational) largely determined the courses he or she would take (Lucas, in press). As "formal tracks were abolished . . . the reality of tracking has been preserved in many schools through a variety of new mechanisms" (Moore and Davenport, 1988:11-12). Within-school grouping contin- ues, although less rigidly than in the past. For example, although many schools retain the familiar three-tiered system, some assign most students to the middle group, with relatively few being placed in higher- or lower- level classes (Gamoran, 1989).

The secondary school schedule also tends to promote tracking. "Be- cause students assigned to a high-level class for one subject tended to be assigned to a similar level in other subjects, the end result was a set of curricular tracks as distinct as in the past. Sometimes students were actually assigned to sets of classes at the same ability level all at once" (Oakes et al., 1992:575).[3]

Parental intervention also operates to preserve curricular differentia- tion in public secondary schools. "Middle-class parents intervene to obtain advantageous positions for their children even over and against school personnel. . . . Middle-class parents are the protectors of the existing in-school stratification system" (Lucas, in press:206). Especially in schools with racially and socioeconomically diverse student popula- tions, these parental influences serve to replace formal tracking with "a more hidden in-school stratification system" (Lucas, in press:205; Meier et al., 1989).

The secondary curriculum is differentiated by subject—students typi- cally have more electives than in elementary school—as well as by track. The degree of differentiation in secondary mathematics, for example, is considerable. It is common to find within a single high school courses ranging from remedial and "business" math to calculus and statistics, arrayed in as many as four distinct tracks (Linn, 1998a:3, citing McKnight et al., 1987). We note with interest that results from the Second Interna-

---

[3]According to national survey data, 60 to 70 percent of the 10th graders in honors mathematics classes also took honors English, and there was similar overlap of students taking remedial mathematics and remedial English (Gamoran, 1988). We do not know, however, how much of this overlap was due to the school schedule and how much to the correlation of student achievement levels across subjects.

tional Mathematics Study show that the variation in student math performance associated with tracking is far greater in the United States than in most other countries; that is, the difference in average achievement of students in different classes in the same school is far greater in the United States than in most other countries (Linn, 1998a).[4] Even in schools that have tried to reduce or eliminate tracking, however, the practice remains nearly universal in the teaching of mathematics, in part because math teachers and parents believe strongly in its effectiveness.

In sum, tracking in various forms has been and remains an important feature of public elementary and secondary education in the United States.

ROLE OF TESTS IN TRACKING DECISIONS

Tests play a complex role in tracking decisions. On one hand, there is evidence that most within-grade and within-class tracking decisions are not based solely on test scores (Delany, 1991; Selvin et al., 1990; White et al., 1996). Although practice varies considerably, even from school to school, educators consistently report that such decisions are based on multiple sources of information: test scores, teacher and counselor recommendations, grades, and (at secondary levels) student choice (Oakes et al., 1992). Also, as previously noted, parents often play a powerful role.

On the other hand, standardized tests are routinely used in making tracking decisions (Glaser and Silver, 1994; Meisels, 1989). Moreover, they may play an important, even dominant, role in selecting children for exam schools and gifted and talented programs.[5] IQ tests play an important part in the special education evaluation process, and their use contributes to the disproportionate placement of minority students into

---

[4]"The class component of variance accounted for almost half of the total variability in performance in the U.S., whereas the class component accounted for a much smaller fraction of the total variability in most other countries" (Linn, 1998a:3).

[5]The use of traditional IQ tests for such purposes has been criticized, and when IQ test scores are the sole criterion for selection, such use is plainly inconsistent with professional standards. Even when such placement decisions are based on IQ test scores and other criteria, traditional IQ tests have been criticized, both because they measure a fairly narrow range of human qualities (Gardner, 1993; Sternberg, 1990) and because they often serve to exclude minority applicants at significantly higher rates than other available selection standards and procedures for gifted programs (Kornhaber, 1997).

classes for students with mild mental retardation (National Research Council, 1982; Haney, 1993).[6] Even when test scores are just one factor among several that influence tracking decisions, they may carry undue weight by appearing to provide a scientific justification and legitimacy for tracking decisions that such decisions would not otherwise have.[7]

Some standardized test scores can be used appropriately in making tracking decisions, and the following sections of this chapter describe criteria that are relevant in determining whether a particular test use is appropriate. At the same time, research suggests that some other standardized tests commonly employed for tracking are not valid for this purpose. For example, Darling-Hammond (1991) asserts that schools improperly use norm-referenced multiple-choice tests for tracking purposes; she argues that such tests are designed to rank students and not to support instruction, and that linking such test scores to student tracking can seriously limit students' learning.[8] Tests that yield criterion-referenced interpretations may be preferable. Similarly, Glaser and Silver (1994) find evidence of negative consequences from the use of selection tests for placement in tracks.[9] Meisels (1989) also contends that some standardized tests are used inappropriately for tracking purposes and recommends that other, more appropriate standardized tests be used in making tracking decisions.[10] Finally, a recent report prepared for the Na-

---

[6]Although the Individuals with Disabilities Education Act (IDEA) authorizes the use of IQ tests, Congress expressed serious concern about racial disproportions in special education when it reauthorized the IDEA in 1997 (see also *Larry P. v. Riles*, 1984; *PASE v. Hannon*, 1980; and *Hobsen v. Hansen*, 1967).

[7]With regard to between-class and within-class tracking, there appears to be little systematic research on how educators actually weigh test scores with other factors in arriving at placement decisions.

[8]Although it has become common to label tests as "norm-referenced" or "criterion-referenced," these labels are more appropriately applied to the *interpretation of scores*—from any test—rather than to the test instruments themselves. Norm-referenced interpretations compare an examinee's performance to the performance of others; criterion-referenced interpretations indicate the extent to which an examinee's performance demonstrates mastery of specific skills and knowledge (see also Glaser, 1963; Messick, 1989; Feldt and Brennan, 1989; and National Research Council, 1999).

[9]Glaser and Silver report that using tests to place students in low-track classes often means that students learn less than they are capable of learning and less than they would in other available placements.

[10]Meisels contends that readiness tests, which are sometimes used for tracking, are concerned with the knowledge and skills a child has already acquired, and are not appropriate for use in predicting performance in a future placement or track. He recommends that screening tests be used instead.

tional Education Goals panel calls attention to a troubling use of tests to track young children (Shepard et al., 1998:4):

> Recently . . . there has been an increase in formal assessments and testing [of children up through age 8], the results of which are used to make "high-stakes" decisions such as tracking youngsters into high- and low-ability groups . . . . In many cases, the instruments developed for one purpose or even one age group of children have been misapplied to other groups. As a result, schools have often identified as "not yet ready" for kindergarten, or "too immature" for group settings, large proportions of youngsters (often boys and non-English speakers) who would benefit enormously from the learning opportunities provided in these settings. In particular, because the alternative treatment is often inadequate, screening out has fostered inequities.

There is some evidence that students' race or socioeconomic status (SES) may influence the weight that educators accord to their test scores, leading to differential treatment in the tracking process. For example, one case study found "that school counselors and teachers respond to comparable achievement scores of Asian and Hispanic students quite differently, with Asians far more likely to be placed in advanced classes than Hispanics with similar scores" (Oakes et al., 1992:577). Similarly, more than one court decision has established that some school officials assign low-scoring white students to high tracks and high-scoring minority students to low tracks (e.g., *People Who Care v. Rockford Board of Education*, 1997; Oakes, 1995). Previously noted research by Lucas (in press) provides powerful evidence that middle- and higher-income parents intervene in tracking decisions, effectively overriding test scores (and other factors that schools may use in tracking decisions) to produce tracks that are highly stratified by SES and race. The importance of social class in tracking decisions is suggested by a study that controlled for prior achievement, social class, and school, using data from the High School and Beyond survey; Gamoran and Mare (1989) concluded that black students were 10 percent more likely than comparable white students to be placed in high-track classes.

The educational consequences of these practices and trends are considered below. It is clear, however, that the role of tests in tracking decisions justifies consideration of their appropriate use.

PSYCHOMETRICS OF PLACEMENT

Tracking decisions are basically placement decisions, and tests used for this purpose should meet professional test standards regarding placement (American Educational Research Association et al., 1985, 1998; Joint Committee on Testing Practices, 1988).

The main assumption underlying tracking decisions is that particular students will benefit more from certain experiences, resources, or environments than they would from others, and that this benefit is optimized when they are taught with other students like themselves in achievement level. Because of this assumption, valid placement requires evidence that students are likely to be better off in the setting in which they are placed than they would be in a different available setting. Such evidence, in psychometric terms, shows an *aptitude-treatment interaction* in terms of outcome measures of learning and well-being. For example, students who get high scores on a placement test of spatial ability should in fact be found to learn more in a physics course in which the problems are expressed in pictures than they would in a physics course in which similar problems were expressed in numbers.

Other assumptions underlying test use for tracking decisions include: that the test taps the knowlege, skills, or other attributes it is interpreted to measure; that the cutscore chosen is an accurate discriminator of the attribute measured in relation to the associated levels of benefit; and that the test scores have comparable meanings and properties for all students. Depending on the context involved, however, it may not be necessary to gather supporting evidence or documentation for all of these assumptions. For example, some of them may be argued to be plausible on their face or already supported by evidence provided by the test developer or in the testing literature. What will always be required, however, is that the sum of the evidence gathered as part of the test validation process is sufficient to make a credible case that the use of the test for placement is appropriate—that is, both valid and fair.[11]

Validation of Test Use

As previously noted, there is evidence that test scores are routinely used, although rarely as the sole criterion, in making tracking decisions. To the extent that they are used, however, they should be validated by the kinds of information described below (American Educational Research Association et al., 1985; 1998).

---

[11]The types of evidence required to establish validity are elaborated in Chapter 4.

Educational Outcome

Decisions about a student's placement should be based on predictions about which available setting will produce the most beneficial expected educational outcome (National Research Council, 1982). The standard for using a test in this way should be its accuracy in predicting the likely educational effects of each of several alternative future placements. For example, if a student performs in a particular way on a math test, that performance should help predict whether the student will be better served by being placed in one type or level of math course rather than another (American Educational Research Association et al., 1985: Standards 1.20 to 1.23, 8.10, and 8.11; 1998). This is true not only when the possible placements include alternative math courses, but also when the choice is between placement in a gifted and talented class or a more traditional class, or when the choice is between special education and general education.

For example, as an earlier National Research Council report (1982) notes, one of the main validity claims for the use of IQ tests to place students in classes for the educable mentally retarded (EMR) was the test's predictive power. That committee concluded, however, that this prediction alone was insufficient evidence of the test's educational utility. Additional evidence was required that children with scores in the EMR range would actually learn more effectively in a special education program than in other available placements. Research on tests used for placement in early childhood has come to the same conclusion about the type of evidence required for validation (Shepard et al., 1998).

Similar standards are relevant to tests used for course placement decisions in high school. Kane concluded that, to establish the validity of an algebra test used as a prerequisite for calculus, one had to demonstrate that students with low scores "do substantially better in the calculus course if they take the remedial course before taking the calculus course" (1992:531). This evidence would be required in addition to the usual conceptual and empirical verification that the test, when used for differential placement, is in fact a valid measure of algebra skills. In this instance, the hypothesized consequences could be checked by means of a randomized experiment, comparing the calculus performance of low scorers with and without remediation.

As previously stated, however, a test score is seldom used as the sole criterion for making a tracking or placement decision. Rather, it is more likely to be used in combination with other sources of information about the student. Therefore, the strength of the interaction between test scores and placement outcomes should be considered in the context of the availability of other relevant information and its relative weight.

Relevant Content

In general, a test used to make a placement decision is not being used to certify mastery but rather to predict a student's response to alternative future educational settings. Therefore it is not essential to show that the students have already been taught the skills tested. To the extent possible, however, the content of such tests should be relevant to the experiences to which the student will be exposed (American Educational Research Association et al., 1985: Standards 6.1 and 6.4; 1998).

For example, in the case of a math test used to aid in placing a student in a beginning or advanced algebra course, the validity of score interpretation may be enhanced by ensuring that the test adequately covers the relevant content and thought processes in the knowledge domain it is interpreted to measure (that domain could be algebra but might also be general mathematics). As noted earlier, a number of researchers claim that some kinds of tests commonly used in making tracking decisions do not, in fact, provide information on the extent to which individual students are prepared for the content to which they are likely to be exposed in future placements, and they recommend that the use of such tests for tracking purposes be discontinued (Darling-Hammond, 1991; Glaser and Silver, 1994; Meisels, 1989; Shepard, 1991).

In addition to evidence of adequate content coverage, the test should be examined to ensure that it does not contain irrelevant material that could confound or obscure the construct to be measured. For example, a math test should not require an unnecessarily high level of reading proficiency, as this may prevent poor readers from demonstrating their readiness to learn math.

Finally, a low score on the test should not be taken as a lack of readiness with respect to the skills being tested without consideration of alternate explanations for the test taker's performance. Variables such as clinically relevant history, school record, and examiner or test taker differences should be considered in interpreting test scores. Influences associated with socioeconomic status, ethnicity, language, age, gender, or specific disabilities may also be relevant (American Educational Research Association et al., 1985: Standard 6.11; 1998).

Accuracy of Cutscores

Tracking decisions, like those for promotion and graduation, depend to some degree on the setting of cutscores. Cutscores are performance standards dividing acceptable levels of readiness from unacceptable levels. Because setting them is inherently judgmental, their validity depends on the reasonableness of the standard-setting process and of its consequences—not the least of which are passing rates and classification errors, especially if they vary by gender, racial, or language minority group.

For example, consider the reasonableness of the widely used Angoff (1971) method of standard setting. In this procedure, expert judges are asked to estimate the probability that a minimally competent respondent will answer each item correctly. The average estimate for each item provides a kind of minimum passing level for the item. These estimates are summed to determine a passing or cutscore for the test. Modified versions of the Angoff method are typically used to set nonminimum standards, such as the basic, proficient, and advanced levels of the National Assessment of Educational Progress (NAEP). The reasonableness of the procedures depends on many factors, including the expertise of the judges. The judges should be knowledgeable not only about the subject tested but also about the expected performance on each item of persons exhibiting various levels of proficiency in the field.

Other procedures have been developed to improve the reasonableness of the standard-setting process (e.g., Jaeger et al., 1996) and to offset some of the vulnerabilities of the Angoff method (Messick, 1995).[12] Several new approaches are being examined to make cutscore judgments by various stakeholders both more reasonable and more defensible.[13]

---

[12]For example, a major weakness of item-level judgmental procedures such as the Angoff method occurs precisely because judgments are made for each item separately. When each item is considered in isolation, item-specific variance looms large compared with construct variance. This tends to distort probability estimates that are supposed to reflect levels of construct competence. This distortion could be reduced by obtaining judgments of the probability of success on sets of items scaled together, because at the scale level construct variance cumulates across items, becoming more salient, whereas item-specific variance does not.

[13]For example, if various points on the scale were benchmarked by exemplary items, along with associated descriptions of the cognitive processes involved in item performance, cutscores could be set directly as points on the scale. This would involve judgments about what level of process complexity (and of associated benchmark exercises) is appropriate for performance at minimal, basic, proficient, or advanced levels. Thus, if

The importance of the cutscore may be lessened by the extent to which other information is used in making placement decisions. Whenever cutscores are used, the quality of the standard-setting process should be documented and evaluated—including the qualification of the judges, the method or methods employed, and the degree of consensus reached (American Educational Research Association et al., 1985: Standard 6.9; 1998).

Test Fairness

Chapter 4 discussed the issue of fairness in terms of comparable validity across individuals, groups, and contexts. Test scores should have comparable meanings and properties for all groups of students. Accordingly, in assessing the fairness of test use in tracking, it is important to determine the extent to which the test is measuring the same construct—and hence has similar meaning—for different populations.

The racial and socioeconomic stratification that often accompanies tracking is discussed below. For the present purpose, the important question is whether the use of tests in tracking contributes to negative outcomes for particular groups of students. For example, in the case of a math test used to assign students to a beginning or advanced algebra class, it may be found that the test consistently assigns higher numbers of males than females or whites than blacks to the advanced class—more so than assignments based on other factors, such as grades or recommendations. This disproportion may be due to bias in certain test items that make them easier for males or white students.[14] Alternatively, the reason may

---

the scale is well structured (such as one based on item-response theory) and if it is well described in terms of the cognitive processes required for item performance at different scale levels, then cutscores can be set directly on the scale rather than indirectly by cumulating item judgments. More work is required up front by the test developer in constructing the scale and in developing benchmarks and process descriptions for scale levels, but then the subsequent cutscore judgments by test users become both more informed and more straightforward.

[14]During the stages of test design and development, judgmental review and statistical procedures are employed by many test publishers as a way to detect and eliminate biased items or tasks. Differential item functioning (DIF) analysis (Holland and Wainer, 1993) is one such statistical procedure. It is important to note that DIF procedures are not, by themselves, adequate to detect bias (Cole and Moss, 1989). For example, DIF procedures are not useful if the entire test is biased, because they operate at the item level. DIF

lie in inequities in the testing process itself, such as differential access to test preparation materials and different physical conditions on the day of testing. Even if the disproportionate outcome is an accurate representation of the degree to which different groups of students have mastered the skills measured by the test, the use of the test for tracking purposes would be improper if students were subsequently exposed to instruction that differed substantially in quality—resulting in higher proportions of females or minority students failing an end-of-course algebra test that is a prerequisite for high school graduation.[15]

Although this type of adverse impact is not automatic evidence of test invalidity, such questions should be part of the validity investigation (Messick, 1989). According to Messick, if adverse impact is traceable to construct over- or underrepresentation, it signals a validity problem. If it is not so traceable, it signals a policy problem. For example, if a test designed to assess algebra skills places a heavy emphasis on complicated word problems, English-language learners will be at a disadvantage in demonstrating their knowledge of algebra. If the resulting scores are weighted heavily in placement, some English-language learners are likely to be placed inappropriately in lower-level classes. Although studies of these types of side effects may not often be part of initial test development, the test user should include a well-designed evaluation component to monitor the intended and unintended consequences of tracking on all students and on significant subgroups of students, including minorities, English-language learners, and students with disabilities.

EFFECTS OF LOW-TRACK PLACEMENT

"Decisions about a student's track placement," a previous National Research Council report concluded, "should be based on predictions about what track will produce the most beneficial expected educational

---

procedures are also problematic with performance-type assessments due to the small number of items involved, which makes it difficult to match students. There is a recognized need for the development of more sophisticated techniques for the detection of DIF and/or bias in performance-type items, since these are not immune from fairness concerns (Linn et al., 1991a). Absent such techniques, greater reliance must be placed on judgmental review of items or tasks.

[15]This is not an unlikely scenario. Shepard (1991:282) made a similar observation about the outcome of tests used to make placement decisions: "Two students who are initially indistinguishable from each other except for measurement error will become more like the mean of their respective ability groups."

outcome for the student" (National Research Council, 1982). It is beyond the committee's mandate to speculate on what track placements are educationally optimal, as a general matter or for particular students.

Under the committee's definition of appropriate test use (National Research Council, 1982), however, it is inappropriate to use tests to place students in settings that are demonstrably ineffective educationally. As tracking is currently practiced, students assigned to typical low-track classes are worse off than they would be in other placements. The most common reasons for this disadvantage are the failure to provide students in low-track classes with high-quality curriculum and instruction and the failure to convey high expectations for such students' academic performance. Unless these conditions are changed, and there is evidence that students will benefit more from such placements than from others, we recommend that low-track placements be eliminated, whether based on test scores or other information.

This is not to say that grouping students by achievement or skill level is in general a bad practice. Some forms of tracking, such as proficiency-based placement in foreign language classes or other classes for which there is a demonstrated need for prerequisites, may be beneficial. We know, morever, that researchers have found some schools and programs in which students in low-track classes received beneficial, high-quality instruction. These, however, involved not typical public schools but Catholic schools (Lee, 1985; Valli, 1986; Page and Valli, 1990), alternative schools, dropout programs (Wehlage, 1982), magnet programs (Mitchell and Benson, 1989), and a school that had recently undergone a thorough restructuring of staff and curriculum (Gamoran and Weinstein, 1998). And what made some of these low-track classes educationally beneficial appears to have been such factors as high teacher expectations, small class size, extra resources that permitted individualized instruction, strong intellectual leadership, a rigorous academic curriculum, extra efforts by teachers to promote extensive class discussion, the capacity to choose students and teachers, and "no system of assigning inexperienced or weak teachers to the low-track classes" (Gamoran, 1993:1; Gamoran and Weinstein, 1998).

Unfortunately, however, empirical research demonstrates that there is a very different reality in typical low-track classes. Moreover, there are serious structural and attitudinal barriers to change: "[Trying] to improve the quality of instruction in low tracks . . . fails to address the problem that tracking and ability grouping constitute not merely differentiation but stratification—that is, an unequal distribution of status—which typically leads to an unequal allocation of resources such as curricular materials [and] teaching competencies" (Gamoran and Weinstein, 1998:387). That minority students and low-SES students are disproportionately assigned to low-track classes is further cause for concern. The following sections describe more fully the research on typical low-track classes.

Teacher Distribution

Numerous studies show that students in most low-track classes have less access to well-qualified, highly motivated teachers than do their peers in other tracks. "[T]eachers often prefer instructing high-ability classes" and principals commonly "use class assignments as a reward for teachers judged more powerful or successful and as a sanction against those deemed weaker or undeserving" (Oakes et al., 1992:583, citing Becker, 1953; Hargreaves, 1967; and McPartland and Crain, 1987). "This process may result in a vicious circle for low tracks: Repeated assignment to the bottom of the school's status hierarchy may demoralize teachers, hindering their improvement and perhaps even reducing their competency over time" (Oakes et al., 1992:583, citing Finley, 1984; Gamoran and Berends, 1987; and Hargreaves, 1967). Although the academic backgrounds of elementary school teachers do not appear to differ much by track taught, there are "significant discrepancies among teachers assigned to various classes in secondary schools" (Oakes, 1990). For example, "[t]eachers of low-ability secondary science and mathematics classes are consistently less experienced, less likely to be certified in math or science, hold fewer degrees in those subjects, have less training in the use of computers, and less often report themselves to be 'master teachers'" (Oakes et al., 1992:583).[16]

Access to Knowledge

In elementary school, students in low tracks proceed by design at a slower pace than do students in higher tracks. Consequently, students who have been in high-track classes "are likely to have covered consider-

---

[16]"These differences remain even when qualification differences for teachers among various types of schools (e.g., schools serving various racial and socioeconomic student populations) are controlled" (Oakes et al., 1992:583).

ably more material by the end of elementary school" (Oakes et al., 1992: 583). The type of material they have covered is also different; "low reading groups spend relatively more time on decoding activities, whereas more emphasis is placed on the meanings of stories in high groups" (Oakes et al., 1992:583, citing Alpert, 1974; Hiebert, 1983; McDermott, 1987; and Wilcox, 1982).

"In secondary schools, low-track classes consistently offer greater exposure to less demanding topics and skills, whereas high-track classes typically include more complex material and more difficult thinking and problem-solving tasks" (Oakes et al., 1992:583, citing Burgess, 1983, 1984; Hargreaves, 1967; Keddie, 1971; Metz, 1978; Oakes, 1985; Page, 1989; Powell et al., 1985; Sanders et al., 1987; Squires, 1966; and Trimble and Sinclair, 1986). "At both the elementary and secondary levels, teachers of low-ability classes reported giving less emphasis than teachers of other classes to such matters as students' interest in math and science . . . inquiry skills and problem solving . . . and to preparing students for further study in those subjects" (Oakes et al., 1992:584. "[H]igh-level classes were more often characterized by authentic assignments, student control over work, and high-order cognitive tasks" (Oakes et al., 1992: 584, citing Nystrand and Gamoran, 1988). According to Oakes (1985), low-track classes are characterized by "a dull, isolating curriculum of passive drill and practice with trivial bits of information, whereas the upper-track curriculum encompass[es] imaginative, engaging assignments with 'high-status knowledge' such as Shakespeare or calculus" (Oakes et al., 1992:585, citing Oakes, 1985).

In sum, the research suggests that instruction in low-track classes is far less demanding than in high-track classes (Welner and Oakes, 1996; McKnight et al., 1987) and far less oriented to the higher-order knowledge and thinking skills that are strongly associated with future success (Linn, 1998a).

Equally important, low-track placements do not serve a remedial function, in that they do not help low-track students catch up with students in other tracks. Instead, "numerous studies provide evidence of the increasing disparity between high- and low-track students over time" (Oakes et al., 1992:591, citing Gamoran and Berends, 1987; Murphy and Hallinger, 1989; Gamoran, 1987; Gamoran and Mare, 1989; Hotchkiss and Dorsten, 1987; Lee and Bryk, 1988; and Vanfossen et al., 1987). Track effects are large, moreover; Gamoran (1987) has estimated that "the academic track advantage was larger than the gap between students in school and dropouts" (Oakes et al., 1992:591). Not surprisingly, there-fore, mobility between low tracks and higher tracks is limited: "Children in the lowest groups are rarely moved to the highest groups; the disparity . . . grows greater over time . . . . [E]ach subsequent assessment of ability is, in part, a product of the assessments that preceded it" (Oakes et al., 1992:596, citing Goodlad and Oakes, 1988).

Finally, students in low-track classes would learn more if they re-ceived high-quality teaching and a demanding curriculum, as research demonstrates (Slavin et al., 1996; Levin, 1988; Oakes et al., 1992). The weight of the evidence has been recognized by the Congress. In its 1994 amendments to Title I, the Congress expressly found that: "[a]ll children can master challenging content and complex problem-solving skills. Research clearly shows that children, including low-achieving children, can succeed when expectations are high and all children are given the opportunity to learn challenging material" (Title I, Elementary and Sec-ondary Education Act, 20 U.S.C. section 6301(c)(1)). Based on this conclusion, other provisions of Title I require that eligible students re-ceive "accelerated," "enriched," and "high-quality" curricula, "effective instructional strategies," "highly qualified instructional staff," and "high-quality" staff development (20 U.S.C. sections 6314(b)(1), 6315(c)(1), and 6320(a)(1)).

As tracking is currently practiced in the United States, students will need to be educated in settings other than typical low-track classes if they are to receive the high-quality curriculum and instruction they need to "master challenging content and complex problem solving skills."

Disproportions Based on Race, National Origin, Language, and SES

Research on patterns of student stratification has found dispropor-tionate percentages of low-SES students and minority students in cur-ricula designed for low-ability and noncollege-bound students (Gamoran and Mare, 1989; Moore and Davenport, 1988; National Center for Edu-cational Statistics, 1985; Oakes, 1990; Braddock, 1990). High School and Beyond survey data from 1982 provide an illustration. "African American students participated in the vocational education track at a rate 34 percent higher than . . . the rate for white students . . . . The participation rate in academic programs among African American stu-dents was 88 percent of the rate for whites, and, in the general track, the

African American student participation rate was 84 percent of the rate for whites" (Braddock, 1990:2). Similar statistics were found for Hispanic students (Braddock, 1990).

Minority students in racially mixed schools are disproportionately placed in low-track classes (Oakes et al., 1992) and consistently underrepresented in programs for the gifted and talented (Darling-Hammond, 1985). The same holds true for advanced placement classes; in Milwaukee for example, whites make up 24 percent of the total student population but 54 percent of those enrolled in advanced placement courses, whereas black students constitute 61 percent of the student population but only 17 percent of those in advanced placement courses (interview with Lynn Krebs, guidance director, Milwaukee School District).

There is evidence that tests used for tracking contribute to these disproportions: lower test scores by minority students and low-SES students undergird these patterns (Oakes et al., 1992). Tests used for tracking are not unique in this respect: "Gaps between average scores of minority and nonminority individuals show up not just on so-called intelligence or ability tests and general achievement tests. They also show up on competency tests used for grade promotion and high-school graduation [and tests used for other purposes]" (Haney, 1993:50, citing National Commission on Testing and Public Policy, 1990). At the same time, disproportionate placement rates are also due to factors other than test use; placement differences by race and social class seem to occur whether test scores, counselor and teacher recommendations, or student and parent choices are the basis for placement (Oakes et al., 1992).

Whether it is due to test scores or other information, the committee sees cause for concern in the fact that minority students and low-SES students are proportionately overrepresented in a classes typically characterized by an exclusive focus on basic skills, low expectations, and less-qualified teachers.

The committee's findings and recommendations about tracking are reported in Chapter 12.

REFERENCES

Alpert, J.L.
  1974   Teacher behavior across ability groups: A consideration of the mediation of Pygmalion effects. *Journal of Educational Psychology* 66(3):348-353.

American Educational Research Association, American Psychological Association, and National Council on Measurement in Education
 1985   *Standards for Educational and Psychological Testing*. Washington, DC: American Psychological Association.
 1998   *Draft Standards for Educational and Psychological Testing*. Washington, DC: American Psychological Association.
Angoff, W.H.
 1971   Scales, norms, and equivalent scores. Pp. 508-600 in *Educational Measurement*, 2nd Edition), R.L. Thorndike, ed. Washington, DC: American Council on Education.
Becker, Henry S.
 1953   The teacher in the authority system of the school. *Journal of Educational Sociology* 27(3):128-141.
Braddock, J.H. II
 1990   *Tracking: Implications for Student Race-Ethnic Subgroups*. Baltimore, MD: Center for Research on Effective Schooling for Disadvantaged Students.
Burgess, Robert G.
 1983   *Experiencing Comprehensive Education: A Study of Bishop McGregor School*. London: Methuen.
 1984   It's not a proper subject: It's just Newsom. Pp. 181-200 in *Defining the Curriculum*, J. Goodson and S. Ball, eds. London: Falmer.
Cole, N., and P.A. Moss
 1989   Bias in test use. *Educational Measurement*, 3rd Edition, R. Linn, ed. New York: American Council on Education.
Darling-Hammond, L.
 1985   *Equality and Excellence: The Educational Status of Black Americans*. New York: College Entrance Examination Board.
 1991   The implications of testing policy for quality and equality. *Phi Delta Kappan* 73(3):220-225.
Delany, B.
 1991   Allocation, choice, and stratification within high schools: How the sorting machine copes. *American Journal of Education* 99(2):181-207.
Feldt, L.S., and R.L. Brennan
 1989   Reliability. Pp. 105-146 in *Educational Measurement*, 3rd Edition, R.L. Linn, ed. New York: MacMillan.
Finley, Marilee K.
 1984   Teachers and tracking in a comprehensive high school. *Sociology of Education* 57:233-243.
Gamoran, A.
 1987   Organization, instruction, and the effects of ability grouping: Comment on Slavin's best-evidence synthesis. *Review of Educational Research* 57(3):341-345.
 1988   A Multi-level Analysis of the Effects of Tracking. Paper presented at the annual meeting, American Sociological Association, Atlanta, GA.
 1989   Tracking and the Distribution of Status in Secondary Schools. Paper presented at the annual meeting, American Sociological Association, San Francisco, CA.

1993   Alternative uses of ability grouping in secondary schools: Can we bring high-quality instruction to low-ability classrooms? *American Journal of Education* 102(1):1-22.

Gamoran, A., and M. Berends
1987   The effects of stratification in secondary schools: Synthesis of survey and ethnographic research. *Review of Education Research* 57(4):415-435.

Gamoran, A., and R.D. Mare
1989   Secondary school tracking and educational inequality: Compensation, reinforcement or neutrality? *American Journal of Sociology* 94(5):1146-1183.

Gamoran, A., and M. Weinstein
1998   Differentiation and opportunity in restructured schools. *American Journal of Education* 106:385-415.

Gardner, H.
1993   *Frames of Mind: The Theory of Multiple Intelligences.* New York: Basic Books.

Glaser, R.
1963   Instructional technology and the measurement of learning outcomes: Some questions. *American Psychologist,* 18:519-521.

Glaser, R., and E. Silver
1994   *Assessment, Testing, and Instruction: Retrospect and Prospect.* Los Angeles, CA: National Center for Research on Evaluation, Standards, and Student Testing.

Goodlad, J.I., and J. Oakes
1988   We must offer equal access to knowledge. *Educational Leadership* 45:16-22.

Haney, W.
1993   Testing and minorities. In *Beyond Silence: Class, Race, and Gender in United States Schools,* edited by L. Weiss, and M. Finne. Albany: State University of New York Press.

Hargreaves, D.H.
1967   *Social Relations in a Secondary School.* London: C. Tinling.

Hiebert, E.
1983   An examination of ability grouping for reading instruction. *Reading Research Quarterly* 18(2):231-255.

Holland, P.W., and H. Wainer
1993   *Differential Item Functioning.* Hillsdale, NJ: Erlbaum.

Hotchkiss, L., and L. Dorsten
1987   Curriculum effects on early post high school outcomes. Pp. 191-219 in *Sociology of Education and Socialization,* R.G. Corwin, ed. Greenwich, CT: JAI Press.

Jaeger, R.M., I.V.S. Mullis, M.L. Bourque, and S. Shakrani
1996   Setting performance standards for performance assessments: Some fundamental issues, current practice, and technical dilemmas. Pp. 79-115 in *Technical Issues in Large-scale Performance Assessment,* G.W. Phillips, ed. Washington, DC: U.S. Goverment Printing Office.

Joint Committee on Testing Practices
1988   *Code of Fair Testing Practices in Education.* Washington, DC: National Council on Measurement in Education.

Kane, M.T.
  1992   An argument-based approach to validity. *Psychological Bulletin* 112:527-535.
Keddie, N.
  1971   Classroom knowledge. Pp. 133-150 in *Knowledge and Control*, M.F.D. Young, ed. London: Collier-Macmillan.
Kornhaber, M.
  1997   Seeking Strengths: Equitable Identification for Gifted Education and the Theory of Multiple Intelligences. Doctoral dissertation, Harvard Graduate School of Education.
Lee, V.E.
  1985   Investigating the Relationship Between Social Class and Academic Achievement in Public and Catholic Schools: The Role of the Academic Organization of the School. Doctoral dissertation, Harvard Graduate School of Education.
Lee, V.E., and A.S. Bryk
  1988   Curriculum tracking as mediating the social distribution of high school achievement. *Sociology of Education* 62:78-94.
Levin, H.
  1988   *Accelerated Schools for At-Risk Students.* New Brunswick, NJ: Center for Policy Research in Education.
Linn, R.
  1998a   Assessments and Accountability. Paper presented at the annual meeting, American Educational Research Association, San Diego, CA.
  1998b   Validating inferences from National Assessment of Educational Progress Achievement-Level Reporting. *Applied Measurement in Education* 11(1):23-47.
Linn, R.L., E.L. Baker, and S.B. Dunbar
  1991a   Complex, performance-based assessment: Expectations and validation criteria. *Educational Researcher* 20(8):15-21.
Linn, R.L., D. Koretz, E.L. Baker, and L. Burstein
  1991b   *The Validity and Credibility of the Achievement Levels for the 1990 National Assessment of Educational Progress in Mathematics.* Tech. Rep. No. XX. Los Angeles: University of California, Center for the Study of Education.
Lipsky, D., and A. Gartner
  1989   *Beyond Separate Education: Quality Education for All.* Baltimore, MD: Brookes.
Lucas, S.
  in press *Tracking Inequality: Stratification and Mobility in American Schools.* New York: Teachers College Press.
Lynn, L., and A. Wheelock
  1997   Making detracking work. *The Harvard Education Letter* 13(1):1-4.
McDermott, R.P.
  1987   The explanation of minority school failure, again. *Anthropology and Education Quarterly* 18(4):361-364.

McKnight, C.C., and F.J. Crosswhite, J.A. Dossey, E. Kifer, S.O. Swafford, K. Travers, and T. J. Cooney
   1987   *The Underachieving Curriculum: Assessing U.S. School Mathematics from an International Perspective.* Champaign, IL: Stipes Publishing.
McPartland, J.M., and R.L. Crain
   1987   Evaluating the trade-offs in student outcomes from alternative school organization policies. Pp. 131-156 in *The Social Organization of Schools: New Conceptualizations of the Learning Process*, Maureen T. Hallinan, ed. New York: Plenum.
Meier, R., J. Stewart, and R. England
   1989   *Race, Class, and Education: The Politics of Second-Generation Discrimination.* Madison: University of Wisconsin Press.
Meisels, S.J.
   1989   *Testing, Tracking, and Retaining Young Children: An Analysis of Research and Social Policy.* Commissioned paper for the National Center for Education Statistics.
Messick, S.
   1989   Validity. Pp. 13-103 in *Educational Measurement*, 3rd Edition, R. Linn, ed. New York: American Council on Education.
   1995   Standards-based score interpretation: Establishing valid grounds for valid inferences. *Joint Conference on Standard Setting for Large-Scale Assessments: Proceedings* (Vol. 2: 291-305). Washington, DC: US Government Printing Office.
Metz, M.H.
   1978   *Classrooms and Corridors: The Crisis of Authority in Desegregated Secondary Schools.* Berkeley: University of California Press.
Mitchell, V., and C. Benson
   1989   *Exemplary Urban Career-oriented High Schools.* Berkeley, CA: National Center for Research in Vocational Education.
Moore, D., and S. Davenport
   1988   *The New Improved Sorting Machine.* Madison, WI: National Center on Effective Secondary Schools.
Mosteller, F., R. Light, and J. Sachs
   1996   Sustained inquiry in education: Lessons from skill-grouping and class size. *Harvard Educational Review* 66 (4):797-843.
Murphy, J., and P. Hallinger
   1989   Equity as access to learning: Curricular and instructional treatment differences. *Journal of Curiculum Studies* 21(2):129-149.
National Center for Education Statistics
   1985   *High School and Beyond: An Analysis of Course-taking Patterns in Secondary Schools as Related to Student Characteristics.* Washington, DC: US Department of Education.
National Commission on Testing and Public Policy
   1990   *From Gatekeeper to Gateway: Transforming Testing in America.* Chestnut Hill, MA: National Commission on Testing and Public Policy.

National Research Council
  1982   *Placing Children in Special Education: A Strategy for Equity*, K.A. Heller, W.H.
          Holtzman, and S. Messick, eds. Committee on Child Development Research
          and Public Policy. Washington, DC: National Academy Press.
  1999   *Uncommon Measures: Equivalence and Linkage Among Educational Tests*, M.J.
          Feuer, P.W. Holland, B.F. Green, M.W. Bertenthal, and F.C. Hemphill, eds.
          Committee on Equivalency and Linkage of Educational Tests, Board on Test-
          ing and Assessment. Washington, DC: National Academy Press.
Nystrand, M., and A. Gamoran
  1988   *A Study of Instruction as Discourse*. Madison: Wisconsin Center for Educa-
          tion Research.
Oakes, J.
  1985   *Keeping Track: How Schools Structure Inequality*. New Haven, CT: Yale
          University Press.
  1986   Keeping track, part I: The policy and practice of curriculum inequality. *Phi
          Delta Kappan* 68(1):12-17.
  1990   *Multiplying Inequalities: The Effects of Race, Social Class, and Tracking on
          Opportunities to Learn Math and Science*. Santa Monica, CA: Rand.
  1995   Two cities' tracking and within-school segregation. *Teachers College Record*
          96(4):681-693.
Oakes, J., A. Gamoran, and R. Page
  1992   Curriculum differentiation: Opportunities, outcomes, and meanings. In P.
          Jackson, ed., *Handbook of Research on Curriculum*. New York: MacMillan
          Publishing Company.
Page, R.
  1989   The lower-track curriculum at a "heavenly" high school: "Cycles of preju-
          dice." *Journal of Curriculum Studies* 21(3):197-221.
Page, R., and L. Valli, eds.
  1990   *Curriculum Differentiation: Interpretive Studies in U.S. Secondary Schools*. New
          York: State University of New York Press.
Powell, A., E. Farrar, and D.K. Cohen
  1985   *The Shopping Mall High School*. Boston: Houghton Mifflin.
Sanders, N., N. Stone, and J. LaFollette
  1987   *The California Curriculum Differtiation: Paths Through High School*. Sacra-
          mento: California State Department of Education.
Selvin, M.J., J. Oakes, S. Hare, K. Ramsey, and D. Schoeff
  1990   *Who Gets What and Why: Curriculum Decisionmaking at 3 Comprehensive High
          Schools*. Santa Monica, CA: Rand.
Shepard, L.
  1991   Negative policies for dealing with diversity: When does assessment and diag-
          nosis turn into sorting and segregation? E. Hiebert, ed., *Literacy for a Diverse
          Society: Perspectives, Practices and Policies*. New York: Teachers College
          Press.
Shepard, L., et al.
  1993   Evaluating test validity. *Review of Research in Education* 19:405-450.

Shepard, L., S. Kagan, and E. Wurtz, eds.
  1998   *Principles and Recommendations for Early Childhood Assessments.* Washington DC: National Education Goals Panel.
Slavin, R.E., J. Braddock, C. Hall, and R. Petza
  1989   *Alternatives to Ability Grouping.* Baltimore, MD: Center for Research on Effective Schooling for Disadvantaged Students.
Slavin, R.E., et al.
  1996   *Every Child, Every School: Success for All.* Thousand Oaks, CA: Corwin Press.
Squires, J.R.
  1966   National study of high school English programs: A school for all seasons. *English Journal* 55(2):282-290.
Sternberg, R.
  1990   *Metaphors of Mind: Conceptions of the Nature of Intelligence.* New York: Cambridge University Press.
Trimble, K., and R.L. Sinclair
  1986   *Ability Grouping and Differing Conditions for Learning: An Analysis of Content and Instruction in Ability-grouped Classes.* Amherst: University of Massachusetts Center for Curriculum Studies.
Valli, L.
  1986   Tracking: Can It Benefit Low-achieving Students? Paper presented at the annual meeting of the American Educational Research Association, San Franciso, CA.
Vanfossen, B.E., J.D. Jones, and J.Z. Spade
  1987   Curriculum tracking and status maintenance. *Sociology of Education* 60(2): 104-122.
Wehlage, G.
  1982   The purpose of generalization in field study research. Pp. 211-226 in *The Myth of Educational Reform: A Study of School Response to a Program of Change,* Thomas Popkewitz, Robert Tabachnick, and Gary Wehlage, eds. Madison: University of Wisconsin Press.
Welner, K.G., and J. Oakes
  1996   (Li)Ability grouping: The new susceptibility of school tracking systems to legal challenges. *Harvard Educational Review* 66(3):451-470.
White, P., A. Gamoran, J. Smithson, and A. Porter
  1996   Upgrading the high school math curriculum: Math course-taking patterns in seven high schools in California and New York. *Educational Evaluation and Policy Analysis* 18(4):285-307.
Wilcox, K.
  1982   Differential socialization in the classroom: Implications for equal opportunity. Pp. 268-309 in *Doing the Ethnography of Schooling,* George Spindler, ed. New York: Holt, Rinehart, and Winston.

LEGAL REFERENCES

Hobson v. Hansen, 269 F. Supp. 401 (D.D.C. 1967), *aff'd sub nom. Smuck v. Hansen*, 408 F.2d 175 (D.C. Cir. 1969) (*en banc*).

The Improving America's Schools Act of 1994, P.L. 103-382 (1994).

Larry P. v. Riles, 793 F.2d 969 (9th Cir. 1984).

PASE v. Hannon, 506 F. Supp. 831 (N.D. Ill. 1980).

People Who Care v. Rockford Board of Education, 111 F.3d 528 (7th Cir. 1997).

Title I, Elementary and Secondary Education Act, 20 U.S.C. section 6301(c)(1).

6

Promotion and Retention

The typical organization of American schools into grades by the ages of their students is challenged by large variations in achievement within ages and grades. The resulting tension is reduced somewhat by overlap in the curriculum from one grade to the next. It is also reduced by strategies for grouping students by observed levels of readiness or mastery: these include special education placement, academic tracking, extended kindergarten, and grade retention. The uses of tests in tracking and with students with disabilities are discussed in Chapters 5 and 8, respectively. The use of testing to support the strategies of extended kindergarten and grade retention is treated in this chapter.

SOCIAL PROMOTION, RETENTION, AND TESTING

Much of the current public discussion of high-stakes testing of individual students is motivated by calls for "an end to social promotion." The committee therefore began by looking for data on the actual extent of promotion and retention, on the prevalence of test use for making those decisions, and at trends and differentials in those data.

In a memorandum for the secretary of education, President Clinton (1998:1-2) wrote that he had "repeatedly challenged States and school districts to end social promotions—to require students to meet rigorous academic standards at key transition points in their schooling career, and to end the practice of promoting students without regard to how much they have learned. . . . Students should not be promoted past the fourth grade if they cannot read independently and well, and should not enter high school without a solid foundation in math. They should get the help they need to meet the standards before moving on."

The administration's proposals for educational reform strongly tie the ending of social promotion to early identification and remediation of learning problems. The president calls for smaller classes, well-prepared teachers, specific grade-by-grade standards, challenging curriculum, early identification of students who need help, after-school and summer school programs, and school accountability. He also calls for "appropriate use of tests and other indicators of academic performance in determining whether students should be promoted" (Clinton, 1998:3). The key questions are whether testing will be used appropriately in such decisions and whether early identification and remediation of learning problems will take place successfully.

The president is by no means alone in advocating testing to end social promotion. Governor Bush of Texas has proposed that "3rd graders who do not pass the reading portion of the Texas Assessment of Academic Skills would be required to receive help before moving to regular classrooms in the 4th grade. The same would hold true for 5th graders who failed to pass reading and math exams and 8th graders who did not pass tests in reading, math, and writing. The state would provide funding for locally developed intervention programs" (Johnston, 1998). New York City Schools Chancellor Rudy Crew has proposed that 4th and 7th graders be held back if they fail a new state reading test at their grade level, beginning in spring 2000. Crew's proposal, however, would combine testing of students with "a comprehensive evaluation of their course work and a review of their attendance records," and the two-year delay in implementation of the tests would permit schools "to identify those students deemed most at risk and give them intensive remedial instruction" (Steinberg, 1998a).

Test-based requirements for promotion are not just being proposed; they are being implemented. According to a recent report by the American Federation of Teachers (1997b), 46 states either have or are in the process of developing assessments aligned with their content standards. Seven of these states, up from four in 1996, require schools and districts to use the state standards and assessments in determining whether students should be promoted into certain grades.[1] At the same time, Iowa and, until recently, California have taken strong positions against grade retention, based on research or on the reported success of alternative intervention programs (George, 1993; Iowa Department of Education, 1998).

In 1996-1997 the Chicago Public Schools instituted a new program to end social promotion. Retention decisions are now based almost entirely on student performance on the Iowa Test of Basic Skills (ITBS) at the end of grades 3, 6, and 8. Students who fall below specific cutoff scores at each grade level are required to attend highly structured summer school programs and to take an alternative form of the test at summer's end.[2] At the end of the 1996-1997 school year, 32 percent, 31 percent, and 21 percent of students failed the initial examination at grades 3, 6, and 8, respectively. Out of 91,000 students tested overall, almost 26,000 failed. After summer school, 15 percent, 13 percent, and 8 percent of students were retained at the three grade levels (Chicago Public Schools, 1998a).[3]

The current enthusiasm for the use of achievement tests to end social promotion raises three concerns. First, much of the public discussion and some recently implemented or proposed testing programs appear to ignore existing standards for appropriate test use. For that reason, much of this chapter is devoted to a review and exposition of the appropriate use

---

[1]The states are Arkansas, Florida, Louisiana, New Mexico, North Carolina, South Carolina, and West Virginia. A report from the Council of Chief State School Officers (1998) lists five states with required testing for promotion: Louisiana, North Carolina, New York, South Carolina, and Virginia. The committee has not attempted to reconcile this discrepancy.

[2]The *1997-1998 Guidelines for Promotion in the Chicago Public Schools* also list minimum report card requirements and a minimum attendance requirement, but "students who score at or above grade level on both the Reading and Mathematics sections of the ITBS are excepted from the latter requirement" (Chicago Public Schools, 1997a). This use of the ITBS appears to be in conflict with the publisher's recommendations about "inappropriate purposes" of testing: "If a retention decision is to be made, classroom assessment data gathered by the teacher over a period of months is likely to be a highly relevant and accurate basis for making such a decision. A test score can make a valuable contribution to the array of evidence that should be considered. However, a test score from an achievement battery should not be used alone in making such a significant decision" (Hoover et al., 1994).

[3]Between 2 and 3 percent of students failed the initial exam at each grade level but were ultimately "waived" into the next grade.

of standardized achievement testing in the context of promotion or retention decisions about individual students.

Second, there is persuasive research evidence that grade retention typically has no beneficial academic or social effects on students.[4] The past failures of grade retention policies need not be repeated. But they provide a cautionary lesson: making grade retention—or the threat of retention—an effective educational policy requires consistent and sustained effort.

Third, public discussion of social promotion has made little reference to current retention practices—in which a very large share of American schoolchildren are already retained in grade. In part, this is because of sporadic data collection and reporting, but far more consistent statistical data are available about the practice of grade retention than, say, about academic tracking. It is possible to describe rates, trends, and differentials in grade retention using data from the U.S. Bureau of the Census, but these data have not been used fully to inform the public debate. For this reason, the committee has assembled and analyzed the available data. Our findings about grade retention are summarized here and elaborated in the appendix to Chapter 6.

TRENDS AND DIFFERENTIALS IN GRADE RETENTION

No national or regional agencies monitor social promotion and grade retention. Occasional data on retention are available for some states and localities, but coverage is sparse, and little is known about the comparability of these data (Shepard and Smith, 1989). The committee asked every state education agency to provide summaries of recent data on grade retention, but only 22 states, plus the District of Columbia, provided data on retention at any grade level. Many states did not respond, and 13 states collect no data at all on grade retention. Among responding states, retention tends to be high in the early primary grades—although not in kindergarten—and in the early high school years, and retention rates are highly variable across states.

---

[4]The failure of past programs is recognized in President Clinton's initiative to end social promotion: "Ending social promotions by simply holding more students back is the wrong choice. Students who are required to repeat a year are more likely to eventually drop out, and rarely catch up academically with their peers. The right way is to ensure that more students are prepared to meet challenging academic standards in the first place" (Clinton, 1998).

The committee's main source of information on levels, trends, and differentials in grade retention is the Current Population Survey (CPS) of the U.S. Bureau of the Census. Using published data from the annual October School Enrollment Supplement of the CPS, it is possible to track the distribution of school enrollment by age and grade each year for groups defined by sex and race/ethnicity. These data have the advantage of comparable national coverage from year to year, but they say nothing directly about educational transitions or about the role of high-stakes testing in grade retention. We can only infer the minimum rate of grade retention by observing changes in the enrollment of children below the modal grade level for their age from one calendar year to the next. Suppose, for example, that 10 percent of 6-year-old children were enrolled below the 1st grade in October 1994. If 15 percent of those children were enrolled below the 2nd grade in October 1995, when they were 7 years old, we would infer that at least 5 percent were held back in the 1st grade between 1994 and 1995.

Extended Kindergarten Attendance

Over the past two decades, attendance in kindergarten has been extended to two years for many children in American schools,[5] with the consequence that age at entry into graded school has gradually crept upward and become more variable. There is no single name for this phenomenon, nor are there distinct categories for the first and second years of kindergarten in Census enrollment data. As Shepard (1991) reports, the names for such extended kindergarten classrooms include "junior-first," "prefirst," "transition," and "readiness room." Fragmentary reports suggest that, in some places, kindergarten retention may have been as high as 50 percent in the late 1980s (Shepard, 1989, 1991). The degree to which early retention decisions originate with parents—for example, to increase their children's chances for success in athletics—rather than with teachers or other school personnel is not known. Moreover, there are no sound national estimates of the prevalence of kindergarten retention, and none of the state data in Appendix Table 6-1 indicate exceptionally high kindergarten retention rates.

The Census Bureau's statistics show that, from the early 1970s to the

---

[5] Another relevant factor is change in state or local requirements about the exact age a child must reach before entering kindergarten or first grade.

late 1980s, age at entry into 1st grade gradually increased, but for the past decade there has been little change. Among 6-year-old boys, only 8 percent had not yet entered the 1st grade in 1971; in 1987 the number was 22 percent, and in 1996 it was almost that high—21 percent. Among 6-year-old girls, only 4 percent had not yet entered 1st grade in 1971; the number grew to 16 percent in 1987 and to 17 percent in 1996. Although boys are consistently more likely than girls to enter 1st grade after age 6, there are only small differences among the rates for blacks, whites, and Hispanics.

One contributing factor to the rising age at entry into 1st grade has been a rising age at entry into kindergarten, which is not related to retention.[6] Although it is not known how widely tests are used in assigning students to extended kindergarten, there is substantial professional criticism of the practice. According to Shepard (1991), such decisions may be based on evidence of "immaturity or academic deficiencies." Shepard adds, "Tests used to make readiness and retention decisions are not technically accurate enough to justify making special placements. . . . Readiness tests are either thinly disguised IQ tests (called developmental screening measures) or academic skills tests. . . . Both types of tests tend to identify disproportionate numbers of poor and minority children as unready for school" (1991:287). Other educators, however, believe that such tests may appropriately be used for placement decisions about young children.

An advisory group of the National Educational Goals Panel has recommended against the use of standardized achievement measures to make decisions about young children or their schools: "Before age 8, standardized achievement measures are not sufficiently accurate to be used for high-stakes decisions about individual children and schools" (Shepard et al., 1998:31). This committee has reached a similar conclusion. At the same time, the advisory group encouraged one type of testing of young children: "Beginning at age 5, it is possible to use direct measures, including measures of children's learning, as part of a comprehensive early childhood system to monitor trends. Matrix sampling procedures should be used to ensure technical accuracy and at the same time protect against the misuse of data to make decisions about individual children" (Shepard

---

[6]National statistics do not indicate exactly how much extended kindergarten may have contributed to the rise in age at entry into graded school because they do not provide direct information about transitions between grade levels (or retention in grade) from year to year.

et al., 1998:27).[7] With young children, it is especially important to distinguish between uses of tests to monitor the progress of large groups and to make decisions about the future of individual students.

Research on kindergarten retention suggests that it carries no academic or social benefits for students. Shepard's (1991:287) review of 16 controlled studies found "no difference academically between unready children who spent an extra year before first grade and at-risk controls who went directly on to first grade." She did, however, find evidence that most children were traumatized by being held back (Shepard, 1989, 1991; Shepard and Smith, 1988, 1989). Shepard further reports that "matched schools that do not practice kindergarten retention have just as high average achievement as those that do but tend to provide more individualized instruction within normal grade placements" (Shepard, 1991:287).

In some cases, even with special treatment for retained students, they were no better off than similar students who had been promoted and given no exceptional treatment. Leinhardt (1980) compared at-risk children in a transition room who received individualized instruction in reading with a group of at-risk children who had been promoted and received no individualized instruction. The two groups performed comparably at the end of first grade, but both performed worse than a second comparison group that had been promoted and given individualized reading instruction.

Retention in the Primary and Secondary Grades

"Age-grade retardation" is a term that refers to enrollment below the modal grade level for a child's age—and no broader meaning is either intended or implied. For example, consider children who were 6 to 8 years old in 1987—the most recent birth cohort whose history can be traced all the way from ages 6 to 8 up through ages 15 to 17. At ages 6 to 8, 21 percent were enrolled below the modal grade for their age; some of this below-grade enrollment reflects differentials in age at school entry, but some represents early grade retention. By 1990, when this cohort reached ages 9 to 11, age-grade retardation grew to 28 percent, and it was 31 percent in 1993, when the cohort reached ages 12 to 14. By 1996,

---

[7]In matrix sampling, each child takes part of a test, and performance levels are estimated statistically for groups of students.

when the cohort reached ages 15 to 17, the percentage who were either below the modal grade level (or had left school) was 36 percent. Almost all of the growth in retardation after ages 12 to 14, however, was due to school dropout, rather than grade retention among the enrolled. In most birth cohorts, age-grade retardation occurs mainly between ages 6 to 8 and 9 to 11 or between ages 12 to 14 and 15 to 17.

Age-grade retardation increased in every cohort that reached ages 6 to 8 from the early 1970s through the mid- to late 1980s. It increased at ages 15 to 17 for cohorts that reached ages 6 to 8 after the mid-1970s, despite a slow decline in its dropout component throughout the period. That is, grade retention increased while dropping out decreased. Among cohorts entering school after 1970, the proportion enrolled below the modal grade level was never less than 10 percent at ages 6 to 8, and it exceeded 20 percent for cohorts of the late 1980s. Age-grade retardation has declined slightly for cohorts that reached ages 6 to 8 after the mid-1980s, but rates have not moved back to the levels of the early 1970s. Overall, a large number of children are held back during elementary school. Among cohorts who reached ages 6 to 8 in the 1980s and early 1990s, age-grade retardation reached 25 to 30 percent by ages 9 to 11.

Retention After School Entry

Age-grade retardation cumulates rapidly after age 6. For example, among children who were 6 years old in 1987, enrollment below the modal grade increased by almost 5 percentage points between ages 6 and 7 and by 5 percentage points more between ages 7 and 9. The trend appears to be a decline in retention between ages 6 and 7 after the early 1980s. That is, there appears to have been a shift in elementary school grade retardation downward in age from the transition between ages 6 and 7 to somewhere between ages 4 and 6.

How much retention is there after ages 6 to 8? And does the recent growth in grade retardation by ages 6 to 8 account for its observed growth at older ages? Age-grade retardation grows substantially after ages 6 to 8 as a result of retention in grade. For example, among children who reached ages 6 to 8 between 1972 and 1985, almost 20 percent more were below the modal grade for their age by the time they were 15 to 17 years old. Among children who reached ages 6 to 8 between the mid-1970s and the mid-1980s, age-grade retardation grew by about 10 percentage points by ages 9 to 11, and it grew by close to 5 percentage points more by ages 12 to 14. Relative to ages 6 to 8, age-grade retardation at ages 9 to 11 and at ages 12 to 14 increased for cohorts who were 6 to 8 years old in the early 1970s; it was stable from the mid-1970s to the mid-1980s; and it has declined since then. However, the gap between retention at ages 15 to 17 and that at ages 6 to 8 has been relatively stable—close to 20 percentage points—with the possible exception of a very recent downward turn. Thus, the rise in age at entry into 1st grade—which is partly due to kindergarten retention—accounts for much of the overall increase in age-grade retardation among teenagers.

In summary, grade retention is pervasive in American schools. Ending social promotion probably means retaining even larger numbers of children. Given the evidence that retention is typically not educationally beneficial—leading to lower achievement and higher dropout—the implications of such a policy are cause for concern.

Social Differences in Retention

Boys are initially more likely than girls to be placed below the typical grade for their age, and they fall farther behind girls as they move through school. Overall, the sex differential gradually increases with age from 5 percentage points at ages 6 to 8 to 10 percentage points at ages 15 to 17.

Differences in age-grade retardation by race and ethnicity are even more striking than the gender differential. Rates of age-grade retardation are very similar among whites, blacks, and Hispanics at ages 6 to 8. But by ages 9 to 11, 5 to 10 percent more blacks and Hispanics than whites are enrolled below the modal grade level. The differentials continue to grow with age, and, at ages 15 to 17, rates of age-grade retardation range from 40 to 50 percent among blacks and Hispanics, and they have gradually drifted up from 25 percent to 35 percent among whites.

Gender and race/ethnic differentials in recent years result mainly from retention, not differences in age at school entry. By age 9, there are sharp social differentials in age-grade retardation favoring whites and girls relative to blacks or Hispanics and boys. By ages 15 to 17, close to 50 percent of black males have fallen behind—30 percentage points more than at ages 6 to 8—but age-grade retardation has never exceeded 30 percent among 15- to 17-year-old white girls.

PSYCHOMETRICS OF CERTIFICATION

This section addresses the underlying rationale for using tests in promotion decisions and then describes the evidence required to validate such use.

Logic of Certification Decisions

Promotion can be thought of in two ways: First, as recognition for mastering the material taught at a given grade level. In this case, a test used to determine whether a student should be promoted would certify that mastery. Second, promotion can also be thought of as a prediction that the student would profit more by studying the material offered in the next grade than by studying again the material in the current grade. In this case, the test is a placement device. At present, most school districts and states having promotion policies use tests as a means of assessing mastery (American Federation of Teachers, 1997a). Furthermore, retention in grade is the most common consequence for students who are found to lack this mastery (Shepard, 1991).

Validating a particular test use includes making explicit the assumptions or claims that underpin that use (Kane, 1992; Shepard, 1991, 1997). On one hand, the most critical assumption in the case of a promotion test certifying mastery is that it is a valid measure of the important content, skills, and other attributes covered by the curriculum of that grade. If, on the other hand, the test is used as a placement device, the most critical assumption is that the assigned grade (or intervention, such as summer school) will benefit the student more than the alternative placement.

In either case, the scores should be shown to be technically sound, and the cutoff score should be a reasonably accurate indication of mastery of the skills in question. As explained in Chapter 4, not every underlying assumption must be documented empirically, but the assembled evidence should be sufficient to make a credible case that the use of the test for this purpose is appropriate—that is, both valid and fair.

Validation of Test Use

Tests used for promotion decisions should adhere, as appropriate, to professional standards for placement, and more generally, to professional standards for certifying knowledge and skill (American Educational Research Association et al., 1985, 1998; Joint Committee on Testing Practices, 1988). These psychometric standards have two central principles:

(1) A test score, like any other source of information about a student, is subject to error. Therefore, high-stakes decisions like promotion should not be made automatically on the basis of a single test score. They should also take into account other sources of information about the student's skills, such as grades, recommendations, and extenuating circumstances. This is especially true with young children (Shepard and Smith, 1987; Darling-Hammond and Falk, 1995). According to a recent survey, most districts report that they base promotion decisions in elementary school on grades (48 percent), standardized tests (39 percent), developmental factors (46 percent), attendance (31 percent), and recommendations (48 percent). The significance of these factors varies with grade level. It appears that achievement tests are more often used for promotion decisions in the elementary grades than in secondary school: at the high school level, they are used by only 26 percent of districts (American Federation of Teachers, 1997a:12).

(2) Assessing students in more than one subject will improve the likelihood of making valid and fair promotion decisions.[8]

Content Coverage

The choice of construct used for making promotion decisions will not only determine, to a large extent, the content and scoring criteria, but it will also potentially disadvantage some students. Depending on whether the construct to be measured is "readiness for the next grade level" or "mastery of the material taught at the current grade level," the content and thought processes to be assessed may be quite different. The first construct might be adequately represented by a reading test *if* readiness for the next grade level is determined solely by a student's ability to read the material presented at that level. With the second construct, however, the number of subjects to be assessed is expanded, along with the type of evidence needed to validate the test use.

In the case of a promotion test being used to certify mastery, it is

---

[8]For example, in 1997 the Florida legislature set forth several new requirements supporting higher student standards. These include a requirement that student progression from one grade to the next be determined by proficiency in three areas: reading, writing, and mathematics (National Coalition of Advocates for Students, 1998).

important that the items employed be generally representative of the content and skills that students have actually covered at their current grade level. For example, in the case of a reading test, evidence of content-appropriateness might be the degree of alignment between the reading curriculum for that grade level and the test. Evidence that the test measures relevant cognitive processes might be obtained by asking a student to think aloud while completing the items or tasks.[9] In addition, the suitability of the scoring criteria could be assessed by examining the relative weighting given to the content and skills measured by the reading test and comparing this to the emphasis given these areas in the curriculum. Some of this information may be collected during test development and documented in the user's manual, or it may be obtained by the user during testing.

Whether the test is being used to certify mastery or predict readiness, students' scores on the test should be interpreted carefully. Plausible rival interpretations of low scores need to be discounted (Messick, 1989). For example, a low score might be interpreted as showing lack of competence, but it could in fact be caused by low motivation or sickness on the day of the test. Or the low score could result from lack of alignment between the test and what was taught in class. Language or disabilities may also be relevant. One way to discount plausible rival interpretations of low scores is to take into account other sources of information about the student's skills, such as grades, recommendations, and extenuating circumstances (American Educational Research Association et al., 1985, 1998).

Setting the Cutoff Score

Chapter 5 described different procedures for setting cutoff scores (cutscores) on tests used for tracking, as well as some of the difficulties involved. With promotion tests, the validity of the cutscore similarly depends on the reasonableness of the standard-setting process and its consequences—especially if they differ by gender, race, or language-mi-

---

[9]This same kind of evidence can illuminate possible differences in meaning or interpretation of test scores across subgroups of examinees, and it can help determine the extent to which capabilities irrelevant or ancillary to the construct may be differentially affecting their performance (American Educational Research Association et al., 1985, 1998).

nority groups (American Educational Research Association et al., 1985, 1998).

Different methods often yield very different standards (Berk, 1986; Mehrens, 1995). Shepard reports that these "discrepancies between standards are large enough to cause important differences in the percentage of students who pass the test" (1980). For example, in many states, fewer students attain the cutscore for the "proficient" level on the 4th grade reading test in the National Assessment of Educational Progress (NAEP) than attain the cutscore for the "proficient" level on the state's own 4th grade reading test (U.S. Department of Education, 1997). This is because the NAEP standards for "basic," "proficient," and "advanced" achievement are generally more challenging than those of the states. Even using the current "basic" achievement level on NAEP as a cutscore for a 4th grade reading test could lead to failure rates of 40 percent (U.S. Department of Education, 1997).

Because of such inconsistencies and their possible impact on students, it is generally recommended that the particular method and rationale for setting the cutscore on a test, as well as the qualifications of the judges, be documented as part of the test validation process.

When a score falls within the range of uncertainty around the cutoff,[10] other information should be examined to reduce the likelihood of placement or certification error. Current professional standards recommend that a student's score on a test be used only in conjunction with other information sources in making such important decisions as promotion to the next grade. This concern applies not only to students who score near or below the cutoff; there can also be students who "pass" the test but have not really mastered the material (Madaus, 1983).

Choosing a cutoff score on a test is a substantive judgment. More than a purely technical decision, it also involves social concerns, politics, and maintaining credibility with the public (Ellwein and Glass, 1989). Public relations played a role in the setting of cutscores on the Iowa tests that are part of Chicago's bid to end social promotion. The cutscores on

---

[10]As discussed in Chapter 4, test reliability may be envisioned as the stability or consistency of scores on a test. An important aspect of the reliability of a test is its standard error of measurement. A small standard error around a student's score is especially important in relation to the setting of cutscores on a test because these may function as decision mechanisms for the placement of students in different grades. A small standard error of measurement for scores near the cutscore gives us more confidence in decisions based on the cutscores.

the reading and mathematics tests were set at what were perceived to be relatively reasonable levels (2.8 for third graders, 5.3 for sixth graders, and 7.2 for eighth graders) with the intention of raising them later (interview with Joe Hahn, director, Research, Assessment, and Quality Review, Chicago school district).[11]

"We decided to be credible to the public," Chicago Chief Accountability Officer Philip Hansen told the committee. "If that 3rd grader doesn't get a 2.8 in reading, the public and the press and everyone understands clearly, more clearly than educators, that, gee, that's a problem, so they can see why that child needs to be given extra help . . . . Our problem comes with explaining it to educators as to why we don't use other indicators."

Educational Outcomes

As mentioned earlier, tests used for student promotion are usually thought to measure mastery of material already taught, but a promotion test may also be interpreted as indicating a student's readiness for the next grade. In the latter case, it would be relevant to obtain evidence that there is a relationship between the test score and certain pertinent criterion measures at the next grade level.[12]

For example, in the case of a reading test, it may be useful to demonstrate that there is a relationship between students' scores on the promotion test and their scores on a reading test taken at the end of the next school year. Such evidence of predictive validity would, however, not usually be enough to justify use of the test for making promotion decisions. Additional evidence would be needed that the alternative treatments (i.e., promotion, retention in grade, or some other intervention)

---

[11]These cutscores are strictly adhered to; failure to reach them results in mandatory summer school. Upon completion of the six-week summer program, students may retake the test in a different form. If they reach the cutscore, they go on to the next grade. Some students who come close to the cutoff (e.g., passing in one subject and coming very close in another) may be retested in January (Chicago Public Schools, 1997a).

[12]Evidence about relations to other variables can also be used to investigate questions of differential prediction for groups. A finding that the relation of test scores to a relevant criterion variable differs from one group to another may imply that the meaning of the scores is not the same for members of the different groups, perhaps due to construct underrepresentation or construct-irrelevant variables (American Educational Research Association et al., 1985, 1998).

were more beneficial to the students assigned to them than would be the case if everyone got the same treatment (American Educational Research Association et al., 1985, 1998; Haney, 1993; Linn, 1997).

This evidence of an "aptitude-by-treatment interaction" could be gathered by taking a group of students who fall just below the cutoff score on the reading test and randomly retaining or promoting them. At the end of the first year, students who were promoted could be given a reading test and their scores recorded. The same test would be given a year later to the students who were retained—after they had been promoted and had spent a year at the next grade level. The results of the two groups could then be compared to see which group benefited the most—if "benefit" is defined as scoring higher on the test. In addition, because reading is necessary for learning other subjects, another potential benefit to examine is differential subject matter learning.[13]

Effects of Retention

Determining whether the use of a promotion test produces better overall educational outcomes requires weighing the intended benefits against unintended negative consequences for individual students and groups of students (American Educational Research Association et al., 1985; Cronbach, 1971; Joint Committee on Testing Practices, 1988; Messick, 1989).

Most of the relevant research focuses on one outcome in particular—retention in grade. Although retention rates can change even when tests are not used in making promotion decisions, there is evidence that using scores from large-scale tests to make such decisions may be associated with increased retention rates (Hendrie, 1997).

---

[13]According to a recent American Federation of Teachers report (1997a:9), "in the early 1980s, partly in response to A Nation at Risk's (U.S. Department of Education, 1983) dire message about low student achievement, many districts passed stringent policies requiring retention of students based on their performance on standardized tests (Roderick, 1995). Chicago, New York City, Boston, Philadelphia, and Dade County, Fla., all instituted policies to retain students who failed standardized tests at various transitional points along the K-12 continuum. By the late 1980s, however, those policies were rescinded when research studies indicated that student achievement of retained students was not improved compared to students with similar reading scores who were socially promoted, but the retained student's dropout rate was higher (Gampert and Opperman, 1988; Olson, 1990; Darling-Hammond and Falk, 1995)."

Increased retention is not a negative outcome if it benefits students. But are there positive consequences of being held back in school because of a test score? Does the student do better after repeating the grade, or would he have fared just as well or better if he had been promoted with his peers? Research data indicate that simply repeating a grade does not generally improve achievement (Holmes, 1989; House, 1989); moreover, it increases the dropout rate (Gampert and Opperman, 1988; Grissom and Shepard, 1989; Olson, 1990; Anderson, 1994; Darling-Hammond and Falk, 1995; Luppescu et al., 1995; Reardon, 1996).

For example, Holmes (1989) reports a meta-analysis of 63 controlled studies of grade retention in elementary and junior high school through the mid-1980s. When promoted and retained students were compared one to three years later, the retained students' average levels of academic achievement were at least 0.4 standard deviations below those of promoted students. In these comparisons, promoted and retained students were the same age, but the promoted students had completed one more grade than the retained students. Promoted and retained students were also compared after completing one or more grades, that is, when the retained students were a year older than the promoted students but had completed equal numbers of additional grades. Here, the findings were less consistent, but still negative. When the data were weighted by the number of estimated effects, there was an initially positive effect of retention on academic achievement after one more grade in school, but it faded away completely after three or more grades. When the data were weighted by the number of independent studies, rather than by the estimated number of effects on achievement, the average effects were negligible in every year after retention. Of the 63 studies reviewed by Holmes, 54 yielded overall negative effects of retention, and only 9 yielded overall positive effects. Some studies had better statistical controls than others, and those with subjects matched on IQ, achievement test scores, sex, and/or socioeconomic status showed larger negative effects of retention than studies with weaker designs. Holmes concluded, "On average, retained children are worse off than their promoted counterparts on both personal adjustment and academic outcomes" (1989:27). A more recent study of Baltimore schoolchildren concludes that grade retention does increase the chances of academic success (Alexander et al., 1994), but a detailed reanalysis of those findings yields no evidence of sustained positive effects (Shepard et al., 1996).

Anderson (1994) carried out an extensive large-scale national study of the effect of grade retention on high school dropout rates. He analyzed data from the National Longitudinal Study of Youth for more than 5,500 students whose school attendance was followed annually from 1978-1979 to 1985-1986. With statistical controls for sex, race/ethnicity, social background, cognitive ability, adolescent deviance, early transitions to adult status, and several school-related measures, students who were currently repeating a grade were 70 percent more likely to drop out of high school than students who were not currently repeating a grade.

There are also strong relationships between race, socioeconomic status (SES), and the use of tests for promotion and retention. A recent national longitudinal study, using the National Education Longitudinal Study database, shows that certain students are far likelier than others to be subject to promotion tests in the 8th grade (Reardon, 1996:4-5):

> [S]tudents in urban schools, in schools with high concentrations of low-income and minority students, and schools in southern and western states, are considerably more likely to have [high-stakes] test requirements in eighth grade. Among eighth graders, 35 percent of black students and 27 percent of Hispanic students are subject to [a high-stakes test in at least one subject] to advance to ninth grade, compared to 15 percent of white students. Similarly, 25 percent of students in the lowest SES quartile, but only 14 percent of those in the top quartile, are subject to eighth grade [high-stakes test] requirements.

Moreover, the study found that the presence of high-stakes 8th grade tests is associated with sharply higher dropout rates, especially for students at schools serving mainly low-SES students. For such students, early dropout rates—between the 8th and 10th grades—were 4 to 6 percentage points higher than for students from schools that were similar excepting the high-stakes test requirement (Reardon, 1996).

What does it mean that minority students and low-SES students are more likely to be subject to high-stakes tests in the 8th grade? Perhaps, as Reardon points out, such policies are "related to the prevalence of low-achieving students—the group proponents believe the tests are most likely to help" (1996). Perhaps the adoption of high-stakes test policies for individuals serves the larger social purpose of ensuring that promotion from 8th to 9th grades reflects acquisition of certain knowledge and skills. Such tests may also motivate less able students and teachers to work harder or to focus their attention on the knowledge domains that test developers value most highly. But if retention in grade is not, on balance, beneficial for students, as the research suggests (Shepard and Smith, 1989), it is cause for concern that low-SES children and minority students are disproportionately subject to any negative consequences.

Those who leave school without diplomas have diminished life chances. High dropout rates carry many social costs. It may thus be problematic if high-stakes tests lead individual students who would not otherwise have done so to drop out. There may also be legal implications if it appears that the public is prepared to adopt high-stakes test programs chiefly when their consequences will be felt disproportionately by minority students[14] and low-SES students.

Negative findings about the effects of grade retention on dropout rates are reported by Grissom and Shepard (1989), based on data for several localities including the 1979 to 1981 freshman classes from the Chicago Public Schools. Another Chicago study, of students in 1987, by Luppescu et al. (1995), showed that retained students had lower achievement scores. Throughout this period, the Chicago Public Schools cycled through successive policies of loose and restrictive promotion policies, and it is not clear how long, and with what consequences, the present strict policies will hold (Chicago Public Schools, 1997a).

New York City appears to be following a similar cycle of strict and loose retention policies, in which the unsuccessful Promotional Gates program of the 1980s was at first "promising," then "withered," and was finally canceled by 1990, only to be revived in 1998 by a new central administration (Steinberg, 1998a, 1998b). This cycle of policies, combining strict retention criteria with a weak commitment to remedial instruction, is likely to reconfirm past evidence that retention in grade is typically harmful to students.

Another important question is whether the use of a test in making promotion decisions exacerbates existing inequalities or creates new ones. For example, in their case study of a school district that decided to use tests as a way to raise standards, Ellwein and Glass (1989) found that test information was being used selectively in making promotion and retention decisions, leading to what was perceived as negative consequences for certain groups of students.[15] Thus, although minorities accounted for 59 percent of the students who failed the 1985 kindergarten test, they made up 69 percent of the students who were retained and received

---

[14]For a discussion of possible claims of discrimination based on race or national origin, see Chapter 3.

[15]Ellwein and Glass (1989) assumed that the intervention, i.e., retention, was not as beneficial as promotion to the next grade level.

transition services. A similar pattern was observed at grade 2. In this instance, disproportionate retention rates stemming from selective test use constitutes evidence of test invalidity (National Research Council, 1982).

In addition, there may be problems with using a test as the *sole* measure of the effectiveness of retention or other interventions (summer school, tutoring, and so on). This concern is related to the fact that the validity of test and retest scores depends in part on whether the scores reflect students' familiarity with actual test items or a particular test format. For example, there is some evidence to indicate that improved scores on one test may not actually carry over when a new test of the same knowledge and skills is introduced (Koretz et al., 1991).

The current reform and test-based accountability systems of the Chicago Public Schools provide an example of high-stakes test use for individual students that raises serious questions about "teaching to the test." Although Chicago is developing its own standards-based, course-specific assessment system, it is committed to using the Iowa Test of Basic Skills as the yardstick for student and school accountability. Teachers are given detailed manuals on preparing their students for the tests (Chicago Public Schools, 1996a, 1996b). Student test scores have increased substantially, both during the intensive summer remedial sessions—the Summer Bridge program—and between the 1996-1997 and 1997-1998 school years (Chicago Public Schools, 1997b, 1998b), but the available data provide no means of distinguishing true increases in student learning from artifactual gains. Such gains would be expected from the combined effects of teaching to the test, repeated use of a similar test, and, in the case of the Summer Bridge program, the initial selection of students with low scores on the test.[16]

Alternatives to Retention

Some policymakers and practitioners have rejected the simplistic alternatives of promoting or retaining students based on test scores. Instead, they favor intermediate approaches: testing early to identify students whose performance is weak; providing remedial education to help such students acquire the skills necessary to pass the test; and giving

---

[16]In the Chicago Public Schools, each retest is based on an alternative form of the Iowa Test of Basic Skills.

students multiple opportunities to retake different forms of the test in the hope that they will pass and avoid retention. Here, testing can play an important and positive role in early diagnosis and targeted remediation.

Intervention strategies appear to be particularly crucial from kindergarten through grade 2 (Shepard et al., 1998; American Federation of Teachers, 1997a). Some of the intensive strategies being used at this level include preschool expansion, giving children who are seriously behind their age-level peers opportunities to accelerate their instruction, and putting children in smaller classes with expert teachers.[17] Such strategies are being implemented in school districts across the country.[18] Data on their effectiveness are as yet unavailable.

It is the committee's view that these alternatives to social promotion and simple retention in grade should be tried and evaluated. In our judgment, however, the effectiveness of such approaches will depend on the quality of the instruction that students receive after failing a promotion test, and it will be neither simple nor inexpensive to provide high-quality remedial instruction. At present only 13 states require and fund such intervention programs to help low-performing students reach the state standards, and 6 additional states require intervention but provide no resources for carrying it out.[19]

---

[17]General intervention strategies employed throughout grades K-12, as described to the committee by James Watts of the Southern Regional Education Board, include clear core-content standards for each grade and course, clear communication of these standards to teachers and parents, having expert faculty, professional development for teachers, and extra instruction beyond the regular school day.

[18]In the Long Beach School District in California, children are assessed beginning in kindergarten. When problems are found, interventions include parent-teacher conferences and mandatory summer school after grade 2. If after completing the 3rd grade and subsequent summer school a student has not reached the 1st grade reading level, he or she is retained in the 3rd grade until reaching the 1st grade reading level. No single test holds students back (interview with Lynn Winters of the Long Beach School District). Cincinnati uses grouping and intervention as well as intensive instruction and smaller classes to help children who appear to be having difficulty staying at grade level (American Federation of Teachers, 1997a).

[19]In Chicago, there is a standard summer program for students who fail the Iowa test at designated grades. Many schools also offer extended-day programs aimed at helping students pass the test. The decision to offer these programs, as well as their content, is made at the school level. Funds for such programs must be found in each school's annual lump-sum allotment (American Federation of Teachers, 1997a).

Issues of Fairness

As discussed in Chapter 4, a fair promotion test is one that yields comparably valid scores from person to person, from group to group, and from setting to setting. This means that if a promotion test results in scores that systematically underestimate or overestimate the knowledge and skill of members of a particular group, then the test would be considered unfair. Or if the promotion test claims to measure a single construct across groups but in fact measures different constructs in different groups, it would also be unfair. The view of fairness as equitable treatment of all examinees in the testing process requires that examinees be given a comparable opportunity to demonstrate their understanding of the construct(s) the promotion test is intended to measure. This includes such factors as appropriate testing conditions on the day of the test, opportunity to become familiar with the test format, and access to practice materials.

The view of fairness as opportunity to learn is particularly relevant in the context of a promotion test used to certify mastery of the material taught. In this regard, when assessing the fairness of a promotion test, it is important that test users ask whether certain groups of students are doing poorly on the test due to insufficient opportunities to learn the material tested. Thus there is a need for evidence that the content of the test is representative of what students have been taught. Chapter 7 discusses several ways of demonstrating that the test measures what students have been taught in the context of graduation tests, although much of this discussion is also relevant to promotion tests. For example, to enhance the fairness of promotion tests linked to state-wide standards and frameworks, states should develop and widely disseminate a specific definition of the domain to be tested; try to analyze item-response patterns on the test by districts, schools within a district, or by student characteristics (for example, race, gender, curriculum tracks in high school, and so on); and plan and, when feasible, carry out a series of small-scale evaluations on the impact of the test on the curriculum and on teaching (Madaus, 1983).[20] Taken together, these steps should increase the chance that these tests give students a fair opportunity to demonstrate what they know and are able to do.

---

[20]Judgmental methods for the review of tests and test items are often supplemented by statistical procedures for identifying items that function differently across identifiable subgroups of examinees.

Finally, the validity and fairness of test score interpretations used in promotion decisions can be enhanced by employing the following sound educational strategies:

(1) identifying at-risk or struggling students early so they can be targeted for extra help;

(2) providing students with multiple opportunities to demonstrate their knowledge through repeated testing with alternate forms or other appropriate means; and

(3) taking into account other relevant information about individual students (American Educational Research Association et al., 1985).

The committee's findings and recommendations about promotion and retention are reported in Chapter 12.

TECHNICAL APPENDIX
Social Promotion and Age-Grade Retardation

Current public discussion of social promotion has made little reference to current retention practices—in which a very large share of American schoolchildren are already retained in grade. In part, this is because of sporadic data collection and reporting, but far more consistent statistical data are available about the practice of grade retention than, say, about academic tracking. These data have not been used fully to inform the public debate. For this reason, and to support its analyses of high-stakes testing for promotion and retention, the committee has assembled and analyzed data on rates, trends, and differentials in grade retention. Some of the available data have been collected by state education agencies, but the most uniform, long-term data have been collected by the U.S. Bureau of the Census in connection with its Current Population Survey (CPS), the same monthly household survey that produces important economic statistics, like the unemployment rate. This appendix presents the details of the committee's analysis.

No national or regional agency monitors social promotion and grade retention. Occasional data on retention are available for some states and localities, but coverage is sparse, and little is known about the comparability of these data (Shepard and Smith, 1989). For example, the denominators of retention rates may be based on beginning-of-year or end-of-year enrollment figures. The numerators may include retention as of the end of an academic year or as of the end of the following summer session. Some states include special education students in the data; others exclude them. In the primary grades, retention is usually an all-or-nothing matter; in high school, retention may imply that a student has completed some requirements but has too few credits to be promoted.

Table 6-1 shows all of the state data collected by Shepard and Smith (1989:7-8) from the late and mid-1980s, updated with data from 1993 to 1996 that other states have provided. Although we have inquired of every state education agency, 15 states have not responded. Some states do not collect retention data at all, or collect very limited data. For example, 13 states—Colorado, Connecticut, Illinois, Kansas, Montana, Nebraska, Nevada, New Hampshire, New Jersey, North Dakota, Pennsylvania, Utah, and Wyoming—collect no state-level data on grade retention. Another 22 states, plus the District of Columbia, provided data on retention at some grade levels, but in some cases the data were very limited. For example, New York State collects such data only at the 8th grade.

We can offer few generalizations from the table. Retention rates are highly variable across states. They are unusually high in the District of Columbia, most of whose students are black. Rates are relatively low in some states, like Ohio, including states with relatively large minority populations, like South Carolina and Georgia. Retention rates tend to be relatively high in the early primary grades—although not in kindergarten—and in the early high school years. Perhaps the most striking fact from this effort to bring together available data is that—despite the prominence of social promotion as an issue of educational policy—very little information about it is available.

The committee's main resource for information about levels, trends, and differentials in grade retention is the CPS. Using published data from the annual October School Enrollment Supplement of the CPS, it is possible to track the distribution of school enrollment by age and grade each year for population groups defined by sex and race/ethnicity. These data have the advantage of comparable national coverage from year to year, but they say nothing directly about educational transitions. We can only infer the minimum rate of grade retention by observing trends in the enrollment of children below the modal grade level for their age from one calendar year to the next. Suppose, for example, that 10 percent of 6-year-old children were enrolled below the 1st grade in October 1994. If 15 percent of those children were enrolled below the 2nd grade in October 1995, when they were 7 years old, we would infer that at least 5 percent were held back in the 1st grade between 1994 and 1995.

EXTENDED KINDERGARTEN ATTENDANCE

Historically, there has been great variation in age at school entry in the United States, which had more to do with the labor demands of a farm economy and the availability of schooling to disadvantaged groups than with readiness for school. The variability declined as school enrollment completed its diffusion from middle childhood into younger and older ages (Duncan, 1968; National Research Council, 1989).

Contrary to the historic trend, age at entry into graded school has gradually crept up and again become more variable over the past two decades, partly through selective extension of kindergarten to two years,

TABLE 6-1 Percentages of Students Retained in Grade in Selected States by Grade-Level and Year

Grade Level	PK	K	1	2	3	4	5
Alabama							
1994-95	NA	4.6	7.7	2.8	2.4	2.1	2.1
1995-96	NA	4.4	7.9	2.9	2.3	2.3	2.4
1996-97	NA	5.1	8.5	3.3	2.5	2.1	2.0
Arizona							
1979-80	NA	5.2	7.7	4.0	2.4	1.9	1.4
1985-86	NA	8.0	20.0	8.0	5.0	4.0	4.0
1994-95	18.0	1.4	2.4	0.9	0.6	0.4	0.4
1995-96	18.9	1.6	2.4	1.0	0.6	0.4	0.4
1996-97	14.8	1.7	2.2	1.0	0.7	0.5	0.5
California							
1988-89		5.7	4.4	1.8	1.1	0.6	0.5
Delaware							
1979-80	NA	NA	11.4	5.1	2.9	2.4	3.1
1985-86	NA	5.4	17.2	4.9	2.8	2.3	3.0
1994-95	NA	2.1	5.8	2.1	1.1	0.7	0.6
1995-96	NA	1.6	5.3	2.0	1.9	0.8	0.9
1996-97	NA	2.0	5.0	2.4	1.4	0.9	1.0
District of Columbia							
1979-80	NA	NA	15.3	10.0	7.2	7.2	6.3
1985-86	NA	NA	12.7	8.4	7.4	5.4	4.6
1991-92	NA	NA	12.9	10.8	8.9	6.9	6.5
1992-93			10.4	8.2	7.4	8.0	6.2
1993-94			11.1	7.9	6.3	6.1	5.3
1994-95			12.7	8.5	6.2	5.9	5.8
1995-96			11.4	8.7	7.4	7.0	5.5
1996-97			14.7	11.3	10.8	8.0	6.1
Florida							
1979-80	NA	6.1	13.7	7.4	7.0	5.9	4.6
1985-86	NA	10.5	11.2	4.7	4.5	3.8	2.6
1994-95	3.1	3.0	3.3	1.5	1.1	0.8	0.6
1995-96	1.8	3.1	3.6	1.9	1.2	0.9	0.7
1996-97	3.6	3.6	4.1	2.2	1.5	1.0	0.7

6	7	8	9	10	11	12	Total
3.2	7.3	5.8	13.1	7.2	6.1	3.8	5.4
2.9	6.7	5.4	12.1	7.2	6.2	3.5	5.2
2.9	6.1	4.4	12.6	6.7	5.2	3.1	5.1
1.3	3.1	2.3	4.4	·2.4	2.5	6.9	3.5
4.0	8.0	7.0	6.0	3.0	2.0	14.0	7.2
1.0	2.5	2.2	5.3	3.5	2.3	8.7	2.3
0.9	2.3	2.2	5.4	3.5	2.6	9.7	2.4
1.1	2.7	2.3	7.0	5.0	3.1	10.2	2.8
0.5	1.0	0.7					
2.4	7.9	8.1	13.1	12.6	7.7	6.6	7.0
3.2	9.6	7.7	15.6	16.8	8.7	7.5	8.1
1.4	3.4	1.7	NA	NA	NA	NA	NA
1.3	2.8	1.6	NA	NA	NA	NA	NA
1.9	3.4	2.8	NA	NA	NA	NA	NA
3.1	NA	NA	20.5	NA	NA	16.6	NA
2.8	10.6	6.6	NA	NA	NA	NA	7.3
3.0	17.3	17.6	15.2	22.1	18.3	11.8	
3.3	18.5	16.4	16.5	26.0	23.8	12.7	
3.5	15.6	15.2	19.5	23.7	18.6	14.1	
2.4	12.2	13.6	16.1	22.1	15.1	13.9	
2.3	11.9	12.1	16.2	24.3	15.9	13.3	
4.1	15.4	16.5	18.7	21.8	21.7	13.6	
5.5	10.4	8.3	10.2	11.5	7.5	4.4	8.0
3.5	7.9	5.8	12.1	11.9	8.9	3.5	7.2
3.3	4.7	3.6	11.1	9.3	7.8	5.3	4.1
3.7	4.7	3.6	12.8	10.8	7.8	5.2	4.4
4.4	4.9	4.0	14.3	12.1	8.6	5.7	5.0

TABLE 6-1 Continued

Grade Level	PK	K	1	2	3	4	5
Georgia							
1979-80	NA	NA	11.0	4.7	3.8	2.8	2.5
1985-86	NA	8.0	12.4	6.7	7.8	5.2	3.9
1994-95	NA	3.8	3.5	1.5	1.1	0.7	0.6
1995-96	NA	3.7	3.7	1.9	1.2	1.0	0.7
1996-97	NA	3.6	3.8	2.1	1.5	1.0	0.8
1997-98	NA	3.7	4.0	2.4	1.7	1.3	1.1
Hawaii							
1979-80	NA	NA	1.1	0.7	0.5	0.4	0.4
1985-86	NA	2.0	1.6	1.0	0.7	0.5	0.4
Indiana							
1994-95							
1995-96							
1996-97							
Kentucky							
1979-80	NA	2.3	12.6	5.7	3.4	2.2	1.8
1985-86	NA	4.0	5.3	4.9	3.0	2.3	1.9
1994-95	NA	NA	NA	NA	NA	1.1	0.7
1995-96	NA	NA	NA	NA	NA	1.1	0.8
Louisiana							
1995-96		8.7	11.0	5.4	4.4		
Maryland							
1979-80	NA	NA	7.6	3.5	3.3	2.5	2.5
1985-86	NA	NA	NA	NA	NA	NA	NA
1994-95	NA	0.8	2.0	1.1	0.7	0.5	0.2
1995-96	NA	0.9	2.3	1.2	0.7	0.5	0.3
1996-97	NA	1.1	2.8	1.5	1.0	0.7	0.4
Massachusetts							
1994-95						0.3	0.2
1995-96						0.3	0.2
Michigan							
1994-95							
1995-96							

6	7	8	9	10	11	12	Total
2.6	5.3	7.4	13.3	10.8	7.9	4.0	6.5
5.3	6.7	7.5	18.1	12.2	8.7	4.5	8.5
1.5	1.8	1.9	11.6	7.5	5.0	3.0	
1.7	2.1	2.2	12.6	7.7	5.2	3.2	
1.9	2.4	2.2	13.1	8.2	5.6	3.4	
2.1	2.5	2.1	12.4	8.7	5.4	3.5	
0.4	0.2	2.3	13.1	10.1	8.5	5.2	3.8
0.5	2.1	2.8	8.9	6.9	5.5	0.8	2.6
							1.4
							1.6
							1.4
1.9	4.2	3.6	5.8	4.2	2.8	3.2	4.4
2.7	5.4	3.8	9.6	6.3	4.6	3.4	5.3
1.9	2.7	1.6	10.7	6.9	4.0	2.3	3.6
1.8	2.7	1.9	10.7	6.8	4.1	2.2	3.6
1.8	8.5	7.6	8.6	11.3	6.2	4.4	5.8
NA	NA	NA	NA	NA	NA	NA	5.5
2.1	3.2	2.4	13.1	7.1	4.8	4.7	3.1
2.3	3.3	2.3	12.2	6.6	4.7	5.3	3.2
2.5	3.7	2.6	10.3	6.1	4.3	5.5	3.2
0.6	1.5	1.5	6.3	4.5	3.3	2.2	
0.6	1.4	1.5	6.3	4.5	3.6	1.9	
			7.8	5.6	3.8	2.0	
			4.8	3.9	2.7	1.7	

TABLE 6-1 Continued

Grade Level	PK	K	1	2	3	4	5
Mississippi							
1979-80	NA	NA	15.1	6.9	4.8	5.0	5.6
1985-86	NA	1.4	16.1	7.0	5.3	5.7	6.0
1994-95	0.0	4.9	11.9	6.1	4.9	6.2	7.1
1995-96	22.2	4.8	11.6	5.8	4.6	5.6	6.3
1996-97	16.7	5.4	11.9	6.6	5.4	6.1	6.6
New Hampshire							
1979-80	NA	NA	8.6	3.3	2.0	1.3	1.1
1985-86	NA	4.4	9.1	3.7	1.5	1.1	1.0
New Mexico							
1990-91	2.2	6.1	2.8	1.5			
1991-92	1.6	4.8	2.0	1.1			
1992-93	1.5	4.3	1.7	1.2			
1993-94	1.3	4.2	1.9	1.0			
New York							
1994-95	NA	NA	NA	NA	NA	NA	
1995-96	NA	NA	NA	NA	NA	NA	
1996-97	NA	NA	NA	NA	NA	NA	
North Carolina							
1979-80	NA	4.5	9.8	6.0	4.5	3.2	2.8
1985-86	NA	6.0	9.3	5.0	5.7	2.7	2.1
1987-88	NA	7.4	7.7	3.8	2.8	2.0	1.3
1988-89	NA	6.8	7.2	2.9	2.7	1.6	1.1
1989-90	NA	5.3	5.5	2.1	2.0	1.1	0.8
1990-91	NA	3.7	4.0	1.6	1.4	0.8	0.6
1991-92	NA	2.9	4.1	1.9	1.5	0.7	0.6
1992-93	NA	3.0	4.1	2.0	1.6	0.7	0.5
1993-94	NA	3.3	4.8	2.4	1.9	0.9	0.7
1994-95	NA	3.5	4.7	2.4	1.9	1.0	0.7
1995-96	NA	3.8	5.0	2.8	2.1	1.3	0.8
1996-97	NA	4.2	5.7	3.1	2.5	1.4	1.0
Ohio							
1994-95	NA	NA	4.0	1.6	1.2	0.9	0.9
1995-96	NA	NA	4.1	1.7	1.1	0.8	0.7
1996-97	NA	NA	4.7	2.0	1.8	1.1	0.9

6	7	8	9	10	11	12	Total		
5.1	13.5	11.1	12.4	11.7	8.1	6.0	8.9		
5.6	11.2	9.3	12.9	12.6	9.0	5.7	8.9		
8.3	15.4	13.2	21.0	13.5	9.5	6.5	9.6		
7.5	14.2	11.5	20.9	12.9	7.9	5.5	9.5		
7.7	15.6	12.9	19.7	12.8	7.7	5.2	9.8		
0.9	2.5	2.8	7.7	4.9	3.6	3.6	3.6		
7.0	3.3	3.2	10.5	5.5	4.2	4.9	4.2		
NA	NA	NA	NA	16.2	NA	NA	NA	NA	
NA	NA	NA	NA	18.2	NA	NA	NA	NA	
NA	NA	NA	NA	19.5	NA	NA	NA	NA	
3.4	6.8	7.1	14.1	14.8	8.6	4.2	6.9		
8.1	7.9	11.0	13.9	13.2	9.3	3.9	7.7		
2.2	3.6	3.0	9.0	7.6	4.5	2.2	4.5		
2.3	3.5	2.8	9.6	7.8	4.5	1.8	4.2		
1.6	2.6	2.2	10.4	7.4	4.3	1.7	3.6		
1.5	2.7	2.0	10.8	7.9	4.6	1.9	3.3		
1.4	2.4	1.9	11.3	7.8	4.6	1.7	3.2		
1.3	2.4	1.8	12.8	8.3	4.9	1.8	3.4		
1.6	2.5	2.1	13.4	10.0	5.7	2.0	3.8		
1.7	2.6	1.8	15.0	10.2	5.9	1.9	4.0		
2.2	3.2	2.3	15.7	10.2	6.1	2.2	4.3		
2.6	3.4	2.8	15.8	10.3	6.8	2.1	4.7		
1.9	2.9	2.3	9.1	5.2	2.9	4.4			
1.6	2.1	1.8	8.1	4.8	2.7	3.9			
1.8	2.9	3.1	11.4	5.9	3.2	4.2			

TABLE 6-1 Continued

Grade Level	PK	K	1	2	3	4	5
South Carolina							
1977-78	NA	NA	8.3	4.4	3.5	2.7	2.6
1994-95			7.0	2.2	1.9	1.4	1.7
1995-96			6.8	2.6	2.0	1.4	1.6
1996-97			7.0	2.9	2.1	1.7	1.8
Tennessee							
1979-80	NA	2.4	10.7	5.6	3.9	3.1	3.3
1985-86	NA	3.9	10.9	5.1	3.9	3.3	3.2
1991-92							
1992-93							
1993-94							
1994-95							
1995-96							
1996-97	NA	4.3	5.5	2.5	1.8	1.2	1.4
Texas							
1992-93	1.6	7.7	2.5	1.5	1.2	1.1	2.3
1993-94	1.4	6.0	2.1	1.2	0.9	0.8	2.0
1994-95	1.5	5.8	2.2	1.3	1.0	0.9	1.7
1995-96	1.7	5.9	2.6	1.5	1.0	0.8	1.7
Vermont							
1994-95	1.9	1.7	1.0	0.5	0.6	0.3	0.3
1995-96	1.5	1.6	1.1	0.7	0.3	0.2	0.3
1996-97	2.1	2.4	1.2	0.6	0.5	0.4	0.4
Virginia							
1979-80	NA	6.2	11.0	6.3	5.3	4.4	4.2
1985-86	NA	8.3	10.2	4.8	4.2	3.7	2.9
1993-94	NA	3.0	3.9	2.0	1.3	1.1	0.7
1994-95	NA	3.5	4.2	2.1	1.5	1.2	0.7
1995-96	NA	3.9	4.3	2.4	1.9	1.6	1.1
West Virginia							
1979-80	NA	1.7	10.8	3.4	2.2	1.9	1.8
1985-86	NA	4.4	7.5	3.3	2.7	2.3	2.2
1994-95	NA	4.7	4.9	2.0	1.5	0.9	0.9
1995-96	NA	4.7	5.4	2.2	1.4	0.8	0.7
1996-97	NA	5.8	6.7	3.7	2.5	2.0	2.1

6	7	8	9	10	11	12	Total
3.5	3.8	2.6	NA	NA	NA	NA	2.6
2.4	3.3	2.2					
2.4	3.8	2.7					
2.8	3.9	2.9					
2.8	7.3	5.6	8.5	6.3	4.1	6.1	5.4
3.2	8.1	6.1	9.6	8.6	7.0	5.9	6.2
							4.2
							3.9
							3.9
							3.5
							3.4
2.7	7.2	5.7	13.4	9.5	7.0	5.8	5.2
3.2	2.3	16.7	8.5	6.1	4.1	4.4	
3.0	2.2	16.5	8.2	5.7	3.8	4.0	
2.7	1.9	16.8	7.9	5.4	3.9	4.0	
2.9	2.1	17.8	7.9	5.5	4.2	4.3	
1.5	1.6	3.9	2.6	2.2	4.8	1.7	
1.5	1.3	4.9	3.0	2.2	3.4	1.7	
1.5	1.3	4.8	2.6	2.2	4.4	1.8	
4.2	7.7	12.6	11.5	8.3	6.3	7.4	7.4
3.4	8.1	9.7	13.9	8.8	6.1	7.0	7.2
3.1	5.4	6.2	12.2	8.3	6.3	6.6	4.6
3.4	5.2	6.3	13.4	8.6	6.6	6.5	4.9
3.6	5.3	6.0	13.2	8.4	6.2	6.4	4.9
1.4	3.5	2.5	NA	NA	NA	NA	3.4
1.8	4.6	2.5	NA	NA	NA	NA	3.5
1.3	3.7	3.0	NA	NA	NA	NA	2.6
1.3	3.5	2.7	NA	NA	NA	NA	2.6
3.5	4.6	2.9	NA	NA	NA	NA	3.8

TABLE 6-1 Continued

Grade Level	PK	K	1	2	3	4	5
Wisconsin							
1993-94							
1994-95							
1995-96							
1996-97	1.2	2.2	1.0	0.5	0.3	0.2	0.6

NOTE: The following states do not collect these data: CO, CT, IL, KS, MO, MT, NE, NH, NJ, ND, NV, PA, UT, WY.

SOURCES: Shepard and Smith (1991:7-8) and individual state reports to the committee.

rather than a single year prior to graded schooling.[21] This is a diffuse phenomenon and there is no single name for it, nor are there distinct categories for the first and second years of kindergarten in the Census enrollment data. Fragmentary reports suggest that, in some places, kindergarten retention may have been as high as 50 percent in the late 1980s (Shepard, 1989; Shepard, 1991). We do not know the degree to which early retention decisions originate with parents—for example, to increase their children's chances for success in athletics—rather than with teachers or other school personnel. Moreover, there are no sound national estimates of the prevalence of kindergarten retention, and none of the state data in Table 6-1 indicate exceptionally high kindergarten retention rates.

The Census Bureau's statistics on grade enrollment by age show that, from the early 1970s to the late 1980s, entry into 1st grade gradually came later in the development of many children, but for the past decade there has been little change in age at school entry. Figure 6-1 shows percentages of 6-year-old children who had not yet entered the 1st grade as of October of the given year.[22] Among 6-year-old boys, only 8 percent had

---

[21]Another relevant factor is change in state or local requirements about the exact age a child must reach before entering kindergarten or the 1st grade.

[22]Percentages shown in Figure 6-1 are 3-year moving averages and do not agree exactly with the annual estimates reported in the text.

6	7	8	9	10	11	12	Total
							2.2
							2.1
							2.3
1.0	0.8	8.5	7.9	6.3	4.4	2.8	

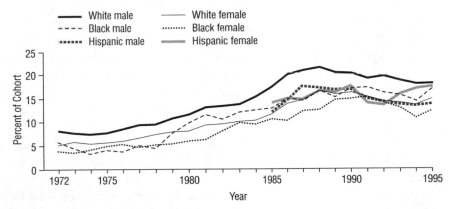

FIGURE 6-1   Percentage of 6-year-old children who have not entered 1st grade. SOURCE: U.S. Bureau of the Census, Current Population Reports, Series P-20 for various years. NOTE: Entries are 3-year moving averages.

not yet entered the 1st grade in 1971,[23] but 22 percent were not yet in the 1st grade in 1987, and 21 percent were not yet in the 1st grade in 1996. Among 6-year-old girls, only 4 percent had not yet entered the 1st grade in 1971, but 16 percent were not yet in the 1st grade in 1987, and 17

---

[23]The percentages include those enrolled below 1st grade level and a small share of 6-year-olds who were not enrolled in school. The data are virtually unchanged if nonenrolled children are eliminated from the analysis; neither the trends nor the differences by race-ethnicity and sex are affected.

percent were not yet in the 1st grade in 1996. Although boys are consistently more likely than girls to enter 1st grade after age 6, there are only small differences between blacks and whites in age at entry into graded school, and these differences consistently favor black children. That is, 6-year-old black children are slightly less likely than white children of the same age and sex to be enrolled below the 1st grade or not enrolled in school. Also, 6-year-old Hispanic boys are consistently more likely than white boys to have entered the 1st grade, but 6-year-old Hispanic girls are less likely than white girls to have entered the 1st grade.

One of the contributing factors to the rising age at entry into 1st grade has been a rising age at entry into kindergarten, which need have nothing to do with kindergarten-level retention and would presumably reduce rates of developmental immaturity among kindergartners.[24] Since the early 1970s, as shown in Figure 6-2, enrollment of 5-year-olds below the kindergarten level—that is, in nursery school—grew from about 2 percent in 1972 to 7 percent in 1992.[25] During the same period, the percentage of nonenrolled children fluctuated around 8 percent, so the combined percentages of 5-year-olds who were either not enrolled or who were enrolled in nursery school grew in parallel with nursery school enrollment. However, there is no firm relationship between these trends and enrollment below the 1st grade at age 6. Children may enter first grade without first attending kindergarten, and, in many of the early years, the share of 5-year-olds who were not enrolled or were in nursery school exceeded the share of 6-year-olds who were enrolled below the 1st grade in the following year.

National statistics do not tell us exactly how much extended kindergarten has contributed to the rise in age at entry into graded school because they do not provide direct information about transitions between grade levels (or retention in grade) from year to year. However, there is a clear downward trend in the ratio of 1st grade enrollment of 5-year-olds in each October to the kindergarten enrollment of 4-year-olds one year earlier. For example, among white males, this ratio declined almost linearly from 0.9 in 1972 to 0.4 in 1987. There is reason to doubt the

---

[24]However, the possibility of retention in kindergarten could lead some parents to hold their youngsters in nursery school a year longer.

[25]There is a very large increase in the enrollment of 5-year-olds below kindergarten in 1994, but this may be attributable to changes in the mode of data collection in the Current Population Survey.

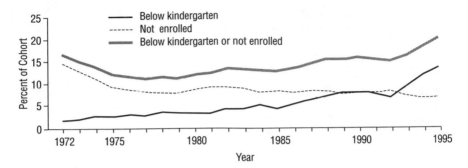

FIGURE 6-2 Percentage of 5-year-old children enrolled below kindergarten or not enrolled. SOURCE: U.S. Bureau of the Census, Current Population Reports, Series P-20. NOTE: Entries are 3-year moving averages.

accuracy with which parents report kindergarten rather than nursery school attendance, but the declining ratio suggests that kindergarten retention has increased.

The Census Bureau's enrollment data are even less informative about the rate at which children who entered kindergarten at age 5 were retained for an additional year at age 6. For example, in 1996, 15 percent of 6-year-old boys and 12 percent of 6-year-old girls were enrolled in kindergarten. The data on enrollment of 5-year-olds in 1995 and of 6-year-olds in 1996 are consistent with the possibility that all of the 6-year-old kindergartners in 1996 were in their second year. The enrollment data are equally consistent with the possibility that all of those children had been in nursery school or had not attended school at all in fall 1995. That is, all we can learn from national statistics is that retention in kindergarten affected no more than 15 percent of 6-year-old boys and no more than 12 percent of 6-year-old girls in 1996.[26]

RETENTION IN THE PRIMARY AND SECONDARY GRADES

Age-grade retardation refers to enrollment below the modal grade level for a child's age—and no broader meaning is either intended or

---

[26]These inferences are based on the assumptions that immigration and mortality between ages 5 and 6 can be ignored and that no children move down in grade between school years, i.e., from kindergarten to nursery school or from 1st grade to kindergarten or nursery school.

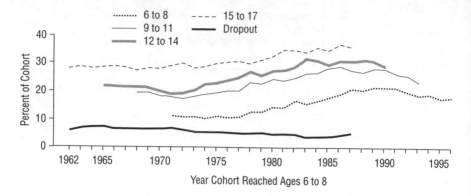

FIGURE 6-3 Percentage of children enrolled below modal grade for age by age group and year in which cohort was ages 6 to 8. SOURCE: U.S. Bureau of the Census, *Historical Statistics*, Table A-3, Persons 6 to 17. NOTE: Dropout series represents the percentage of the age cohort that had dropped out by ages 15-17. Dropouts are included in the series at ages 15 to 17.

implied. The committee has looked at national rates of age-grade retardation by age, sex, and race/ethnicity for three-year age groups at ages 6 to 17 from 1971 to 1996 and also at parallel tabulations for young children by single years of age from 1971 to 1996. In each case, we have organized the data by birth cohort (year of birth) rather than by calendar year, so it is possible to see the evolution of age-grade retardation throughout the schooling of a birth cohort, as well as changes in age-grade retardation rates from year to year.[27]

The recent history of age-grade retardation is summarized in Figure 6-3. It shows age-grade retardation at ages 6 to 8, 9 to 11, 12 to 14, and 15 to 17 among children who reached ages 6 to 8 between 1962 and 1996. The horizontal axis shows the year in which an age group reached ages 6

---

[27]These data have been assembled from *Historical Statistics*, Table A-3, "Persons 6 to 17 Years Old Enrolled Below Modal Grade, 1971 to 1995," which is available from the U.S. Bureau of the Census at www.census.gov/population/socdemo/school/report95/taba-3.txt, and from selected publications in the P-20 series of *Current Population Reports*, "School Enrollment: Social and Economic Characteristics of Students," from the U.S. Bureau of the Census (Nos. 241, 260, 272, 286, 303, 319, 333, 346, 360, 400, 408, 413, 426, 439, 443, 452, 460, 469, 474, 479, 487, and 492). Unpublished data for 1996, as well as corrections in the *Historical Statistics*, Table A-3, were kindly provided by Census Bureau staff.

to 8, so vertical comparisons among the trend lines at a given year show how age-grade retardation cumulated as a birth cohort grew older.

For example, consider children who were 6 to 8 years old in 1987—the most recent cohort whose history can be traced all the way from ages 6 to 8 up through ages 15 to 17. At ages 6 to 8, 21 percent were enrolled below the modal grade for their age. By 1990, when this cohort reached ages 9 to 11, age-grade retardation grew to 28 percent, and it was 31 percent in 1993, when the cohort reached ages 12 to 14. By 1996, when the cohort reached ages 15 to 17, the percentage who were either below the modal grade level or had left school was 36 percent. Almost all of the growth in retardation after ages 12 to 14, however, was due to dropout (5 percent), rather than grade retention among the enrolled.

One could read the rate of enrollment below the modal grade at ages 6 to 8 as a baseline measure, that is, as if it did not necessarily indicate that grade retention had taken place. Relative to that baseline, increases in enrollment below the modal grade at older ages clearly show the net effects of retention in grade. This reading of the data would suggest that, in most birth cohorts, retention occurs mainly between ages to 6 to 8 and 9 to 11 or between ages 12 to 14 and 15 to 17.[28] This way of looking at the data surely understates the prevalence of grade retention, for much of it occurs within or below ages 6 to 8.

The series for ages 15 to 17 includes early school dropout, which is also shown as a separate series along the bottom of the figure. Dropout, rather than retention, evidently accounts for a substantial share of the increase in age-grade retardation between ages 12 to 14 and ages 15 to 17.

The trend in age-grade retardation at ages 6 to 8, 9 to 11, 12 to 14, and 15 to 17 can be read across Figure 6-3 from left to right. Age-grade retardation increased in every age group from cohorts of the early 1970s through those of the mid- to late 1980s. Age-grade retardation increased at ages 15 to 17 after the mid-1970s, despite the slow decline in its early school dropout component throughout the period. That is, grade retention increased while dropout decreased. Peak rates occurred earlier at older than at younger ages, suggesting that policy changes occurred in specific calendar years, rather than consistently throughout the life of successive birth cohorts. Among cohorts entering school after 1970, the

[28]We ignore the logical possibility that age-grade retardation at younger ages could be counterbalanced by double promotion at older ages.

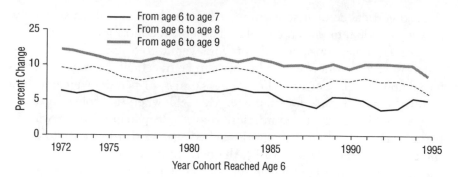

FIGURE 6-4 Differences in age-grade retardation between age 6 and ages 7 to 9 by year when cohort was age 6. SOURCE: U.S. Bureau of the Census, Current Population Reports, Series P-20. NOTE: Entries are 3-year moving averages.

percentage enrolled below the modal grade level was never less than 10 percent at ages 6 to 8, and it exceeded 20 percent for cohorts of the late 1980s. The trend lines suggest that age-grade retardation has declined slightly for cohorts entering school after the mid-1980s, but rates have not moved back to the levels of the early 1970s.

Overall, a large share of each birth cohort now experiences grade retention during elementary school. Among children ages 6 to 8 from 1982 to 1992, age-grade retardation has reached 25 to 30 percent by ages 9 to 11.

RETENTION AFTER SCHOOL ENTRY

Enrollment below the 1st grade at age 6 is a convenient baseline against which to assess the effects of later grade retention. The comparisons of age-grade retardation at ages 7 to 9 with that at age 6 are shown in Figure 6-4. There are two main patterns in the series. First, grade retention continues through the elementary years at each successive age. Retention cumulates rapidly after age 6. For example, among children who were 6 years old in 1987, enrollment below the modal grade increased by almost 5 percentage points between ages 6 and 7 and by 5 more percentage points between ages 7 and 9. Second, there appears to have been a decline in retention between ages 6 and 7 after the early 1980s. That is, comparing Figure 6-1 with Figure 6-4, we can infer a shift in elementary school age-grade retardation downward in age from the transition between ages 6 and 7 to somewhere between ages 4 and 6.

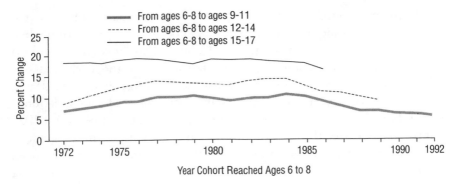

FIGURE 6-5 Differences in age-grade retardation between ages 6 to 8 and ages 9 to 17 by year when cohort was ages 6 to 8. SOURCE: U.S. Bureau of the Census, Historical Statistics, Table A-3, Persons 6 to 17. NOTES: Dropouts are included in the series at ages 15 to 17. Entries are 3-year moving averages.

How much grade retention is there after ages 6 to 8? And does the recent growth in age-grade retardation by ages 6 to 8 account for its observed growth at older ages? Figure 6-5 shows changes in age-grade retardation between ages 6 to 8 and each of the three older age groups.[29] Age-grade retardation grows substantially after ages 6 to 8 as a result of retention in grade. For example, among children who reached ages 6 to 8 between 1972 and 1985, almost 20 percent more were below the modal grade for their age by the time they were 15 to 17 years old. Among children who reached ages 6 to 8 between the mid-1970s and the mid-1980s, age-grade retardation grew by about 10 percentage points by ages 9 to 11, and it grew by close to 5 percentage points more by ages 12 to 14. Relative to ages 6 to 8, age-grade retardation at ages 9 to 11 and ages 12 to 14 increased for cohorts who were 6 to 8 years old in the early 1970s; it was stable from the mid-1970s to the mid-1980s, and it has declined since then. However, the gap between retention at ages 15 to 17 and that at ages 6 to 8 has been relatively stable—close to 20 percentage points—with the possible exception of a very recent downward turn. Thus, the rise in age at entry into 1st grade—which is partly due to kindergarten retention—accounts for much of the overall increase in age-grade retardation among teenagers.

---

[29] Again, early school dropout (at ages 15 to 17) is counted as age-grade retardation.

In summary, grade retention is pervasive in American schools. It is important to consider the implications of ending social promotion when ages at school entry are increasing, and a large share of each new cohort of youth already experiences grade retention after the early years of schooling. To be sure, the temporal location of age-grade retardation appears to have changed over time. Cumulative rates of age-grade retardation have increased for cohorts entering school since the early 1970s, but this has occurred through a combination of later entry into 1st grade—possibly involving retention in nursery school or kindergarten—reduced retention between ages 6 and 7, and variable patterns of retention in the preadolescent and adolescent years.

SOCIAL DIFFERENCES IN RETENTION

Not only are there similarities in the pattern of age-grade retardation among major population groups—boys and girls and majority and minority groups—but there are also substantial differences in rates of age-grade retardation among them, many of which develop well after school entry. Figure 6-6 shows differences in grade-retardation between boys and girls at ages 6 to 8 and ages 15 to 17. Overall, the sex differential gradually increases with age, from 5 percentage points at ages 6 to 8 to 10 percent-

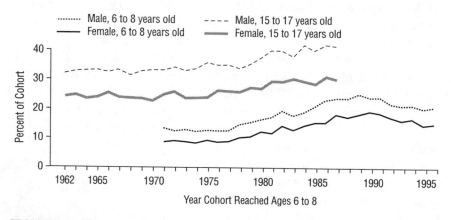

FIGURE 6-6 Percentage enrolled below modal grade at ages 6 to 8 and at ages 15 to 17 by sex and year cohort reached ages 6 to 8. SOURCE: U.S. Bureau of the Census, Historical Statistics, Table A-3, Persons 6 to 8 and 15 to 17.

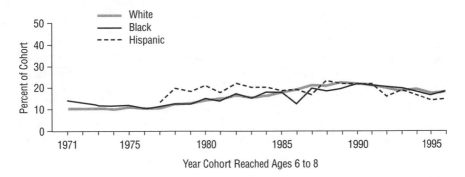

FIGURE 6-7 Percentage enrolled below modal grade at ages 6 to 8 by race/ethnicity and year. SOURCE: U.S. Bureau of the Census, Historical Statistics, Table A-3, Persons 6 to 8.

age points at ages 15 to 17. That is, boys are initially more likely than girls to be placed below the modal grade for their age, and they fall further behind girls as they pass through childhood and adolescence.

The differentiation of age-grade relationships by race and ethnicity is even more striking than that by gender. Figures 6-7 to 6-10 show trends in the development of age-grade retardation by race/ethnicity in each of the four age groups: 6 to 8, 9 to 11, 12 to 14, and 15 to 17. Here, unlike the case of gender differentiation, the rates of age-grade retardation are very similar among whites, blacks, and Hispanics at ages 6 to 8. However, by ages 9 to 11, the percentages enrolled below modal grade levels are typically 5 to 10 percentage points higher among blacks or Hispanics than among whites. The differentials continue to grow with age, and at ages 15 to 17, rates of grade retardation range from 40 to 50 percent among blacks and Hispanics, and they have gradually drifted up from 25 percent to 35 percent among whites. By ages 15 to 17, there is a differential between Hispanics and blacks favoring the latter, and this appears to follow from high rates of early school dropout among Hispanics. Figure 6-11 shows the rates of school dropout among whites, blacks, and Hispanics ages 15 to 17. There is almost no difference in the dropout rates between whites and blacks,[30] but Hispanics are much more likely to leave

---

[30]Dropout by ages 15 to 17 does not indicate ultimate rates of failure to complete high school because large numbers of youth complete regular schooling through age 19 or, alternatively, pass the GED exam through their late 20s (Hauser, 1997).

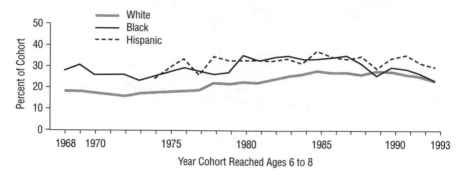

FIGURE 6-8 Percentage enrolled below modal grade at ages 9 to 11 by year cohort reached ages 6 to 8 by race/ethnicity. SOURCE: U.S. Bureau of the Census, Historical Statistics, Table A-3, Persons 9 to 11.

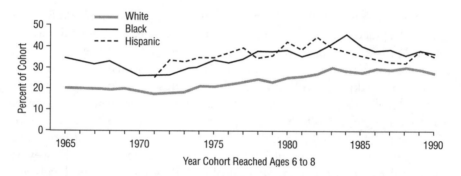

FIGURE 6-9 Percentage enrolled below modal grade at ages 12 to 14 by year cohort reached ages 6 to 8 by race/ethnicity. SOURCE: U.S. Bureau of the Census, Historical Statistics, Table A-3, Persons 12 to 14.

school at an early age. Thus, early high school dropout contributes very little to the observed difference in age-grade retardation between blacks and whites, which is mainly due to retention in grade. Early dropout does account in part for the difference in age-grade retardation between Hispanics and whites or blacks.

In recent years, gender and race/ethnic differentials in age-grade retardation, even at young ages, are a consequence of school experience and not primarily of differentials in age at school entry. Social differentials in age-grade relationships are vague at school entry, but a hierarchy

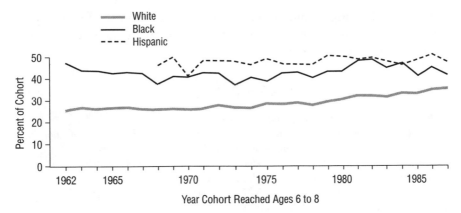

FIGURE 6-10 Percentage enrolled below modal grade or dropping out by ages 15 to 17 by year cohort reached ages 6 to 8 by race/ethnicity. SOURCE: U.S. Bureau of the Census, Historical Statistics, Table A-3, Persons 15 to 17.

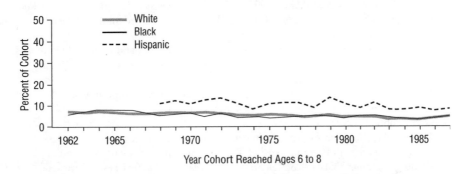

FIGURE 6-11 Percentage dropping out by ages 15 to 17 by year cohort reached ages 6 to 8 by race/ethnicity. SOURCE: U.S. Bureau of the Census, Historical Statistics, Table A-3, Persons 6 to 17.

is clearly established by age 9, and it persists and grows through the end of secondary schooling. This growth can only be explained by grade retention. By age 9, there are sharp social differentials in age-grade retardation, favoring whites and girls relative to blacks or Hispanics and boys. By ages 15 to 17, close to 50 percent of black males have fallen behind in school—30 percentage points more than at ages 6 to 8—but age-grade retardation has never exceeded 30 percent among white girls of the same age. If these rates and differentials in age-grade retardation are characteristic of a schooling regime in which social promotion is perceived to be the norm, it is important to consider what we might observe when that norm has been eliminated.

REFERENCES

Alexander, K.L., D.R. Entwisle, and S.L. Dauber
  1994   On the Success of Failure: A Reassessment of the Effects of Retention in the Primary Grades. Cambridge, England: Cambridge University Press.
American Educational Research Association, American Psychological Association, and National Council on Measurement in Education
  1985   Standards for Educational and Psychological Testing. Washington, DC: American Psychological Association.
  1998   Draft Standards for Educational and Psychological Testing. Washington, DC: American Psychological Association.
American Federation of Teachers
  1997a   Passing on Failure: District Promotion Policies and Practices. Washington, DC: American Federation of Teachers.
  1997b   Making Standards Matter 1997: An Annual Fifty-State Report on Efforts to Raise Academic Standards. Washington, DC: American Federation of Teachers.
Anderson, D.K.
  1994   Paths Through Secondary Education: Race/Ethnic and Gender Differences. Unpublished doctoral thesis, University of Wisconsin-Madison.
Berk, R.
  1986   A consumer's guide to setting performance standards on criterion-referenced tests. Review of Educational Research 56:137-172.
Chicago Public Schools
  1996a   Preparing Your Elementary Students to Take Standardized Tests. Chicago: Chicago School Reform Board of Trustees, Bureau of Student Assessment.
  1996b   Preparing Your High School Students to Take Standardized Tests. Chicago: Chicago School Reform Board of Trustees, Bureau of Student Assessment.
  1997a   1997-1998 Guidelines for Promotion in the Chicago Public Schools. Chicago: Chicago School Reform Board of Trustees, Bureau of Student Assessment.
  1997b   CPS Ninth Grade Students Excel in Summer School. Press release. Chicago: Chicago Public Schools.
  1998a   The Summer Bridge: Helping Chicago's Public School Students Bridge the Gap. Chicago: Chicago Public Schools.
  1998b   CPS Test Results of Individual Schools Show Improvements. Press release. Chicago: Chicago Public Schools.
Clinton, W.J.
  1998   Memorandum to the Secretary of Education. Press release. Washington, DC: The White House.
Council of Chief State School Officers
  1998   Survey of State Student Assessment Programs. Washington, DC: Council of Chief State School Officers.

Cronbach, L.J.
  1971   Test validation. In *Educational Measurement*, 2nd Edition, R.L. Thorndike,
          ed. Washington, DC: American Council on Education.
Darling-Hammond, L., and B. Falk
  1995   Using standards and assessments to support student learning: Alternatives to
          grade retention. In *Report to the Chancellor's Committee on Grade Transition
          Standards. National Center for Restructuring Education, Schools and Teaching.*
          New York: Teachers College, Columbia University.

Duncan, B.
  1968   Trends in output and distribution of schooling. In *Indicators of Social Change*,
          E.B. Sheldon and W.E. Moore, eds. New York: Russell Sage Foundation.
Ellwein, M.C., and G.V. Glass
  1989   Ending social promotion in Waterford: Appearances and reality. Pp. 151-173
          in *Flunking Grades: Research and Policies on Retention*, L.A. Shepard and M.L.
          Smith, eds. London, England: Falmer Press.
Gampert, R., and P. Opperman
  1988   Longitudinal Study of the 1982-83 Promotional Gates Students. Paper pre-
          sented at the Annual Meeting of the American Educational Research Asso-
          ciation. New Orleans, LA.

George, C.
  1993   *Beyond Retention: A Study of Retention Rates, Practices, and Successful Alterna-
          tives in California, Summary Report*. Sacramento: California Department of
          Education.
Grissom, J.B., and L.A. Shepard
  1989   Repeating and dropping out of school. Pp. 34-63 in *Flunking Grades: Re-
          search and Policies on Retention*, L.A. Shepard and M.L. Smith, eds. London:
          Falmer Press.
Haney, W.
  1993   Testing and minorities. In *Beyond Silence: Class, Race and Gender in United
          States Schools*. L. Wise and M. Fine, eds. Albany: State University of New
          York Press.
Hauser, R.M.
  1997   Indicators of high school completion and dropout. Pp. 152-184 in *Indicators
          of Children's Well-Being*, R.M. Hauser, B.V. Brown, and W.R. Prosser, eds.
          New York: Russell Sage Foundation.
  1998   Trends in black-white test score differences: I. Uses and misuses of NAEP/
          SAT data. Pp. 219-249 in *The Rising Curve: Long-Term Gains in IQ and
          Related Measures*, U. Neisser, ed. Washington, DC: American Psychological
          Association.
Hendrie, C.
  1997   Do or die. *Education Week* (August 6).
Holmes, C.T.
  1989   Grade level retention effects: A meta-analysis of research studies. Pp. 16-33
          in *Flunking Grades: Research and Policies on Retention*, L.A. Shepard and M.L.
          Smith, eds. London: Falmer Press.

Hoover, H., A. Hieronymus, D. Frisbie, et al.
   1994   *Interpretive Guide for School Administrators: Iowa Test of Basic Skills, Levels 5-14*. University of Iowa, Iowa City: Riverside Publishing Company.
House, E.R.
   1989   Policy implications of retention research. Pp. 202-213 in *Flunking Grades: Research and Policies on Retention*, L.A. Shepard and M.L. Smith, eds. London: Falmer Press.
Iowa Department of Education, Early Childhood Network, The Primary Program, Position Statements
   1998   Retention, Tracking, and Extra Year Programs. Available: http://www.state.ia.us [July 13].
Johnston, R.C.
   1998   Texas governor has social promotion in his sights. *Education Week* (February 11).
Joint Committee on Testing Practices
   1988   *Code of Fair Testing Practices in Education*. American Psychological Association. Washington, DC: National Council on Measurement in Education.
Jones, L.V.
   1984   White-black achievement differences: The narrowing gap. *American Psychologist* 39(November 11):1207-213.
Kane, M.T.
   1992   An argument-based approach to validity. *Psychological Bulletin* 112:527-535.
Koretz, D.
   1986   *Trends in Educational Achievement*. Prepared for the Congress of the United States by the Congressional Budget Office. Washington, DC: Government Printing Office.
Koretz, D.M., R.L. Linn, S.B. Dunbar, and L.A. Shepard
   1991   The Effects of High-Stakes Testing on Achievement: Preliminary Findings About Generalization Across Tests. Paper presented at the annual meeting of the American Educational Research Association and the National Council on Measurement in Education. Chicago, IL (April).
Leinhardt, G.
   1980   Transition rooms: Promoting maturation or reducing education. *Journal of Educational Psychology* 72:55-61.
Linn, R.L.
   1997   Evaluating the validity of assessments: The consequences of use. *Educational Measurement: Issues and Practice* 16(2):14-16.
Luppescu, S., A.S. Bryk, P. Deabster, et al.
   1995   *School Reform, Retention Policy, and Student Achievement Gains*. Chicago: Consortium on Chicago School Research.
Madaus, G.F., ed.
   1983   *The Courts, Validity, and Minimum Competency Testing*. Hingham, MA: Kluwer-Nijhoff Publishing.
Mehrens, W.A.
   1995   Methodological issues in standard setting for educational exams. Pp. 221-263 in *Proceedings of the Joint Conference on Standard Setting for Large-Scale Assessments of the National Assessment Governing Board (NAGB) and the National*

Center for Education Statistics (NCES), II. Washington, DC: National Assessment Governing Board and National Center for Education Statistics.

Messick, S.
1989   Validity. Pp. 13-103 in *Educational Measurement*, 3rd Edition, R. Linn, ed. Washington, DC: American Council on Education.

National Coalition of Advocates for Students
1998   *A Gathering Storm: How Palm Beach County Schools Fail Poor and Minority Children*. Report by the National Coalition of Advocates for Students. Boston: Shea Brothers.

National Research Council
1982   *Placing Children in Special Education: A Strategy for Equity*, K. A. Heller, W.H. Holtzman, and S. Messick, eds. Committee on Child Development Research and Public Policy, National Research Council. Washington, DC: National Academy Press.
1989   *A Common Destiny: Blacks and American Society*, G.D. Jaynes and R.M. Williams, Jr., eds. Committee on the Status of Black Americans, Commission on Behavioral and Social Sciences, National Research Council. Washington, DC: National Academy Press.

Olson, L.
1990   Education officials reconsider policies on grade retention. *Education Week* (May 16).

Reardon, S.
1996   Eighth-Grade Minimum Competency Testing and Early High School Dropout Patterns. Paper presented at the annual meeting of the American Educational Research Association. New York, NY, April.

Roderick, M.
1995   Grade retention and school dropout: Policy debate and research questions. *Research Bulletin* 15. Center for Evaluation, Development, and Research.

Shepard, L.A.
1980   An evaluation of the regression discrepency method for identifying children with learning disabilities. *Journal of Special Education* 14(1):79-91.
1989   A review of research on kindergarten retention. Pp. 64-78 in *Flunking Grades: Research and Policies on Retention*, L.A. Shepard and M.L. Smith, eds. London: Falmer Press.
1991   Negative policies for dealing with diversity: When does assessment and diagnosis turn into sorting and segregation? Pp. 279-298 in *Literacy for a Diverse Society: Perspectives, Practices, and Policies*, E. Hiebert, ed. New York: Teachers College Press.
1997   The Centrality of Test Use and Consequences for Test Validity. *Educational Measurement: Issues and Practice* Summer:5-8.

Shepard, L.A., and M.L. Smith
1987   Effects of kindergarten retention at the end of first grade. *Psychology in the Schools* 24:346-357.
1988   Escalating academic demand in kindergarten: Counterproductive policies. *Elementary School Journal* 89:135-145.

1989   Academic and emotional effects of kindergarten retention in one school district. Pp. 79-107 in *Flunking Grades: Research and Policies on Retention*, L.A. Shepard and M.L. Smith, eds. London, England: Falmer Press.

Shepard, L.A., M.L. Smith, and S.F. Marion
1996   Failed evidence on grade retention. *Psychology in the Schools* 33(3):251-261.

Shepard, L.A., S.L. Kagan, and E. Wurtz, eds.
1998   *Principles and Recommendations for Early Childhood Assessments*. Prepared for the National Educational Goals Panel by the Goal 1 Early Childhood Assessments Resource Group. Washington, DC: Government Printing Office.

Smith, M.S., and J. O'Day
1991   Educational equality: 1966 and now. Pp. 53-100 in *Spheres of Justice in Education: The 1990 American Education Finance Association Yearbook*, D. Verstegen and J. Ward, eds. New York: Harper Collins.

Steinberg, J.
1998a   Chancellor vows to fail students lacking in skills. *New York Times*, (April 21).
1998b   Crew's plan to hold back failing students has familiar ring. *New York Times*, (April 26).

U.S. Bureau of the Census
1971-   *Current Population Reports* P-20 Series, "School Enrollment: Social and Eco-
1995   nomic Characteristics of Students."

U.S. Department of Education
1983   *A Nation at Risk: The Imperative for Educational Reform*. Washington, DC: U.S. Department of Education.

U.S. Department of Education, State Department of Education, National Education Goals Panel
1997   Table Attachment to Secretary Riley's April 29, 1997 Statement on Voluntary National Tests for Reading and Math.

7
Awarding or Withholding High School Diplomas

Certification exams based on externally developed standards of performance are routinely administered in the United States to prospective nurses, doctors, pilots, plumbers, and insurance adjusters. It is no wonder, then, that the idea of requiring students to pass a test before graduating from high school has great appeal. In the 1970s, several states implemented minimum competency testing as a partial requirement for high school graduation. A single test, consisting of multiple-choice items, was thought to measure accurately whether students had mastered the basic skills that should be required of a high school graduate.

Florida was one of the first states to develop a minimum competency graduation test and was also one of the first to have to defend its testing program in court. As described in Chapter 3, in *Debra P. v. Turlington* (1981), a U.S. court of appeals ruled that (1) students have a legally recognized property interest in receiving a high school diploma; (2) the graduation test must be a fair measure of what students have been taught; and (3) students must have adequate advance notice of the high-stakes test requirement.

The current emphasis on standards-based educational reform is shifting the nature of assessments. Instead of focusing on multiple-choice measures of minimum competencies, assessments are emphasizing more challenging tasks that are aligned with demanding content standards (American Federation of Teachers, 1997). Although many states have begun to look critically at the level of skills assessed in their high school graduation tests, they face dilemmas in trying to raise standards on these tests (Bond and King, 1995).

For example, states wanting to test complex skills in their graduation exams face the challenge of ensuring that all schools are teaching those skills. Bond and King describe this as a catch-22. Before using a graduation test for high-stakes purposes (awarding or denying a diploma), a state must ensure that curriculum and instruction are aligned with what the test measures. Some proponents of reform, however, see the test as a tool for inducing changes in the content and methods of teaching. "Clearly, a test cannot both lead the curriculum and reflect the curriculum at the same time," Bond and King conclude (1995:3). One possible way around this dilemma is for test users to plan a gap of several years between the introduction of new tests and the attachment of high stakes to individual student performance, during which time schools may achieve the necessary alignment between tests, curriculum, and instruction.

In addition, lower-level skills are easier to test, whereas more advanced skills are not as well defined, and ways to assess them are not well established. Moreover, there is evidence that "any of the high standards that are now being touted . . . would fail an unacceptably large fraction of the students" if used for making high-stakes decisions such as awarding or withholding high school diplomas (Linn, 1998a:23). Thus, as states move toward assessment of more rigorous standards, there are numerous challenges in the context of graduation testing that remain to be worked out.

CURRENT GRADUATION TESTING PRACTICES

In most states, students earn high school diplomas by accumulating Carnegie units, which are based on the number of hours spent in class. The system also ensures that students have passed certain courses, but this is an imprecise and nonuniform measure of what students actually have learned. Many states are therefore requiring that students also pass one or more competency exams in order to graduate (Mehrens, 1993). According to the most recent Council of Chief State School Officers survey (1998), 18 states have high school exit exams.[1] In fact, graduation

---

[1]The states are Alabama, Florida, Georgia, Hawaii, Louisiana, Maryland, Minnesota, Mississippi, Nevada, New Jersey, New Mexico, New York, North Carolina, Ohio, South Carolina, Tennessee, Texas, and Virginia.

tests are the most popular type of individual accountability mechanism aimed at students.[2]

Bond and King (1995) provide a summary of state high school graduation testing practices as of 1995. State programs typically assessed 10th and 11th grade students, with some states starting as early as 6th grade. In most states, the student was allowed an unlimited number of chances to retake the exam, even several years after completing high school course work. All states assessed reading and math; the next most frequently assessed subject was writing. Every state used a multiple-choice test, often in combination with a writing sample, and all but one state used criterion-referenced tests.[3] Of the 18 states that currently have high school exit exams, 9 use tests that could be considered to measure minimum competency in that they are based on 9th grade or lower standards.[4]

Two models are commonly used to combine data from multiple requirements and assessments: *conjunctive* and *compensatory*. A conjunctive model requires adequate performance on each measure, whereas a compensatory model allows performance on one measure to offset, or compensate for, substandard performance on another. Phillips (1991) points out that test-based graduation decisions typically follow a conjunctive model—students do not receive diplomas until they complete all required course work satisfactorily *and* pass the test(s). So although graduation decisions do not rest on test scores alone, passing the test is still a necessary condition of earning a diploma.

Some critics argue that the model chosen for these decisions should be compensatory rather than conjunctive (e.g., Mehrens, 1986). In a compensatory model, students with low test scores would be able to earn a diploma if they met or exceeded other requirements, such as getting good to excellent grades in required course work. Such an approach is

---

[2]In 1984, 19 states had high school exit exams. This suggests that the prevalence of this practice has not changed much over the last decade (Reardon, 1996).

[3]Only Nevada used a norm-referenced graduation test at the time of the Bond and King survey. This test was to be replaced by a new criterion-referenced high school proficiency test in math and reading, which was to be pilot-tested during the 1996-1997 school year.

[4]This definition of a minimum competency graduation test is taken from the 1997 AFT report, *Making Standards Matter 1997: An Annual Fifty-State Report on Efforts to Raise Academic Standards*. The nine states listed in this report as employing minimum competency-type graduation tests are Hawaii, Maryland, Minnesota, Mississippi, North Carolina, Ohio, Tennessee, Texas, and Virginia.

more compatible with current professional testing standards, which state that "in elementary or secondary education, a decision or characterization that will have a major impact on a test taker should not automatically be made on the basis of a single test score. Other relevant information . . . should also be taken into account" (American Educational Research Association et al., 1985:54, Standard 8.12).

LOGIC OF CERTIFICATION DECISIONS

High school graduation decisions are inherently certification decisions: the diploma certifies that the student has attained an acceptable level of learning. A test is one of many types of evidence that may be used in certification; to be valid, the test must be an accurate measure of the student's degree of mastery of the relevant knowledge and skills (American Educational Research Association et al., 1985: Standard 8.7; 1998).

As discussed in Chapters 5 and 6, the psychometric requirements for tests used for placement and certification decisions overlap considerably, but not completely. For example, the setting of cutoff scores is important to both types of decisions. Tests used for certification, however, have some distinct psychometric requirements. In particular, there is a greater need for evidence that the test's content represents the student's school experience—because a high school graduation test is presumably a measure of achievement rather than readiness (Green, 1973).

The most important assumptions underlying the use of a test for certification decisions are (1) that the test taps the knowledge, skills, or other attributes it is interpreted to measure and (2) that the cutoff score is an accurate discriminator of mastery or nonmastery in the domain. These assumptions and the evidence required to support them are addressed in more detail below. Other assumptions may arguably be plausible on their face or may already be supported by evidence provided by the test developer or in the testing literature (e.g., that the test scores are sufficiently reliable). A persuasive argument for test use will not require that *every* assumption be documented empirically, but that the assembled evidence be sufficient to make a credible case that the use of the test for a particular certification decision is appropriate—that is, both valid and fair (see Chapter 4 for an explanation of the kinds of evidence pertinent to this judgment).

Validation of Test Use

Content Coverage

Because not everything can be measured in a graduation test, the choice of constructs is critical, as is setting the boundaries of the content domain to be included in the test. Should a graduation test cover only reading and math, or should it also include writing, social studies, and a foreign language? Depending on the answer to this question, the content and cognitive demands of the test will differ, as will the consequences of using the test score to make graduation decisions. For example, as mentioned earlier, graduation rates for males and females, as well as for English-language learners, would be quite different if the test emphasized reading and writing as opposed to science and mathematics (Willingham and Cole, 1997).

Should a graduation test be a measure of basic skills, or should it attempt to assess higher-level skills and knowledge? As discussed earlier, several states that employ graduation tests are moving away from minimum competency tests that measure basic skills in a few subject areas, toward tests that measure higher-level skills in several subjects and are aligned with more demanding content standards (American Federation of Teachers, 1997). This move toward more demanding standards for certifying students is significant, not only in terms of what passing the graduation test would represent, but also in terms of the likely effects on graduation rates. For example, since revising their graduation tests in order to align them to rigorous state-level content standards, both Texas and Florida have experienced increased failure rates among their minority student populations (National Coalition of Advocates for Students, 1998; G.I. Forum, 1997). It is unclear at present, however, to what extent these increases are due simply to higher standards. There is also the possibility that the test is not yet representative of what students have actually been taught. This issue is discussed more fully in the section below on test fairness.

Whichever type of graduation test is employed, there are some steps that may be taken—before, during, or after test development—to help ensure the appropriateness of the content and skills measured by the test. For example, the domain to be assessed on the graduation test should be carefully defined and widely publicized. The test content should be representative of what students have actually been taught. Test items should also be reviewed to ensure that they do not tap irrelevant skills or knowledge that could confound the test score interpretation.[5]

Of particular concern is the extent to which construct underrepresentation or construct-irrelevant components may give an unfair advantage or disadvantage to one or more subgroups of examinees. For example, a mathematics test that uses unnecessarily complex vocabulary may disadvantage some English-language learners, leading to lower passing rates that do not constitute a valid measure of these students' mathematics knowledge. Similarly, not providing certain testing accommodations (such as large-print versions) may make it difficult for some students with disabilities to adequately demonstrate what they know and can do.

These are complex issues, which we discuss further in Chapters 8 and 9. Careful review of the construct and content domain by a diverse panel of experts may point to some potential sources of irrelevant difficulty (or easiness) on a test that require further investigation. Taken together, these steps should ensure that evidence of the appropriateness of the content and cognitive processes measured by the graduation test, for individuals and groups, is gathered as part of the validation process (American Educational Research Association et al., 1985, 1998).

Setting Cutoff Scores

Chapter 4 describes different procedures for setting cutoff scores on tests as well as some of the difficulties involved. As with tests used for tracking or promotion decisions, the validity of the cutscore(s) on graduation tests depends on the reasonableness of the standard-setting process and of its outcome and consequences—especially if these differ by gender, race, or language-minority group. Several psychometric standards are relevant here (e.g., American Educational Research Association et al., 1985: Standards 1.24, 2.8 to 2.10, 2.12, 6.9 and 10.9).

Although there are right and wrong ways of setting cutscores, there is no single right answer to the question of where the cutscore should be set on a graduation test—or any other test with high stakes for students. This is partly because of the conceptual problems involved in interpret-

---

[5]In addition, test specifications should include a rationale for the particular weights given to the graduation test's subdomains and show how the actual test items are congruent with both the test specifications and the domain definition (American Educational Research Association et al., 1985: Standards 8.4 to 8.7, 1998; Messick, 1989).

ing the cutscore. As Jaeger has acknowledged: "If competence is a continuous variable, there is clearly no point on the continuum that would separate students into the competent and the incompetent" (1989:492).

This lack of certainty has several implications—not only for the need to document and evaluate the standard-setting process but also for the need to examine the consequences of choosing a particular cutscore. The most obvious consequence is the pass rate on the test.

Three variables interact to influence pass rates on any test: the positioning of the cutscore, the complexity of the content domain, and the difficulty of the items chosen to measure this content. For example, if a low cutscore is combined with easy items measuring simple knowledge, pass rates on the test will probably be high. If any of these variables change, that is, if the cutscore is raised and/or the content becomes more complex, and/or the difficulty of the items is increased, pass rates will decrease, at least in the short term. These issues are important to keep in mind at all stages of test development, but particularly when deciding on the stakes that will be attached to passing or failing the graduation test.

General concern over the lack of a "right answer" in setting cutscores is reflected in the recommendation that, when feasible, multiple standard-setting methods should be used, and that all the results should be considered together when determining a final cutscore on the test (Hambleton, 1980; Shepard, 1984). Concern is also reflected in current psychometric standards, which recommend that a decision that will have a major impact on a test taker should not be made solely or automatically on the basis of a single test score, and that other relevant information about the student's knowledge and skills should also be taken into account (American Educational Research Association et al., 1985: Standard 8.12; 1998). This concern affects not only students who fail the test while performing well on other measures, but also those who pass the test, if their poor performance on other measures suggests the need for extra instruction or other interventions (Madaus, 1983).

New challenges in the setting of cutoff scores for graduation tests have been raised by the proliferation of open-ended items, extended-response items, and performance assessments (which are sometimes mixed with multiple-choice items to increase domain coverage). The minimum competency tests of the past contained mostly multiple-choice items. And there was much debate over the best method for setting standards on these tests, even though the properties of multiple-choice items were well understood. In comparison, systems for determining reliable cutscores for the newer forms of assessment are less well established (Burstein et al., 1996; Linn, 1998b; National Academy of Education, 1996).[6]

As for any test used for making high-stakes decisions, the test developer or user needs to provide evidence that the test score is sufficiently reliable, and that the standard error surrounding scores on the test is sufficiently small for the proposed interpretation and use (American Educational Research Association et al., 1985: Standard 2.1). This is particularly important in relation to student scores that fall around the cutscore on the test, because even a one point difference can lead to the denial of a high school diploma. When feasible, therefore, some experts have recommended that multiple standard-setting methods be used in any given study, and that all the results be considered together when determining a final cutscore on the graduation test (Hambleton, 1980; Shepard, 1984).

Another issue is whether more than one cutscore should be set. Some researchers have concluded that it may be preferable to have more than two options (pass and fail) on graduation tests, either for political reasons (to prevent backlash against high failure rates) or to increase student motivation (by allowing students the opportunity to earn different types of diplomas) (Bishop, 1997a; Costrell, 1994; Kang, 1985). Some states are already doing this: students in Michigan, New York, and Tennessee may receive either a regular or a special "endorsed" diploma, depending on their test performance (Council of Chief State School Officers, 1998). This emerging practice is discussed below as a possible alternative to simply awarding or withholding diplomas.

Making Predictive Inferences

Tests used for granting or denying high school diplomas are often treated as if they were pure certification tests, but some people interpret them as also having an implicit predictive purpose. That is, a low score on a graduation test may be thought to reflect not only lack of mastery of

---

[6]In a current lawsuit, discussed below, the plaintiffs have alleged that lack of reliability is a problem in the writing section of the Texas Assessment of Academic Skills. As a result, the plaintiffs contend, a student who receives a certain score on the writing assessment cannot be reliably distinguised from a student whose score is one point higher—yet one point can lead to the denial of a high school diploma (G.I. Forum, 1977).

what a student has been taught but also a future inability to function successfully in society (Madaus, 1983; Tenopyr, 1977). This was a problem in the *Debra P.* case, in which students who failed a graduation test were labeled "functionally illiterate"—the long-term consequences of which could be as severe as diploma denial itself. A similar issue has arisen in a Texas lawsuit concerning use of a 10th grade test, the Texas Assessment of Academic Skills (TAAS), to make decisions regarding high school graduation.[7] The plaintiffs contend that awarding or denying a high school diploma on the basis of a student's score on this test cannot be justified because there is insufficient evidence that TAAS scores predict future success in school or at work (G.I. Forum, 1997). The case has not yet gone to trial, and the validity of this claim has yet to be determined.

Gathering evidence to demonstrate the predictive power of a graduation test would be difficult. In most instances, there is no single criterion or outcome variable that could be applied to all students. Schools might gather multiple sources of information, such as the number of students in college or employed two years after graduating, as a general indication of how students are functioning, but this information might be difficult to obtain as time passed.

Schools that give graduation tests early (sometimes as early as 8th or 9th grade), however, assume that such tests are diagnostic and that students who fail can benefit from effective remedial instruction. For example, in the Charlotte-Mecklenburg school district in North Carolina, students who fail the graduation test (first taken in 8th grade) get remedial assistance. Using these test results to place a pupil in a remedial class or other intervention also involves a prediction about the student's performance—that is, that as a result of the placement, the student's mastery of the knowledge and skills measured by the test will improve. Thus, evidence that a particular treatment (in this case, the remedial program) benefits students who fail the test would be appropriate as part of the test validation process.

---

[7]The test was implemented in 1990. In the 10th grade, students take an exit-level test in three parts and have eight chances to pass before graduation. Student who don't pass the test but pass all their courses are eligible for a certificate specifying that the student has completed all 12 grades but has not completed requirements for a diploma.

Consequences of Graduation Test Use

Test validation includes collecting evidence on the intended and unintended consequences of test use. Determining whether the use of a test for making graduation decisions produces better overall educational outcomes requires that the various intended benefits of test use be weighed against unintended negative consequences for individual students and different kinds of students (American Educational Research Association et al., 1985: Standard 6.5; Joint Committee on Testing Practices, 1988; Messick, 1989). The committee recognizes, however, that decisions about graduation will be made with or without information from standardized tests; the costs and benefits of using test scores to make these decisions should therefore be balanced against the costs and benefits of making the same decisions using other kinds of information.

There is very little research that specifically addresses the consequences of graduation testing. In the absence of substantial empirical evidence, proponents and opponents of minimum competency graduation tests have argued over the probable consequences. Reardon reports that "while proponents of the tests have generally argued that such requirements provide incentives for students and schools, particularly those at the low end of the achievement spectrum, to improve their performance, opponents have argued that the tests lead to a low level basic skills curriculum and increase dropout rates by discouraging students who fail the tests from continuing in school" (1996:1).

Catterall adds, "initial boasts and doubts alike regarding the effects of gatekeeping competency testing have met with a paucity of follow-up research" (1990:1). This is clearly an important area for future research, to which test users should pay particular attention in validating their testing programs, as well as an issue for policymakers when they are considering whether to administer high-stakes graduation tests. The studies reported below generally address the impact of minimum competency graduation testing. The consequences of emerging graduation assessments based on higher standards may well be different. Research is needed to explore the different effects of these two types of programs.

Impact on Instruction

Many proponents and opponents of graduation testing agree that high-stakes minimum competency tests have a substantial impact on instruction and curriculum. They disagree, however, on whether the impact is, on balance, beneficial or detrimental to learning. Much of the literature on high-stakes minimum competency testing (not limited to graduation testing) argues that preparing students for high-stakes tests often results in drill-and-practice teaching methods that fail to develop higher levels of thinking (Darling-Hammond and Wise, 1985; Madaus and Kellaghan, 1991; O'Day and Smith, 1993). A comparison of low- and high-stakes state testing programs found that, as the stakes of testing increase, "there is a point at which district strategies take on the flavor of a single-minded devotion to specific, almost 'game-like' ways to increase the test scores" (Wilson and Corbett, 1991:36).

Other researchers have concluded that the increased emphasis on basic skills may be educationally sound if accompanied by intelligent professional development of teachers that promotes active learning among students (Berger and Elson, 1996). The same study also found that, when schools use tests that carry high stakes for students, teachers are likelier to report a clear understanding of their school's mission but a diminished sense of their own professional autonomy.

Finally, some researchers hold that minimum competency graduation testing has little or no impact on instruction and learning. For instance, some findings suggest that the teachers' selection of topics for instruction does not seem to be influenced by minimum competency testing (Kuhs et al., 1985; Porter et al., 1988). Catterall (1990) interviewed students in four states with high school exit exams and found that half of the students at all performance levels were not even aware of the test, even though the majority had already taken it. Educators explained that the issues surrounding graduation testing had subsided markedly over the years. The numbers now being denied diplomas based on low minimum competency test scores ranged from negligible to none. Catterall concludes: "if a graduation test is ever to contribute to student performance through motivational or diagnostic mechanisms, it might be advantageous for students to know about the test, its use, and its meaning. Large shares of students at all performance levels are not aware of exit testing policies in their own schools, which raises doubts about any such educational contributions" (1990:7).

The findings described thus far have focused on the impact of minimum competency exams. It will become increasingly important to study the impact of emerging graduation assessments based on high standards, because the effects on instruction and learning are likely to be different. In one of the few such studies on this topic, Bishop (1997a) compared the

Third International Mathematics and Science Study (TIMSS) test scores of countries with and without rigorous graduation tests. He found that countries with demanding exit exams outperformed other countries at a comparable level of development. He concluded, however, that such exams were probably not the most important determinant of achievement levels and that more research was needed.

Impact on Dropout Rates

Although the causal connections are unclear, much of the existing research shows that the use of high-stakes tests is associated with higher dropout rates. Kreitzer et al. (1989) compared the testing activities in the 10 states with the highest dropout rates and the 10 states with the lowest dropout rates. They found that 9 of the 10 states with the highest dropout rates had high-stakes graduation tests, and none of the states with low dropout rates used tests for high-stakes purposes.

Using data from the National Educational Longitudinal Study (NELS), Reardon found that high-stakes 8th grade tests were associated with sharply higher dropout rates—6 to 8 percentage points higher just between the 8th and 10th grades. Reardon also found that the schools most likely to have high-stakes testing policies were those with high concentrations of students of low socioeconomic status (SES). His analysis suggests that "it is the concentrated poverty of these schools and their communities, and their concomitant lack of resources, that link [high-stakes testing] policies to higher dropout rates, rather than other risk factors such as student grades, age, attendance, and minority group membership" (1996:5).

Reardon and other researchers acknowledge that these studies do not provide clear evidence of causality. The question therefore remains: Do high-stakes tests cause students to drop out, or do high dropout rates spur policymakers to adopt high-stakes testing programs in the first place? We do not know the answer, though Kreitzer et al. conclude that high-stakes graduation tests may give at-risk students "an extra push out the school door" (1989:146).

In an effort to collect more direct evidence of the relationship between minimum competency graduation tests and students' decisions about dropping out, Catterall (1990) conducted interviews with educators, administrators, and high school students. He found that school administrators tend to believe that high school competency tests are so easy that they pose no real threat to graduation, and that most students consider graduation tests beneficial. Still, students who fail the test at least once are considerably more likely than those who pass to report that they may drop out of school, even after a number of other academic variables are controlled. His results suggest that graduation tests pose no threat to most students, but, among those who fail them, they increase a sense of discouragement and contribute to the likelihood of dropping out. A limitation of this study is that it reports on students' beliefs about the likelihood of their dropping out in the future, but provides no data on whether they actually do drop out.

Cawthorne (1990) interviewed students at two schools in Boston to find out why many good students, who "were doing everything their schools asked of them," had failed Boston's newly implemented graduation test. He found that many of them were minority and/or bilingual students who had received good grades. Although all the students interviewed could read, some said either that they "did not test well" or that they read English too slowly to be able to finish the test, even though they could do well in school by working long hours on their assignments. Many of the students with good grades who failed the graduation test reported that they would not have returned to school for another year simply to pass the test requirement. The need to do so was eliminated, however, as Boston rescinded its graduation test policy that year.

A more recent study suggests that quite different subgroups are most strongly affected by failing a high-stakes test. Griffin and Heidorn (1996) report that failing a minimum competency graduation test significantly increased the likelihood that students would leave school, but only for students who were doing *well* academically. Students with poorer academic records did not appear to be affected by failing the test, and minority students who failed the test did not demonstrate an increased likelihood of leaving school as a result. These researchers speculate that the perceived stigma attached to test failure may cause students with higher grades to experience a substantial drop in self-esteem or a sense of embarrassment before their peers. This study suggests that such experiences might be especially acute for students with records of academic success.

These studies are not inconsistent. Some groups, such as low-SES children, blacks, Hispanics, and English-language learners, are more likely than other students to attend the schools in which high-stakes tests are given, and they are therefore likelier to be subject to high-stakes test policies and their consequences (Reardon, 1996). The same groups are also more likely to attend schools that do not provide high-quality curriculum and instruction. It is thus not surprising that low-SES and minority students tend to fail high-stakes graduation tests at higher rates than do high-SES and white students (Eckland, 1980).[8] What is less clear is whether high-stakes graduation tests lead over time to improved curriculum, instruction, and student performance, which is one of the stated purposes of such tests. Nor is it clear why students with high grades would react more strongly than other students to failing a high-stakes graduation test. These findings and unresolved issues underscore the need for further empirical research in this area.

Societal Effects of Not Earning a High School Diploma

Very little is known about the specific consequences of passing or failing a high school graduation exam, but a good deal is known about whether and how earning a high school diploma affects a student's future life chances. Jaeger (1989) asserts that having a high school diploma, as distinct from having the skills assessed by a minimum competency test, largely determines whether a young person can obtain employment and earn money, as well as the amount of money a person can earn. He bases this conclusion on evidence suggesting that performance on a minimum competency test is not a good predictor of whether a young person will obtain employment or earn a good salary, provided the person receives a high school diploma (Eckland, 1980). Statistics show that in 1997 the unemployment rate of 25- to 34-year-old men who lacked a diploma was more than twice that of men who had diplomas. At the same ages, unemployment was 3 times higher among women who had dropped out of high school than among graduates (National Center for Education Statistics, 1998: Supplemental Table 31-1).

Hauser (1997) provides evidence that the failure to complete high school, whether due to graduation tests or other reasons, is increasingly associated with problems in employment, earnings, family formation and stability, civic participation, and health. For instance, in the last two decades, employment has been very high and stable among male college graduates; it has declined, however, among high school graduates and, to

---

[8]The same holds true for English-language learners and students with disabilities who must take high-stakes tests without appropriate accommodation. These issues are discussed in Chapters 8 and 9.

an even greater extent, among dropouts. Furthermore, the earning power of high school dropouts has fallen relative to that of high school graduates. Over the last two decades, the earnings of white male dropouts declined from 85 percent to less than 75 percent of the earnings of white high school graduates; among black and Hispanic men, there appears to have been a similar decline. Electoral participation by high school dropouts is also lower than among high school graduates. Based on a large collection of such evidence, Hauser concludes: "Failure to obtain at least a high school diploma looks more and more like the contemporary equivalent of functional illiteracy. High school dropout indicates a failure to pass minimum thresholds of economic, social or political motivation, access and competence" (1997:154).

Issues of Fairness

The core meaning of fairness in test use concerns comparable validity. Thus a fair graduation test is one that yields comparably valid scores from person to person, from group to group, and from setting to setting.

There are several ways to assess the comparability, or fairness, of scores. Test items can be checked (using judgmental and statistical methods) to ensure that they are not biased in favor of any particular group. The testing process itself can also be assessed in terms of the extent to which students are given a comparable opportunity to demonstrate their knowledge of the construct(s) the test is intended to measure. For example, all students should have adequate notice of the skills and content to be tested, as well as access to appropriate test preparation materials, and they should be tested under equivalent conditions. Students who are at risk of failing a graduation test should be advised of their situation well in advance and provided with appropriate instruction that would improve their chances of passing. In addition, students who fail a graduation test should be given multiple opportunities to demonstrate their capabilities through repeated testing with alternate forms, or through other construct-equivalent means. The validity and fairness of score interpretations on a graduation test will be enhanced by taking into account other relevant information about individual students (American Educational Research Association et al., 1985: Standards 8.4, 8.5, 8.7, 8.8; 1998).

When assessing the fairness of a graduation test, it is particularly important that test users ask whether certain groups of students are being denied diplomas unfairly due to insufficient opportunities to learn the material tested. Graduation tests should provide evidence of mastery or nonmastery of material taught. Thus there is a need for evidence that the content of the test is representative of what students have been taught.

Measuring What Students Have Been Taught

Not surprisingly, a great deal of research has shown that students learn best what they are taught (Porter, 1998). Thus, an important determinant of the fairness of a graduation test is the degree to which curriculum and instruction are aligned with what the test measures. *Debra P. v. Turlington* (1981), a circuit court decision that has influenced courts and policymakers in other parts of the United States, established the principle that a high-stakes graduation test should be a fair measure of what students have been taught. The court ordered a four-year phase-in period for Florida's graduation test, partly to provide time to bring the test, the curriculum, and instruction into alignment.

Test users can demonstrate the necessary alignment by comparing evidence on test content, curricular coverage, and instructional preparation. Curricular coverage refers to how well test items represent the objectives of the curriculum. Instructional preparation is an appraisal of the extent to which schools equip students with the knowledge and skills that the test measures. McLaughlin and Shepard (1995) state that the effort to assess alignment should (1) focus on the elements of schooling that are directly related to student achievement, (2) focus on the curriculum as enacted rather than as reported or listed in official documents, and (3) identify indicators that can be tried and then evaluated for adequacy. They also recommend that a test not be used to make high-stakes decisions about individual students until test users can show that the content of the test is representative of what the students have actually been taught.

Popham and Lindheim (1981) describe two possible approaches for measuring curricular coverage and instructional preparation. One is to analyze textbooks, syllabi, lesson plans, and other materials to determine the degree to which the planned instruction covers the content of the assessment. The second method is to observe actual classrooms. Madaus (1983) also offers steps that states can take to ensure fairness on graduation tests.[9]

---

[9]One is to develop and publicize a specific definition of the domain to be tested. A second is to assess the degree of alignment between the content of a state test and the

It is neither straightforward nor inexpensive to measure the content of actual instruction (Popham and Lindheim, 1981). As a result, there is little evidence to suggest that exit exams in current use have been validated properly against the defined curriculum and actual instruction; rather, it appears that many states have not taken adequate steps to validate their assessment instruments, and that proper studies would reveal important weaknesses (Stake, 1998).

Finally, today's professional standards for content in such core academic subjects as mathematics and science are much more demanding than the minimum competency standards of the 1970s and 1980s (e.g., National Council of Teachers of Mathematics, 1989; National Research Council, 1996). If a high school graduation test needed to be aligned with these more ambitious content standards and with actual instruction, the task would be more difficult today than it was in 1981, when *Debra P.* was decided. Thus, states and school districts face challenges in demonstrating that the content of a high-standards, high-stakes graduation test is representative of what students have been taught (McLaughlin and Shepard, 1995).

DIPLOMA DENIAL: ALTERNATIVE AND COMPLEMENTARY STRATEGIES

As noted above, current professional testing standards state that "in elementary or secondary education, a decision or characterization that will have a major impact on a test taker should not automatically be made on the basis of a single test score. Other relevant information . . . should also be taken into account" (American Educational Research Association et al., 1985:54, Standard 8.12).

With or without tests, states and school districts must make decisions about which students receive high school diplomas. The decision to award or withhold a high school diploma plainly has a major impact on a young person's future life chances (Hauser, 1997; Jaeger, 1989), however,

state- or district-level curricular frameworks. Third, at the local level, Madaus recommends efforts to ensure that what is being taught corresponds with the test's domain. Fourth, he recommends that, after the test has been given, item-response patterns be analyzed by district, by school, and by student characteristics (e.g., race, gender, and curricular tracks in high school). Finally, he suggests a series of small-scale evaluations on the long-term impact of the program on curriculum and teaching.

and there are alternative ways of making such decisions that do not rely on test scores alone. These include the use of compensatory models for making diploma decisions, the use of differentiated diplomas, and reliance on end-of-course examinations in making high school graduation decisions. In addition, many states, including those with high-stakes graduation tests, have adopted strategies in which students who are at risk of failing a graduation test are advised of their situation well in advance and provided with instruction to improve their chances of passing. For some of these approaches, which are described in more detail below, American experience is limited and research is needed to explore their effectiveness. For instance, we do not know how best to combine advance notice of high-stakes test requirements, remedial intervention, and opportunity to retake graduation tests. Research is also needed to explore the effects of different kinds of high school credentials on employment and other post-school outcomes.

Compensatory Model

As discussed earlier, states that use high-stakes graduation tests typically require students to complete all their course work satisfactorily *and* to pass the graduation test(s) (Phillips, 1991; Council of Chief State School Officers, 1998). This is a conjunctive model. An alternative, compensatory, model (Mehrens, 1986) would allow a student's strong performance on one indicator, such as course work, to offset or compensate for low performance on another, such as the graduation exam. This strategy has its drawbacks, particularly where policymakers and citizens question what it actually means to receive good grades. At the same time, combined with other strategies for promoting high standards in classroom instruction, this model could help satisfy demands that diplomas be based on tangible evidence of achievement while respecting standards of good test practice.

Differentiated Diplomas

Some states offer advanced or endorsed diplomas for students who pass a high-stakes graduation test. The test may thus provide increased incentives for teachers and students. At the same time, students who pass their courses can still graduate with a traditional diploma even if they do not pass the test. This is similar to how high-stakes tests are used in many other countries, including Britain and France, to indicate students' qualifications as they depart secondary school (Broadfoot, 1996). Using tests to indicate qualifications allows high stakes to be attached to tests without the punishing effects of barring graduation to those who fail. On one hand, this approach has potential drawbacks; teacher and student motivation may not be as high if students can graduate without passing the test. On the other hand, this strategy provides some incentives to students and teachers, and it allows states to develop assessments based on higher standards, even if the majority of students do not initially meet them.

Connecticut recently implemented a grade 10 assessment that attaches a certificate of mastery to students' high school diplomas if they meet the state goals. Students have the option of retaking the assessment in grades 11 and 12 to earn the certificate. In the first year, only 11 percent of students statewide earned the certificate in all four subjects; that percentage is climbing gradually, however.

Teacher focus groups conducted after the first two years of the program suggested that the assessment has caused some narrowing of the curriculum. Teachers also reported some positive effects, however, including placing more emphasis on higher-level thinking skills in their instruction, having students write more, and emphasizing problem-solving and open-ended science labs that reflect the activities on the assessment. Teachers also reported having more reason and opportunity to talk to each other about instruction, informally as well as in the context of local and state-sponsored workshops. The study concluded that, although an endorsed diploma has the potential to motivate students, the ways in which the special certificate will serve students in the future must be clear and tangible. Teachers reported widespread ambivalence among students because the state's colleges and businesses had not yet taken a clear position on the use of the certificate in admissions and hiring decisions (Chudowsky and Behuniak, 1999).

End-of-Course Exams

Some states award advanced or endorsed diplomas on the basis of end-of-course exams. There are few data on the effectiveness of these programs, but in general they appear promising and warrant further investigation as a possible alternative basis for graduation decisions.

One of the best-known programs of this kind is New York's Regents examination system. Bishop (1997b) found that, when student demography was held constant, New York did significantly better than other states on the SAT and the NAEP math assessments without experiencing a reduction in high school graduation rates. Bishop attributes these results to the presence of the rigorous Regents examinations that many New York students take prior to graduation.[10]

Virginia is in the process of implementing an end-of-course graduation exam system. Starting in 2004, 12th graders will be required to pass a series of tests—based on Virginia's standards of learning—to earn a standard diploma. Students will be able to earn an advanced studies diploma if they pass additional end-of-course tests. This program also has an accountability component: by 2007, if 70 percent of students in a given school do not pass the exams, the school could lose its state accreditation. The standards of learning, approved in 1995, have won praise from many national experts for their content and rigor.

Virginia's case is an example of standards being introduced well in advance of the high-stakes assessment, providing adequate notice and time to bring tests, curriculum, and instruction into alignment. The large majority of the state's 135 districts have already begun incorporating the standards into their English, math, science, and social studies curricula (*Education Week*, 1998).

Early Intervention and Remedial Instruction

As noted earlier, the rates at which students fail minimum competency graduation exams has declined over the years, in part because states and school districts administer the test early (often in the 10th grade or earlier), provide multiple opportunities for students to retake the test(s) they have failed, and offer remedial education aimed at helping students learn what they need to know to satisfy requirements for graduation. This is sound educational practice; students who fail a high-stakes test should have the opportunity to retake the test, and students who are at risk of failing a graduation test should be apprised of their situation well

---

[10]Not all students are currently required to take these rigorous exams prior to graduation. This will change in the year 2000, when all graduating students must pass the new Regents English exam. It will be interesting to see if this requirement (with passing scores in additional subjects to be required in subsequent years) affects the high school graduation rate.

in advance and provided with effective instruction that will improve their chances of passing. It is also sound practice legally, for effective remedial education is one way of helping to ensure that students have been taught the kinds of knowledge and skills that the graduation test measures (*Debra P. v. Turlington*, 1981). In the committee's judgment, when tests are used to make decisions about graduation, states and school districts should implement programs of early intervention and effective remedial assistance.

This strategy is appealing, and low failure rates on minimum competency graduation tests could mean that the strategy is effective. At the same time, solid evaluation research on the most effective remedial approaches is sparse. Indeed, there are concerns that some existing remedial programs may offer only intense drill and practice, so that they treat the symptom (low test scores) without affecting the underlying condition (low achievement) (Office of Technology Assessment, 1992). There is plainly a need for good research on effective remedial education.

Lack of funding is also a problem for some of these programs and may jeopardize their long-term viability. Only 7 of the 18 states with graduation exams in 1994 earmarked funds to either schools or districts expressly for remedial education (Bond and King, 1995). Many remedial programs therefore rely on alternative sources of funding. Effective remedial education is expensive; whether most states and school districts have the resources needed to provide high-quality remedial instruction for students who have failed high-stakes graduation tests is not known.

The committee's findings and recommendations about awarding or withholding high school diplomas are reported in Chapter 12.

REFERENCES

American Educational Research Association, American Psychological Association, and National Council on Measurement in Education
    1985   *Standards for Educational and Psychological Testing.* Washington, DC: American Psychological Association.
    1998   *Draft Standards for Educational and Psychological Testing.* Washington, DC: American Psychological Association.
American Federation of Teachers
    1997   *Making Standards Matter 1997: An Annual Fifty-State Report on Efforts to Raise Academic Standards.* Washington DC: American Federation of Teachers.

Berger, Noah, and Hilari Hanamaikai Elson
  1996   What Happens When MCTs Are Used as an Accountability Device: Effects on Teacher Autonomy, Cooperation and School Mission. Paper presented at the annual meeting of the American Educational Research Assocation, April, New York.
Bishop, John H.
  1997a   The effect of national standards and curriculum-based exams on achievement. *American Economic Review* 87(2):260-264.
  1997b   *Do Curriculum-based External Exit Exam Systems Enhance Student Achievment?* New York: Consortium for Policy Research in Education and Center for Advanced Human Resource Studies, Cornell University.
Bond, Linda A., and Diane King
  1995   *State High School Graduation Testing: Status and Recommendations.* Oak Brook, IL: North Central Regional Educational Laboratory.
Broadfoot, Patricia M.
  1996   *Education, Assessment and Society.* Buckingham, England: Open University Press.
Burstein, Leigh, Daniel Koretz, Robert Linn, Brenda Sugrue, John Novak, Eva L. Baker, and Elizabeth Lewis Harris
  1996   Describing performance standards: Validity of the 1992 National Assessment of Educational Progress achievement level descriptors as characterizations of mathematics performance. *Educational Assessment* 3(1):9-51.
Catterall, James S.
  1990   A Reform Cooled-Out: Competency Tests Required for High School Graduation. CSE Technical Report 320. UCLA Center for Research on Evaluation, Standards, and Student Assessment.
Cawthorne, John E.
  1990   *"Tough" Graduation Standards and "Good" Kids.* Chestnut Hill, MA: Boston College, Center for the Study of Testing, Evaluation and Educational Policy.
Chudowsky, Naomi, and Peter Behuniak
  1999   Using focus groups to examine the consequences of large-scale assessments. *Educational Measurement: Issues and Practice.*
Costrell, Robert
  1994   A simple model of educational standards. *The American Economic Review* 84(4):956-971.
Council of Chief State School Officers
  1998   *Trends in State Student Assessment Programs.* Washington, DC: Council of Chief State School Officers.
Darling-Hammond, L., and A. Wise
  1985   Beyond standardizaton: State standards and school improvement. *Elementary School Journal* 85(3).
Eckland, Bruce K.
  1980   Sociodemographic implications of minimum competency testing. In *Minimum Competency Achievement Testing: Motives, Models, Measures, and Consequences*, Richard M. Jaeger and Carol K. Tittle, eds. Berkeley, CA: McCutchan Publishing.

EducationWeek
1998   *Quality Counts.* An Education Week/Pew Charitable Trusts report.
G.I. Forum and Image de Tejas
1997   Brief for lawsuit brought against the Texas Education Agency, Dr. Mike
          Moses, and members of the Texas State Board of Education regarding the
          Texas Assessment of Academic Skills.
Green, R.
1973   *The Aptitude Achievement Distinction.* Proceedings of Second CTB/McGraw-
          Hill Conference in Educational Measurement. Monterey, CA: CTB/
          McGraw-Hill.
Griffin, Bryan W., and Mark H. Heidorn
1996   An examination of the relationship between minimum competency test per-
          formance and dropping out of high school. *Educational Evaluation and Policy
          Analysis* 18(3):243-252.
Hambleton, R.K.
1980   Test score validity and standard-setting methods. In *Criterion-Referenced Mea-
          surement: The State of the Art,* R.A. Berk, ed. Baltimore, MD: Johns Hopkins
          University Press.
Hauser, Robert M.
1997   Indicators of high school completion and dropout. In *Indicators of Children's
          Well-Being,* Robert M. Hauser, Brett V. Brown, and William R. Prosser, eds.
          New York: Russell Sage Foundation.
Jaeger, Richard M.
1989   Certification of student competence. In *Educational Measurement,* 3rd Ed., R.
          Linn, ed. New York: Macmillan.
Joint Committee on Testing Practices
1988   *Code of Fair Testing Practices in Education.* American Psychological Associa-
          tion. Washington, D.C.: National Council on Measurement in Education.
Kang, Suk
1985   A formal model of school reward systems. In *Incentives, Learning, and Em-
          ployability,* John Bishop, ed. Columbus, OH: National Center for Research
          in Vocational Education.
Kreitzer, A.E., F. Madaus, and W. Haney
1989   Competency testing and dropouts. Pp 129-152 in *Dropouts from School: Is-
          sues, Dilemmas and Solutions,* L. Weis, E. Farrar, and H.G. Petrie, eds. Al-
          bany: State University of New York Press.
Kuhs, T., A. Porter, R. Floden, D. Freeman, W. Schmidt and J. Schwille
1985   Differences among teachers in their use of curriculum-embedded tests. *El-
          ementary School Journal* 86(2):141-153.
Linn, Robert
1998a   Assessments and Accountability. Paper presented at the annual meeting of
          the American Educational Research Association, April, San Diego.
1998b   Validating inferences from National Assessment of Educational Progress
          achievement-level setting. *Applied Measurement in Education* 11(1):23-47.

Madaus, George, ed.
  1983   The Courts, Validity, and Minimum Competency Testing. Hingham, MA:
          Kluwer-Nijhoff Publishing.
Madaus, G.F., and T. Kellaghan
  1991   Examination Systems in the European Community: Implications for a Na-
          tional Examination System in the U.S. Paper prepared for the Science, Edu-
          cation and Transportation Program, Office of Technology Assessment, U.S.
          Congress, Washington, DC.
McLaughlin, M.W., and L.A. Shepard
  1995   Improving Education Through Standards-Based Reform. A report by the Na-
          tional Academy of Education Panel on Standards-Based Education Reform.
          Stanford, CA: National Academy of Education.
Mehrens, William A.
  1986   Measurement specialists: Motive to achieve or motive to avoid failure? Edu-
          cational Measurement: Issues and Practice 5(4):5-10.
  1993   Issues and Recommendations Regarding Implementaiton of High School Gradua-
          tion Tests. North Central Regional Educational Laboratory.
Messick, Samuel
  1989   Validity. Educational Measurement, 3rd Ed., Robert L. Linn, ed. New York:
          MacMillan.
National Academy of Education
  1996   Quality and Utility: The 1994 Trial State Assessment in Reading, Robert Glaser,
          Robert Linn, and George Bohrnstedt, eds. Panel on the Evaluation of the
          NAEP Trial State Assessment. Stanford, CA: National Academy of Educa-
          tion.
National Center for Education Statistics
  1998   The Condition of Education, 1998. NCES 98-013. Washington, DC: U.S.
          Government Printing Office.
National Coalition of Advocates for Students
  1998   A Gathering Storm: How Palm Beach County Schools Fail Poor and Minority
          Children. A report by the National Coalition of Advocates for Students.
          Boston: Shea Brothers.
National Council of Teachers of Mathematics
  1989   Curriculum and Evaluation Standards for School Mathematics. Reston, VA:
          National Council of Teachers of Mathematics.
National Research Council
  1996   National Science Education Standards. Washington, DC: National Academy
          Press.
O'Day, Jennifer A., and Marshall S. Smith
  1993   Systemic reform and educational opportunity. In Designing Coherent Educa-
          tional Policy, Susan H. Fuhrman, ed. San Francisco: Jossey-Bass.
Office of Technology Assessment
  1992   Testing in American Schools: Asking the Right Questions. OTA-SET-519.
          Washington, DC: U.S. Government Printing Office.
Phillips, S.E.
  1991   Diploma sanction tests revisited: New problems from old solutions. Journal
          of Law and Education 20(2):175-199.

Popham, W. James, and Elaine Lindheim
  1981   Implications of a landmark ruling on Florida's minimum competency test. *Phi Delta Kappan* 63(1):18-20.
Porter, A.C.
  1998   The effects of upgrading policies on high school mathematics and science. In *Brookings Papers on Education Policy*, D. Ravitch, ed. Washington, DC: Brookings Institution Press.
Porter, A., R. Floden, D. Freeman, W. Schmidt, and J. Schwille
  1988   Content determinants in elementary school mathematics. Pp. 96-113 in *Perspectives on Research on Effective Mathematics Teaching*, D.A. Grouws and T.J. Cooney, eds. Hillsdale, NJ: Lawrence Erlbaum Associates.
Reardon, Sean F.
  1996   Eighth Grade Minimum Competency Testing and Early High School Dropout Patterns. Paper presented at the annual meeting of the American Educational Research Assocation, New York, April.
Shepard, Lorrie A.
  1984   Setting performance standards. In *A Guide to Criterion-Referenced Test Construction*, R. A. Berk, ed. Baltimore, MD: Johns Hopkins University Press.
Stake, R.
  1998   Some comments on assessment in U.S. education. *Education Policy Analysis Archives* (on-line serial) 6(14). Available: http://epaa.asu.edu/epaa/v6n14.html.
Tenopyr, M.
  1977   Content-construction confusion. *Personnel Psychology* 30:47-54.
Willingham, W.W., and N.S. Cole
  1997   *Gender Bias and Fair Assessment*. Hillsdale, NJ: Erlbaum.
Wilson, Bruce L., and H. Dickson Corbett
  1991   *Two State Minimum Competency Testing Programs and Their Effects on Curriculum and Instruction*. Philadelphia, PA: Research for Better Schools.

LEGAL REFERENCE

Debra P. v. Turlington, 474 F. Supp. 244 (M.D. Fla. 1979); *aff'd in part and rev'd in part,* 644 F.2d 397 (5th Cir. 1981); *rem'd,* 564 F. Supp. 177 (M.D. Fla. 1983); *aff'd,* 730 F.2d 1405 (11th Cir. 1984).

8

Students with Disabilities

Recent federal and state laws mandate the inclusion of all students in large-scale assessments, even students with special learning and language needs. The federal legislation includes Goals 2000 and Title I of the Improving America's Schools Act of 1994. Several other federal statutes and regulations, including the Individuals with Disabilities Education Act (IDEA), Section 504 of the Rehabilitation Act of 1973, and Title II of the Americans with Disabilities Act (ADA), play a prominent role in determining how students with disabilities will participate in general education, including large-scale assessment programs.

The committee has benefited enormously from recent work in this area by another committee of the Board on Testing and Assessment. The Committee on Goals 2000 and the Inclusion of Students with Disabilities examined in detail the implications of standards-based reforms for students with disabilities. That committee's report, *Educating One and All: Students with Disabilities and Standards-Based Reform* (National Research Council, 1997), discusses systems of accountability and assessment and ways to increase the participation of children with disabilities. We draw on this earlier report throughout this chapter.

The 1997 amendments to the IDEA include several new or expanded assessment provisions likely to increase dramatically the participation of students with disabilities in large-scale assessments. They link decisions about participation to a student's individualized education program (IEP), which is required by law to be developed for each student with a disability. The 1997 amendments provide that:

- As a condition of eligibility, states must have policies and procedures to ensure that students with disabilities are included in general state- and district-wide assessment programs, with appropriate accommodations when necessary.
- Effective July 1, 1998, IEPs must include a statement of any individual modifications in the administration of state- or district-wide assessments of student achievement that are needed in order for the student to participate in such assessments. If the IEP team—which includes parents, the teacher, and others concerned with the child's education—determines that the child will not participate in a particular state-wide or district-wide assessment of student achievement (or part thereof), then the IEP must include a statement of why that assessment is not appropriate for the student and how the student will be assessed.
- For the students whose IEPs specify that they should be excluded from regular assessments, the state must ensure development of guidelines for their participation in alternate assessments, developing and conducting alternate assessments no later than July 1, 2000.
- States must have recording policies and procedures in place that ensure proper reporting of information regarding the performance of students with disabilities on large-scale assessments.

These changes in the law were designed to benefit children with disabilities by promoting high expectations commensurate with their needs and providing a means of holding school systems accountable for attending to those needs. Because about 50 percent of students with disabilities have been excluded from state- and district-wide assessments in the past, there has been a shortage of key indicators of success for many of these children, including performance on assessments, dropout rates, graduation rates, and regular reports to the public on progress toward meeting goals for their educational improvement. Many school systems have therefore not established meaningful educational goals for children who, it is now clear, can achieve at higher levels than society has historically assumed. Changes in the new law also aim to improve reporting to parents and teachers of students with disabilities (and the students themselves) with respect to the progress they are making toward achievement of these goals. The 1997 IDEA amendments also contemplate that state performance goals and indicators will help determine needs for personnel training and development (U.S. Department of Education, October 1997).

STUDENTS WITH DISABILITIES: WHO QUALIFIES?

Describing appropriate assessment policies for students with disabilities is complicated by the wide variation in the characteristics of the 5 million students—10 percent of the school-age population—who qualify for special education services under the IDEA. Cognitive, physical, sensory, and behavioral disabilities are covered.

Educating One and All describes the diversity of this population and their school experiences (National Research Council, 1997):

• Although 13 disabilities are mentioned in the federal IDEA and defined in the regulations, 4 categories of disability account for about 90 percent of all special education students: speech or language impairment, serious emotional disturbance, mental retardation, and specific learning disabilities. The category of learning disabilities, by itself, accounts for more than half of all students identified for special education.

• Identification and classification practices vary widely from place to place. Inconsistencies are particularly common in distinguishing students with mild cognitive disabilities, such as learning disabilities and mild mental retardation, from students who are low achieving but may not have a specific disability. Identification practices and disability definitions vary so greatly, in fact, that a student who is identified in one of these categories in one school district may not be so identified in another (Shepard, 1989). Prevalence rates vary widely across jurisdictions (U.S. Department of Education, 1995). Practices for identifying students with disabilities also vary over time and thus can affect estimates of trends in prevalence rates. The responses of schools to financial incentives (such as increased funding based on the numbers of students who are classified as having a disability) also vary over time and can affect these trends.

• Students with disabilities also vary in terms of their educational experience. Over the past 20 years, students with disabilities have been participating to an increasing extent in general education classrooms and curricula. For example, as of 1993-1994, almost 75 percent of special education students spent at least 40 percent of their school day in regular classrooms (U.S. Department of Education, 1996). Others receive specialized instruction and individualized curricula for some part of their school day or in the area of their disability. For a small number of students, mostly those with severe cognitive impairments, the focus of a predominantly academic general education curriculum is not consistent with their life goals. They experience a highly individualized curriculum that emphasizes independence and self-sufficiency.

Identification for Special Education

To be eligible for special education services under the IDEA, a student must first be found to meet the criteria for at least 1 of 13 recognized disabilities (or the counterpart categories in state law). The second criterion is that the student must be found to require special educational services. A student who needs special education is also entitled to receive related services—that is, other services that enable him or her to benefit from special education. States and school districts must provide each such student with a free, appropriate public education.

This means that not all students with disabilities are eligible to receive services under the IDEA. They must demonstrate educational need. Even those who do not qualify for special education, however, are protected by Section 504 of the Rehabilitation Act of 1973 and by the ADA (1990), which entitle them to reasonable accommodations in school activities to permit them to overcome impairments in one or more major life activities. The number of students in this category is not known.[1] Nevertheless, the legal rights accorded them could affect large-scale assessment programs, especially those with high stakes for individual students, by increasing the number of students receiving accommodations and raising questions about the extent to which the scores of students with disabilities should be aggregated with other students' scores.

Educating One and All describes the provisions of the IDEA designed to ensure the fair, nondiscriminatory use of tests in identifying students who qualify for special education services (National Research Council, 1997:69-70):

---

[1]Data on children with disabilities are collected for IDEA-eligible children and thus do not include other students with disabilities.

The IDEA is explicit and detailed about testing and assessment procedures used to qualify students for special education. A number of legislative provisions are designed to protect students and ensure the fair, nondiscriminatory use of tests. These provisions stipulate that decisions about children must be based on more than a single test, that tests must be validated for the purpose for which they are used, that students must be assessed in all areas related to a suspected disability, and that evaluations must be made by a multidisciplinary team. Children are generally tested in one-to-one situations with various school professionals (e.g., school psychologist, an occupational therapist, a speech and language therapist) on tests that can be individually adapted to match the child's level.

Such highly individualized testing, conducted for the purpose of diagnosis or instructional planning, differs considerably from the large-scale, group-administered assessments of achievement that are the primary focus of this report. The Congress nonetheless expressed serious concern about racial disproportions in special education when it reauthorized the IDEA in 1997.[2]

IEP Process

Testing thus plays a critical role in determining who qualifies for special education services, but traditionally accountability in special education has not relied mainly on assessment. Rather, it has centered on the individualized education program, an essentially private document that lays out the educational goals and curriculum of an individual student. Each IEP is designed to reflect one child's capabilities and to specify the services necessary for the child to benefit from that curriculum. IEPs thus vary considerably from student to student and have varying degrees of relationship with the general curriculum. For example, one IEP may call for a sign-language interpreter to enable a deaf student to participate fully in the general education curriculum; another may establish a set of instructional objectives that focus on the goal of independent living—telling time, personal hygiene, and basic safety skills.

By law the IEP also serves as a device for monitoring a student's progress. Classroom-based assessment, teacher judgment, and other measures that are sensitive to small and specific changes are typically used for

---

[2]As part of this legislation, the Congress requested a National Research Council study to examine issues related to the overrepresentation of minority children in special education.

this purpose. Large-scale assessments have not often been used, because of their emphasis on broad content domains rather than on the specific skills that are usually represented in IEP goals.

In many cases, the IEP is used in making high-stakes decisions about students with disabilities. The IEP team often considers assessment information in conjunction with a student's IEP goals and the progress made toward meeting them when making decisions on placement or retention in grade. In several states, where special education students may be exempt from state or local graduation requirements, completion of IEP goals is a sufficient condition for receipt of a high school diploma or its equivalent (Thurlow et al., 1996). Box 8-1 provides additional detail on state practices with regard to high school graduation and students in special education.

PARTICIPATION IN LARGE-SCALE ASSESSMENT PROGRAMS

For a variety of reasons, many students with disabilities have traditionally been exempted from large-scale achievement tests. Educators and parents have sometimes been confused about the availability of test modifications or accommodations, or they have been concerned about subjecting these children to the stress of testing. Officials sometimes have "excused" children with disabilities from a testing requirement in an effort to raise their schools' average scores. Other concerns include the potential mismatch between test content and student curricula and difficulties in administering certain tests to students with severe disabilities. In any case, exempting these students from assessments, and thus from system accountability measures, has meant that there is less incentive to enhance their educational programs and improve their performance (National Research Council, 1997:152-153). Exclusion from testing may also communicate the message that students are not capable of meeting the expectations represented by the test. Most parents and teachers of students with disabilities say they want these students to meet the same high standards set for the general population (Thurlow et al., 1998).

There are a number of other reasons for including students with disabilities in asssessment systems. A more accurate picture of aggregate student performance is produced when all students are included (Vanderwood et al., 1998); comparisons of test results among schools or districts will not be valid if participation rates of students with disabilities

BOX 8-1
High School Graduation

Educating One and All (National Research Council, 1997) reported that, among states with high school exit exams in 1995, five exempted special education students with IEPs from such tests if course requirements were met; this could be done even through alternative special education courses (Thurlow et al., 1995a). Some analysts have suggested that such policies may inflate special education referrals (Allington and McGill-Franzen, 1992) or lead families to move their children to schools in "easy" graduation states (Thurlow et al., 1995a). A related issue is that students with disabilities who do not graduate are entitled to remain in school and receive special education and related services until the age of 21 or 22—a costly proposition. Receiving a diploma, which terminates IDEA services, constitutes a change in placement requiring parental consent, and some parents may prefer that their children continue to receive services rather than graduate.

Another option practiced in some states is to give students a modified diploma or certificate upon successful completion of IEP goals. This alternative is reserved in some places for students with the most profound disabilities. The various practices reflect differing opinions about how best to meet the needs of students with disabilities. Some argue that differentiated diplomas stigmatize students; others feel that giving a standard diploma to these students devalues the credential and corrupts the educational process (DeStefano and Metzer, 1991). Research evidence on these questions is generally missing.

Educating One and All emphasizes that, because a high school diploma is the minimum requirement for many jobs, graduation testing of students with disabilities raises serious concerns. If graduation standards are increased, more students—including those with disabilities—may well be denied diplomas. The 1997 report makes the following recommendations:

If students receive alternative credentials to the standard high school diploma, parents need to understand the different diplomas and the implications of decisions to modify curriculum and assessments for the type of diploma their child will receive.

Before attaching significant stakes to the performance of individual students, those students should be given an opportunity to learn the skills and knowledge expected of them.

The report also calls for research on the effects of different kinds of high school credentials on employment and other post-school outcomes, as well as research to develop meaningful alternative credentials that can credibly convey the nature of a student's accomplishments and capabilities.

vary from one place to the next. Individual scores also provide important information to students, their parents, and their teachers. In addition, education reforms and the allocation of resources and extra services are increasingly driven by these test results; if students with disabilities were not included, then the resulting reforms would be less likely to meet their needs. Finally, recent federal legislation has mandated that students with disabilities be included in large-scale assessments and that accommodations and alternate assessments be provided when necessary.

Surveys have indicated that the participation of students with disabilities in statewide assessments has generally been minimal, but with extreme variation from one state to another—from 0 to 100 percent (Erickson et al., 1995; Gronna et al., 1998; McGrew et al., 1992; Shriner and Thurlow, 1992). Forty-three states had written guidelines for participation at the time that *Educating One and All* was written. IEP teams helped make the decision in most states, but only about half of those with guidelines required that participation decisions be documented in the IEP (Erickson and Thurlow, 1996). Research suggests that the criteria for making decisions about participation have also varied widely from district to district, even in states with written guidelines (DeStefano, 1998).

One of the ways to increase the participation of students with disabilities in large-scale assessments is to offer accommodations. Four broad categories of accommodations are currently in use (Thurlow et al., 1993):

(1) Changes in *presentation:* for example, braille forms for visually impaired students, taped versions for students with reading disabilities.

(2) Changes in *response mode:* use of a scribe or amanuensis (someone who writes answers for the examinee), computer assistance on tests not otherwise administered by computer.

(3) Changes in *timing:* extra time within a given test session, the division of a session into smaller time blocks.

(4) Changes in *setting:* administration in small groups or alone, in a separate room. Some students with disabilities may take the test in a standard setting with some form of physical accommodation (e.g., a special desk) but with no other change (National Research Council, 1997:159).

Written guidelines on the use of accommodations vary considerably from state to state. States take different approaches regarding what accommodations they allow or prohibit. A change that is explicitly permitted in one state might be prohibited in another (Thurlow et al., 1995b). Little research exists on the impact of specific accommodations on the validity of achievement tests (Thurlow et al., 1995c).

Most students with disabilities have only mild impairments. These students can participate in large-scale assessments, although some will require accommodations. A small percentage of students have disabilities severe enough to require a different assessment, because their curriculum does not match the content of the common test. Section 504 of the Rehabilitation Act of 1973, the ADA, the IDEA, Goals 2000, and Title I all require states and school districts to provide different assessments for these children.

Educating One and All reported that only six states currently offer students with disabilities alternatives to the common assessment (Bond et al., 1996), and that no research exists on "either the ability of alternate assessments to measure students' educational progress validly or to encourage greater accountability for students with disabilities. We do know, however, that the design of alternate assessments poses all the same technical challenges as the development of valid accommodations for the common assessment" (National Research Council, 1997:175).

PSYCHOMETRICS OF ACCOMMODATIONS

Educating One and All reviews the existing evidence on the reliability and validity of test use for students with disabilities, including the logic of providing accommodations, and summarizes the findings as follows (National Research Council, 1997):

> Traditionally, standardization (of content, administrative conditions, scoring, and other features) has been used to make the results of assessments comparable in meaning from one test-taker to the next. For some students with disabilities, however, a standard assessment may yield scores that are not comparable in meaning to those obtained by other students because the disability itself biases the score. In many cases, students with disabilities would get a lower score than they should because the disability introduces construct-irrelevant variance, variations in the scores unrelated to the construct purportedly measured. Therefore, "in the case of students with disabilities, some aspects of standardization are breached in the interest of reducing sources of irrelevant difficulty that might otherwise lower scores artificially" (Willingham, 1988:12).
>
> Accommodations are intended to correct for distortions in a student's true competence caused by a disability unrelated to the construct being mea-

sured. . . . The risk of accommodations is that they may provide the wrong correction. They may provide too weak a correction, leaving the scores of individuals with disabilities lower than they should be, or they may provide an irrelevant correction or an excessive one, distorting or changing scores further and undermining rather than enhancing validity. This risk is explicitly recognized in the guidelines provided by some state education agencies for avoiding these errors, although their guidance is sometimes very general and limited. For example, Maryland's *Requirements and Guidelines for Exemptions, Excuses, and Accommodations for Maryland Statewide Assessment Programs* (Maryland State Department of Education, 1995) says that "accommodations *must not invalidate the assessment for which they are granted*" (p. 2, emphasis in the original). However, the only guidance it provides for meeting this standard is a single pair of examples (p. 3):

> Addressing the issue of validity involves an examination of the purpose of test and the specific skills to be measured. For example, if an objective of the writing test is to measure handwriting ability, that objective would be substantially altered by allowing a student to dictate his/her response. On the other hand, if a writing objective stated that the student was to communicate thoughts or ideas, handwriting might be viewed as only incidental to achieving the objective. In the latter case, allowing the use of a dictated response probably would not appreciably change the measurement of the objective.

Unfortunately, many cases will be far less clear than this, and accommodations may not succeed in increasing validity even when they seem clear and logical on their face (pp. 173, 176-177).

· · ·

Many approaches to the assessment of individuals with disabilities, particularly assessment accommodations, assume that disabilities are not directly related to the construct tested. Case law indicates that rights to accommodations do not apply when the disability is directly related to the construct tested (see Phillips, 1994). In other words, a student with a reading disability might be allowed help with reading (the accommodation) on a mathematics test, since reading is not in the construct being measured, but would not be allowed help with reading on a reading test, since the disability is directly related to the construct of reading.

However, the groups of students with clearly identifiable disabilities (such as motor impairments) that are largely unrelated to the constructs being tested constitute a small number of the identified population of students with disabilities. Most students with disabilities have cognitive impairments that presumably are related to at least some of the constructs tested.

Relationships between disabilities and assessed constructs have important implications for the validity of inferences based on test scores. For example, if a new assessment includes communication skills as an important part of the domain of mathematics, then, to score well in mathematics, students would need to be able to read and write reasonably well . . . . On such an assessment, it is possible that students with reading disabilities might score worse than their proficiency in other aspects of mathematics would warrant, but providing them with accommodations such as the reading of questions or the scribing of answers is likely to undermine the validity of inferences to the broader, more complex domain of mathematics (pp. 170-171).

Legal and Professional Standards[3]

Federal statutes and regulations on educating students with disabilities, including the IDEA, Section 504, and the ADA, require that tests and other evaluation materials be validated for the specific purpose for which they are used. All three also require that, when a test is given to a student with impaired sensory, manual, or speaking skills, the results accurately reflect the child's achievement level or whatever other factors the test purports to measure, rather than reflecting the student's disabilities.

These statutes and regulations also require accommodations. Both Section 504 and the ADA prohibit discrimination on the basis of disability. People with disabilities are guaranteed access to programs and services as effective as those provided to their peers without disabilities. The ADA further requires that public entities make "reasonable modification" in policies, practices, and procedures when "necessary to avoid discrimination on the basis of disability, unless the public entity can demonstrate that making the modifications would fundamentally alter the nature of the service, program, or activity" (28 CFR 35.130(b)(7)). In other words, alternate forms or accommodations in testing are required, provided that the content being tested is the same.

Distinctions among the various purposes of assessments become critical in light of these legal rights. Some assessments, for example, are designed mainly for the accountability of schools and school systems. Others are an integral part of learning, instruction, and curriculum. Some tests are used for making high-stakes decisions about individual students, including tracking, promotion or retention in grade, and awarding of a high school diploma or certificate of mastery. Each use raises its own set of legal issues with different implications. As a general rule, the greater the potential harm to students, the greater the protection to which they

---

[3]The legal discussion in this section is drawn from *Educating One and All*.

are entitled, and the more vulnerable the assessment is to legal challenge (National Research Council, 1997:186-187).

The *Standards for Educational and Psychological Testing* (American Educational Research Association et al., 1985) state that any claims made for a test cannot be generalized to a version of the test that has been altered significantly. The Standards continue: "When tests are administered to people with handicapping conditions, particularly those handicaps that affect cognitive functioning, a relevant question is whether the modified test measures the same constructs" (cited in Phillips, 1993:381).

Scarcity of Research Evidence

The committee that wrote *Educating One and All* concluded that "research on the validity of scores from accommodated assessments is limited, and little of it is directly applicable to the assessments that are central to standards-based reform. Much of the available evidence pertains to college admissions tests and other postsecondary tests (e.g., Wightman, 1993; Willingham et al., 1988)" (National Research Council, 1997:179). From the research reviewed, that committee went on to conclude:

• Different disabilities can cause different distortions in test scores. Predicting how the type of disability will affect test scores is difficult, in part because of the ambiguity of the disability classifications. Research is needed about the relationship of specific disabilities to test score performance in different subject areas (pp. 177-178).

• Some accommodations may inflate scores for some students. Raising scores, however, is not the purpose of accommodations and it is inappropriate to use them merely to raise scores (pp. 179-182).

• A need for additional testing time should not be assumed. The effects on test scores of providing additional time warrant empirical investigation (pp. 180-181).

• Although individuals with disabilities are entitled to reasonable accommodations that do not alter the content being tested, current knowledge and testing technology are not sufficient to allow the design of such accommodations (p. 193).

Recent studies have examined teachers' perceptions of accommodations and their likelihood of use. Gajria et al. (1994) found that teachers were more likely to use modifications involving changes in test design (e.g., large print, braille, response format) than those involving changes in administrative procedures (e.g., extra time, individual administration). Jayanthi and colleagues (1996) reported that most of the 401 general educators they surveyed believed it was unfair to provide testing adaptations only for students with identified disabilities, and that the adaptations teachers considered most helpful (simplified wording for items, individual help with directions) were not easy to make. Schumm and Vaughn (1991) also found that teachers believed all types of accommodations were more desirable than feasible. In that study, teachers favored accommodations that addressed motivational issues over those requiring curricular or environmental adaptations.

Clearly, more research on the validity of scores from accommodated testing is needed—in particular, research tailored directly to the particular assessments and inferences central to high-stakes decision making. In the interim, the existing research, although limited and based largely on different populations and types of assessments, suggests caution. The effects of accommodation cannot be assumed; they may be quite different from what an a priori logical analysis would predict. In addition, policies on the need to "flag" or mark score reports when accommodations are provided raise vexing legal, policy, and ethical questions (see Box 8-2).

The committee that wrote *Educating One and All* made the following broad recommendation to guide policymakers attempting to include more students with disabilities in standards-based assessment programs (p. 204):

> Assessment accommodations should be provided, but they should be used only to offset the impact of disabilities unrelated to the knowledge and skills being measured. They should be justified on a case-by-case basis, but individual decisions should be guided by a uniform set of criteria.

A number of research studies are under way, including efforts to include more students with disabilities in the National Assessment of Educational Progress.[4] A recent report from the National Center for Education Statistics describes many of these efforts (Olson and Goldstein, 1997); they are summarized in the appendix to this chapter.

Another problem raised in *Educating One and All*, which may make scores on large-scale assessments hard to interpret for some students with

---

[4]More complete discussion of the issues of including students with disabilities in the National Assessment of Educational Progress (NAEP) can be found in *Grading the Nation's Report Card: Evaluating NAEP and Transforming the Assessment of Educational Progress* (National Research Council, 1999).

> ## BOX 8-2
> ## Test Score Flagging
>
> Flagging is a concern when a nonstandard administration of an assessment—for example, providing accommodations such as extra time or a reader—may have compromised the validity of inferences based on the student's score. Flagging warns the user that the meaning of the score is uncertain.
>
> Flagged scores are typically not accompanied by any descriptive detail about the individual, or even the nature of accommodations offered. Therefore, flagging may not really help users to interpret scores more appropriately. It does, however, confront them with a decision: Should the score be ignored or discounted because of the possibility that accommodations have created unknown distortions? In the case of scores reported for individual students, flagging identifies the individual as having a disability, raising concerns about confidentiality and possible stigma.
>
> When testing technology is able to ensure that accommodations do not confound the measurement of underlying constructs, score notations will be unnecessary. Until then, however, flagging should be used only with the understanding that the need to protect the public and policymakers from misleading information must be weighed against the equally important need to protect student confidentiality and prevent discriminatory uses of testing information.
>
> SOURCE: National Research Council (1997).

disabilities, is the way in which performance levels are set. A number of new large-scale assessments typically use only a few performance levels, wherein the lowest level is high relative to the average distribution of performance. Consequently, very little information is provided about modest gains by the lowest-performing students, including some students with disabilities. This kind of reporting rubric may also signal that modest improvements are not important unless they bring students above the performance standard. To enable participation of students with disabilities, high-stakes tests should represent performance accurately at all points across a rather broad continuum. This not only implies breadth in terms of difficulty and the content assessed, but also requires that reporting methods provide sufficient and adequate information about all levels of student performance.

New assessment systems are relying heavily on performance assessments, which may decrease the reliability of information about low-achieving students, including some with disabilities. All such assessments should be designed to be informative about the achievement of all students. In particular, task selection and scoring criteria should be designed to accommodate varying levels of performance. These reliability concerns are magnified when high-stakes decisions will be based on individual test score results.

PROMISING APPROACHES IN TEST DESIGN[5]

Research and development in the field of educational testing is continually experimenting with new modes, formats, and technologies. Continued development of new forms of test construction, such as new ways of constructing test items and using computers, may hold promise for accommodating the needs of students with disabilities in large-scale assessment programs.

Item response theory (IRT), which is rapidly displacing classical test theory as the basis for modern test construction, is one promising development. IRT models describe "what happens when an examinee meets an item" (Wainer and Mislevy, 1990:66). They are based on the notion that students' performance on a test should reflect one latent trait or ability and that a mathematical model should be able to predict performance on individual test items on the basis of that trait.[6]

To use IRT modeling in test construction and scoring, test items are first administered to a large sample of respondents. Based on these data, a model is derived that predicts whether a given item will be answered correctly by a given individual on the basis of estimates of the difficulty of the item and the skill of the individual. A good model yields information about the difficulty of items for individuals with differing levels of skill. Items for which the model does not fit—that is, for which students' estimated mastery does not predict performance well—are discarded. This information is later used to score tests given to actual examinees.

Item response theory offers potential for including students with dis-

---

[5]This section is taken from pp. 182-183 of *Educating One and All* (National Research Council, 1997).

[6] Most IRT models are predicated on the notion that a test is unidimensional and that scores should therefore reflect a single latent trait. Recently, however, IRT models have been extended to multidimensional domains as well.

abilities in large-scale assessments. First, in many cases, assessments based on IRT allow for everyone's scores to be placed on a common scale, even though different students have been given different items. Given the wide range of performance levels among students, including students with disabilities, it is unlikely that the same set of items will be appropriate for everyone. Second, IRT makes it possible to assess changes in the reliability of scores as a function of a student's skill in what the assessment is measuring. Thus it is possible to identify an assessment that may not be reliable for low-scoring students with disabilities, even though it is reliable for high-scoring students. Third, IRT provides sophisticated methods for identifying items that are biased for students with disabilities.

Computerized testing also holds promise (Bennett, 1995). One of the accommodations most often given to students with disabilities is extra time. But, as noted earlier, extra time may undermine the validity of scores. Computer-based "adaptive" assessments allow students with a wide range of skills to be tested at a reasonable level of reliability and in a shorter amount of time by adapting items individually. This makes it possible to "give more time to everyone." Computer-based adaptive tests can be shorter than traditional tests but still comply with measurement principles. The need for accommodation in test administration is reduced, thereby circumventing the validity problems.

Finally, computer-based tests may allow students with disabilities to participate in simulated hands-on assessments through adaptive input devices, such as a light pen mounted on a head strap. These can replace assessments requiring manual movements that are impossible for some students. However, as Baxter and Shavelson (1994) have shown, computerized simulations of hands-on tasks can yield results surprisingly unlike those generated by the original tasks, so this approach will require careful evaluation.

The committee's findings and recommendations about students with disabilities are reported in Chapter 12.

APPENDIX

Including Students with Disabilities in Large-Scale Assessments: Summary of Current and Ongoing Research Activities

This appendix is a catalogue of the projects summarized and described in more detail in Olson and Goldstein (1997).

National Center for Education Statistics (NCES)

• *Working Conference on Guidelines for Inclusion of Students with Disabilities and Accommodations in Large-Scale Assessment Programs.* This report (National Center on Educational Outcomes, 1994a) summarizes a conference at which a variety of issues relating to the participation of students with disabilities in large-scale assessments and guidelines for including and accommodating students were discussed. Many recommendations made to NCES were incorporated into National Assessment of Educational Progress (NAEP) procedures for upcoming assessments.

• *Working Paper on Assessing Students with Disabilities and Limited English Proficiency* (Houser, 1995).

National Academy of Education (NAE)

Several studies were conducted for the National Academy of Education by the American Institutes for Research to evaluate the NAEP Trial State Assessment. NAE's evaluation of the 1992 trial state assessment (National Academy of Education, 1993) examined the exclusion of students, and the evaluation of the 1994 assessment (National Academy of Education, 1996) examined the assessibility of English-language learners and those with individual education programs who were excluded.

National Center on Educational Outcomes

This center has issued a collection of reports that include recommendations for the inclusion and accommodation of students with disabilities in state assessments and guidelines for states' use of assessments (National Center on Educational Outcomes, 1994b, 1995a, 1995b, 1996).

Office of Educational Research and Improvement (OERI)

Grants from OERI have helped fund a number of state projects aimed at creating better assessments, providing appropriate accommodations, and modifying assessments for use with students with disabilities or English-language learners.

Office of Special Education and Rehabilitation Services
The Division of Innovation and Development (DID) of the Office of Special Education Programs (OSEP) funds a number of research projects on students with disabilities, including some related to assessment.

Council of Chief State School Officers State Collaboration on Assessment and Student Standards (SCASS)
  • SCASS *Consortium on Assessing Special Education Students.* In this consortium, states share methods and criteria for accommodating special education students in large-scale assessments and plan a research program to develop criteria and procedures to assess the performance of all students.
  • SCASS *Consortium on Technical Guidelines for Performance Assessment (TGPA).* This consortium focuses on designing and implementing research to foster the development of sound performance assessments. The SCASS TGPA "Study 6—The Impact of Adapting Assessments for Special Education Students" examines issues of inclusion.

National Center for Research on Evaluation, Standards and Student Testing (CRESST)
The research being conducted at CRESST focused on assessment of students with disabilities addresses validity issues and the quality of measuring students' performance. Specifically, these studies examine the characteristics of the students, the level of difficulty of assessments for students with disabilities, the types of accommodations that seem reasonable, and the validity of results from accommodated assessments.

Educational Testing Service (ETS)
A book issued in 1988 by ETS (Willingham et al.) contains the findings of several studies that focus on measurement and validity issues in the testing of students with disabilities. These studies examined population characteristics, test performance, use of accommodations, admissions decisions, psychometric characteristics, and effects on validity.

National Academy of Sciences/National Research Council
Several studies have been conducted by the NAS/NRC. The Committee on Goals 2000 and the Inclusion of Students with Disabilities issued a report that examines policy and legislative background on special

education and standards-based reform and implications for research, practice, and policy (National Research Council, 1997). The Committee on the Evaluation of National and State Assessments of Educational Progress reviews NAEP in general and also evaluates the participation of English-language learners and students with disabilities (National Reseach Council, 1999). Two earlier studies are still relevant: *Placing Children in Special Education: A Strategy for Equity* (National Research Council, 1982b) and *Ability Testing for Handicapped People: Dilemma for Government, Science, and the Public* (National Research Council, 1982a).

NAEP Validity Studies (NVS) Expert Panel

The NVS panel planned a study on the validity of testing accommodations and their impact on student performance. "A Proposed Study Design to Examine the Impact of Accommodations of the Performance of Students with Disabilities in NAEP: The Impact of Increased Testing Time on the Performance of Disabled and Non-Disabled Students" is a draft proposal for a study of the impact of extended testing time on students with and without disabilities and across different content areas, as well as of student perceptions of their need for accommodations.

Joint Committee on Testing Practices (JCTP)

Project on Assessing Individuals with Disabilities. Currently, a working group of JCTP is compiling information about what is helpful to test users (e.g., assessment specialists, educators, counselors) and what is useful to policymakers about the assessment of students with disabilities, about interpreting scores from assessments, and about making educational and career decisions.

REFERENCES

American Educational Research Association, American Psychological Association, and National Council on Measurement in Education
  1985   *Standards for Educational and Psychological Testing.* Washington, DC: American Psychological Association.
Allington, R.L., and A. McGill-Franzen
  1992   Unintended effects of educational reform in New York. *Educational Policy* 4:397-414.
Baxter, G.P., and R.J. Shavelson
  1994   Performance assessment. *International Journal of Education Research* 21(3):233-350.

Bennett, R.E.
   1995   *Computer-based Testing for Examinees with Disabilities: On the Road to General-
            ized Accommodation.* Princeton, NJ: Educational Testing Service.
Bond, L.A., D. Braskamp, and E.D. Roeber
   1996   *The Status of State Student Assessment Programs in the United States.* Oak
            Brook, IL: North Central Regional Educational Laboratory and Council of
            Chief State School Officers.
DeStefano, L.
   1998   Translating Classroom Accommodations to Accommodations in Large-Scale
            Assessment. Paper presented at the Annual Meeting of the American Educa-
            tional Research Association, San Diego, CA.
DeStefano, L., and D. Metzer
   1991   High stakes testing and students with handicaps: An analysis of issues and
            policies. Pp. 267-288 in *Advances in Program Evaluation 1*, R.E. Stake, ed.
            Greenwich, CT: JAI Press.
Erickson, R.N., and M.L. Thurlow
   1996   *State Special Education Outcomes 1995.* Minneapolis, MN: National Center
            on Educational Outcomes, University of Minnesota.
Erickson, R.N., M.L. Thurlow, and K. Thor
   1995   *1994 State Special Education Outcomes.* Minneapolis, MN: National Center
            on Educational Outcomes, University of Minnesota.
Gajria, M., S.J. Salend, and M.A. Hemrick
   1994   Teacher acceptability of testing modifications for mainstreamed students.
            Learning Disabilities Research and Practice 9(4):236-243.
Gronna, S.S., A.A. Jenkins, and S.A. Chin-Chance
   1998   Who are we assessing? Determining state-wide participation rates for stu-
            dents with disabilities. *Exceptional Children* 64(3):407-418.
Hambleton, R.K., and H. Swaminathan
   1985   *Item Response Theory: Principles and Applications.* Hingham, MA: Kluwer
            Boston, Inc.
Houser, J.
   1995   *Assessing Students with Disabilities and Limited English Proficiency.* Working
            Paper Number 95-13. Washington, DC: National Center for Education
            Statistics, Policy and Review Branch, Data Development Division.
Jayanthi, M., M.H. Epstein, E.A Polloway, and W.D. Bursuck
   1996   A national survey of general education teachers' perceptions of testing adap-
            tations. *The Journal of Special Education* 30(1):99-115.
Koretz, D., S. Barron, K. Mitchell, and B. Stecher
   1996a   Assessment-Based Educational Reform: A Look at Two States (Kentucky
            and Maryland). Papers presented at the Annual Meeting of the American
            Educational Research Association, New York, NY.
   1996b   *The Perceived Effects of the Kentucky Instructional Results Information System.*
            Santa Monica, CA: RAND.
Maryland State Department of Education
   1995   *Requirements and Guidelines for Exemptions, Excuses, and Accommodations for
            Maryland Statewide Assessment Programs.* Baltimore: Maryland State Depart-
            ment of Education.

McGrew, K.S., M.L. Thurlow, J.G. Shriner, and A.N. Spiegel
  1992   *Inclusion of Students with Disabilities in National and State Data Collection Programs.* Minneapolis, MN: National Center on Educational Outcomes, University of Minnesota.
National Academy of Education
  1993   *The Trial State Assessment: Prospects and Realities.* Stanford, CA: National Academy of Education.
  1996   *Quality and Utility: The 1994 Trial State Assessment in Reading.* Stanford, CA: National Academy of Education.
National Center on Educational Outcomes
  1994a   *Making Decisions about the Inclusion of Students with Disabilities in Large-Scale Assessments.* Synthesis Report 14. Minneapolis, MN: University of Minnesota, National Center on Educational Outcomes.
  1994b   *Recommendations for Making Decisions about the Participation of Students with Disabilities in Statewide Assessment Programs.* Synthesis Report 15. Minneapolis, MN: National Center on Educational Outcomes.
  1995a   *Compilation of State Guidelines for Including Students with Disabilities in Assessments.* Synthesis Report 17. Minneapolis, MN: National Center on Educational Outcomes.
  1995b   *Compilation of State Guidelines for Accommodations in Assessments for Students with Disabilities.* Synthesis Report 18. Minneapolis, MN: National Center on Educational Outcomes.
  1996   *Assessment Guidelines that Maximize the Participation of Students with Disabilities in Large-Scale Assessments: Characteristics and Considerations.* Synthesis Report 25. Minneapolis, MN: National Center on Educational Outcomes.
National Research Council
  1982a   *Ability Testing of Handicapped People: Dilemma for Government, Science and the Public,* S.W. Sherman and N.M. Robinson, eds. Panel on Testing of Handicapped People, Committee on Ability Testing, National Research Council. Washington, DC: National Academy Press.
  1982b   *Placing Children in Special Education: A Strategy for Equity,* K.A. Heller, W.H. Holtzman, and S. Messick, eds. Committee on Child Development Research and Public Policy. Washington, DC: National Academy Press.
  1997   *Educating One and All: Students with Disabilities and Standards-Based Reform,* L.M. McDonnell, M.J. McLaughlin, and Patricia Morison, eds. Committee on Goals 2000 and the Inclusion of Students with Disabilities, Board on Testing and Assessment. Washington, DC: National Academy Press.
  1999   *Grading the Nation's Report Card: Evaluating NAEP and Transforming the Assessment of Educational Progress,* J. Pellegrino, L. Jones, and K. Mitchell, eds. Committee on the Evaluation of National and State Assessments of Educational Progress, Board on Testing and Assessment. Washington, DC: National Academy Press.
Olson, J.F., and A.A. Goldstein
  1997   *The Inclusion of Students with Disabilities and Limited English Proficient Students in Large-scale Assessments: A Summary of Recent Progress.* NCES 97-482. Washington, DC: U.S. Department of Education, Office of Educational Research and Improvement.

Phillips, S.E.
   1993   Testing accommodations for disabled students. *Education Law Reporter* 80:9-32.
   1994   High-stakes testing accommodations. Validity versus disabled rights. *Applied Measurement in Education* 7(2):93-120.
   1995   *All Students, Same Test, Same Standards: What the New Title I Legislation Will Mean for the Educational Assessment of Special Education Students.* Oak Brook, IL: North Central Regional Educational Laboratory.

Schumm, J.S., and S. Vaughn
   1991   Making adaptations for mainstreamed students: General classroom teachers' perspectives. *Remedial and Special Education* 12(4):18-27.

Shepard, L.A.
   1989   Identification of mild handicaps. Pp. 545-572 in *Educational Measurement*, 3rd Ed., R.L. Linn, ed. New York: American Council on Education and Macmillan Publishing Co.

Shriner, J.G., and M.L. Thurlow
   1992   *State Special Education Outcomes 1991.* Minneapolis, MN: National Center on Educational Outcomes, University of Minnesota.

Thurlow, M.L., J.L. Elliott, and J.E. Ysseldyke
   1998   *Testing Students with Disabilities: Practical Strategies for Complying with District and State Requirements.* Thousand Oaks, CA: Corwin Press.

Thurlow, M.L., J.E. Ysseldyke, and C.L. Anderson
   1995a   *High School Graduation Requirements: What's Happening for Students with Disabilities?* Synthesis Report 20. Minneapolis, MN: National Center on Educational Outcomes, University of Minnesota.

Thurlow, M.L., D.L. Scott, and J.E. Ysseldyke
   1995b   *A Compilation of States' Guidelines for Accommodations in Assessments for Students with Disabilities.* Synthesis Report 17. Minneapolis, MN: National Center on Educational Outcomes, University of Minnesota.

Thurlow, M.L., J.E. Ysseldyke, and B. Silverstein
   1993   *Testing Accommodations for Students with Disabilities: A Review of the Literature.* Synthesis Report 4. Minneapolis, MN: National Center on Educational Outcomes, University of Minnesota.
   1995c   Testing Accommodations for Students with Disabilities. *Remedial and Special Education* 16(5):260-270.

Thurlow, M.L., R. Erickson, R. Spicuzza, et al.
   1996   *Accommodations for Students with Disabilities: Guidelines from States with Graduation Exams.* Minnesota Report 5. Minneapolis, MN: National Center on Educational Outcomes, University of Minnesota.

U.S. Department of Education
   1995   *Seventeenth Annual Report to Congress on the Implementation of the Individuals with Disabilities Education Act.* Washington, DC: Office of Special Education Programs.
   1996   *Eighteenth Annual Report to Congress on the Implementation of the Individuals with Disabilities Education Act.* Washington, DC: Office of Special Education Programs.

1997   Nineteenth Annual Report to Congress on the Implementation of the Individuals with Disabilities Education Act. Washington, DC: Office of Special Education Programs.

Vanderwood, M., K. McGrew, and J.E. Ysseldyke
1998   Why we can't say much about students with disabilities during educational reform. Exceptional Children 64(3):359-370.

Wainer, H., and R.J. Mislevy
1990   Item response theory, item calibration and proficiency estimation. Pp. 65-102 in Computerized Adaptive Testing: A Primer, H. Wainer, ed. Mawah, NJ: Erlbaum.

Wightman, L.F.
1993   Test Takers with Disabilities: A Summary of Data from Special Administrations of the LSAT. Research Report 93-03. Newton, PA: Law School Admission Council.

Willingham, W.W.
1988   Introduction. Pp. 1-16 in Testing Handicapped People, W.W. Willingham, M. Ragosta, R.E. Bennett, H. Braun, D.A. Rock, and D.E. Powers, eds. Boston, MA: Allyn and Bacon.

Willingham, W.W., M. Ragosta, R.E. Bennett, H. Braun, D.A. Rock, and D.E. Powers, eds.
1988   Testing Handicapped People. Boston, MA: Allyn and Bacon.

LEGAL REFERENCES

Goals 2000, Educate America Act, 20 U.S.C. sections 5801 et seq.
Individuals with Disabilities Education Act, 20 U.S.C. section 1401 et seq.
Section 504 of the Rehabilitation Act of 1973, 29 U.S.C. sections 794 et seq.
Title I, Elementary and Secondary Education Act, 20 U.S.C. sections 6301 et seq.
Title II, Americans with Disabilities Act of 1990, 42 U.S.C. sections 12131 et seq.

9

English-Language Learners

There is increasing pressure to include in assessment programs larger numbers of students with special language and learning needs. Several federal laws, for example, require the participation of all students in assessments used to gauge student performance. Those that affect English-language learners include Goals 2000, Title I (Helping Disadvantaged Children Meet High Standards) and Title VII (Bilingual Education) of the Improving America's Schools Act of 1994, and the reauthorization of the Office of Educational Research and Improvement (Title IX of Goals 2000). As Chapter 3 notes, English-language learners are also protected by Title VI of the Civil Rights Act of 1964; Title VI regulations forbid various forms of discrimination on the basis of national origin and limited English proficiency (*Lau v. Nichols*, 1974). These laws provide that "standards and assessments are to fully include English-language learners" and that "innovative ways of assessing student performance are encouraged, including modifications to existing instruments for English-language learners" (National Research Council and Institute of Medicine, 1997:132-134).

Given the limitations of time and resources, the committee has taken advantage of recent work in this area by another committee of the National Research Council (NRC) and the Institute of Medicine (IOM). The Committee on Developing a Research Agenda on the Education of Limited-English-Proficient and Bilingual Students considered in detail how best to meet the academic and social needs of children who are English-language learners. That committee's report, *Improving Schooling for Language-Minority Children: A Research Agenda* (National Research Council and Institute of Medicine, 1997), devotes a portion of the discussion to the issue of assessing the language proficiency and subject-matter knowledge and skills of English-language learners. We draw on this earlier report throughout this chapter.

POPULATION OF ENGLISH-LANGUAGE LEARNERS

Defining appropriate assessment policies for English-language learners is complicated by the great diversity of their language backgrounds, previous educational experience, length of time residing in the United States, and current instructional programs. The number of English-language learners in grades K-12 is large and has grown considerably over the last decade (National Research Council and Institute of Medicine, 1997:17-19). A survey conducted in 1991 (Fleischman and Hopstock, 1993) estimated the number of students classified as English-language learners at 2.3 million (or about 6 percent of the school population)—an increase of almost 1 million students over a similar survey in 1984.

About three-fourths of English-language learners in the United States have Spanish as their language background; 27 percent come from other language backgrounds. No other single language is spoken by more than 4 percent of English-language learners. Over half of English-language learners are in the early elementary grades (K-4). A large majority are from disadvantaged socioeconomic backgrounds.

Children who cannot participate meaningfully and equitably in English-only classrooms due to limited English proficiency are eligible by law for special instructional services. The type and range of such programs vary tremendously (see National Research Council and Institute of Medicine, 1997:19-21, for an overview). In addition, English-language learners enter the United States at different ages, and their home and community environments differ in the amount of English used. Some arrive in U.S. schools with limited or interrupted prior schooling. Once here, they may enter English-only instructional programs or bilingual programs; many shift between programs.

A number of methods are used to determine which students are English-language learners, to place these students in special instructional programs, and to monitor their progress. *Improving Schooling for Language-*

Minority Children reported that the use of language-proficiency tests in English was the most common method of identifying English-language learners. More than 80 percent of the affected school districts used such tests, either alone or in combination with other techniques. Large majorities of districts also used these tests to assign English-language learners to specific instructional services and to reclassify students after they had developed English proficiency. About half the districts also used achievement tests in English to identify and assign English-language learners; more than 70 percent used them for reclassification. Other methods include home language surveys, observations, interviews, and enrollment information. But because many states allow districts to choose their assessment methods (usually from a menu of state-approved instruments), there is wide variation in the ways these decisions are made (National Research Council and Institute of Medicine, 1997:115-116). Estimates of trends in the prevalence of English-language learners can be affected by these variations across jurisdictions and over time; variations in the practice of classifying students as English-language learners to increase funding can also affect these trends.

The appropriate use of these assessment methods helps ensure that English-language learners receive the services necessary for learning; their inappropriate use can result in faulty assignment of services—or no services at all—and can lead to the tracking of English-language learners in low-level classes, their retention in grade, and their failure to graduate. For example, researchers have found that lack of language proficiency can lead to low-track placements, particularly in middle and high school. Berman and colleagues (1992) document that it is not unusual for secondary schools to require that students demonstrate proficiency in English before they are given access to grade-level mathematics and science courses; students who are not fluent in English may be barred from regular classes or tracked into remedial or compensatory classes, where instruction proceeds at a slower pace.[1]

Assessing English-language learners who may also have learning disabilities is particularly problematic. A lack of appropriate instruments is exacerbated by the scarcity of personnel with expertise in evaluating both

[1]Note the committee's finding that low-track placements are typically not educationally beneficial (Chapter 5).

linguistically and culturally diverse learners and students with disabilities.

The NRC and IOM report concludes that "most measures used [for assessing English-language proficiency] not only have been characterized by the measurement of decontextualized skills but also have set fairly low standards for language proficiency. Ultimately, English-language learners should be held to high standards for both English language and literacy, and should transition from special language measures to full participation in regularly administered assessments of English-language arts" (1997: 118).

TESTING ENGLISH-LANGUAGE LEARNERS

The central dilemma regarding participation of English-language learners in large-scale assessment programs is that, when students are not proficient in the language of the assessment (English), their scores on a test given in English will not accurately reflect their knowledge of the subject being assessed (except for a test that measures only English proficiency). School officials typically decide first whether to exempt an English-language learner from an assessment altogether and, second, if the student is included, how to modify the test or testing procedures to measure the student's skills more accurately. Official policies about exempting or accommodating English-language learners in assessment programs vary widely from place to place. For example, surveys of statewide assessment systems suggest that states are in various stages of incorporating English-language learners into their statewide assessment programs.[2] The following section describes some of the variation across jurisdictions in policies for exempting and accommodating English-language learners in large-scale achievement testing. It goes on to describe in more detail current assessment systems in one city—Philadelphia—and four states with large numbers of English-language learners—California, Florida, New York, and Texas.[3]

---

[2]Note that some of these assessments may be for accountability purposes and others for examining state trends.

[3]These states were selected partly because they have recently instituted policies (after considerable discussion) that incorporate English-language learners into state assessment systems.

Exempting English-Language Learners Based on Language Proficiency

Recent data from the Council of Chief State School Officers' annual survey of state assessment programs (1998) indicate that nine states do not allow exemptions of English-language learners from one or more of their state assessments. When exemptions are allowed, amount of time in the United States (for 27 assessments) or amount of time in an English as a second language (ESL) program (for 18 assessments) are most often named as criteria. States report using formal (for 4 assessments) and informal (for 5 assessments) testing much less frequently to make exemption decisions. When exemption decisions are made at the local level, it is usually by local committees (26 reported instances) or school districts (25 reported instances) and less frequently by parents (9 reported instances). If exemption decisions are made at the local level, formal assessments tend to be used more frequently than at the state level (11 reported instances), but time in the United States (13) and time in an ESL program (16) are still the most frequently named criteria (pp. 334-338).

Decisions about exemption are thus often made on the basis of some indicator of English proficiency (see Box 9-1). Yet there is considerable variability from place to place in the criterion used and the basis for its choice. California, for example, recently tightened its policy regarding exemptions on the SAT-9, which is required each year for all students in grades 2 through 11. The new policy, which will allow far fewer exemptions, requires all English-language learners who have been in California for more than one year to take the SAT-9 in English. Children may also be assessed in their primary language, if such assessments exist.[4]

This policy is being contested. The superintendent of San Francisco's schools recently filed suit in federal court against California's test policy, arguing that the civil rights of students with limited English proficiency are being violated because they don't know enough English to read the test and show what they know about reading, writing, math, history, and science (*Education Week*, 1998). He argued that a longer time is required before a student is proficient enough to take the test in English—specifically, that students should be enrolled in the city's schools for 30 months

---

[4]The director of bilingual education for the state reports that districts will probably use the Aprenda, the CTBS Espanol, or the SABE for this purpose (see Box 9-1).

BOX 9-1
Examples of Policies on Exemptions and Accommodations

Philadelphia: Exemptions: The SAT-9 and the Aprenda (a reading and math assessment in Spanish) are used to assess math and reading knowledge and skills. Level 1 English-language learners (those who are not literate in their native language) are generally exempt from the SAT-9 and are given the Aprenda. In some schools, the Aprenda is given to all students in bilingual programs. Levels 2 and 3 English-language learners take the SAT-9 with accommodations. Level 4 English-language learners (those who are almost ready to be mainstreamed) take the SAT-9 without accommodations.

Accommodations include extra time; multiple shortened test periods; simplification of directions; reading aloud of questions (for math and science only); translation of words or phrases on the spot (for math and science only); decoding of words upon request (but not for reading); use of gestures and nonverbal expressions to clarify directions and prompts; student use of graphic organizers and artwork, usually in combination with student's oral responses; testing in a separate room or small-group setting; use of a study carrel; and use of a word match glossary.

Philadelphia teachers reported that students generally reacted favorably. Some, however, said that "ungraded" English-language learners tested at their age-appropriate grade level, especially in middle and high school, were frustrated in spite of accommodations. Recommendations include allowing the use of bilingual dictionaries and electronic translators and even more time (interspersed with short breaks and over a series of days).

A few schools in Philadelphia are experimenting with portfolios, which may be used to assess math and reading knowledge and skills of Levels 1, 2, and 3 English-language learners.

Florida: The state requires district norm-referenced achievement tests at grades 4 and 8; Florida Writes, a writing assessment given at grades 4, 8, and 10; and the high school competency test, required for high school graduation. In the coming year, the state will replace the district norm-referenced achievement tests with the Florida comprehensive assessment test, a test of math and reading based on state standards.

Exemptions: The state suggests that English-language learners in an approved limited-English-proficient program for fewer than two years may be exempted from the norm-referenced district testing programs and Florida Writes. Exempted students must be assessed through other means determined by school and district personnel. Students not receiving special language assistance services may not be exempted by virtue of their classification as English-language learners alone. For system accountability purposes, scores for students in the English as a second language program for less than two years are disaggregated but not used to identify critically low-performing schools.

Accommodations: Districts are required to provide accommodations for English-language learners who are currently receiving services in a program operated in accordance with an approved district plan for English-language learners, but the exact combination of accommodations to be offered to any particular student is individually determined, considering the needs of the student.

Texas: The Texas assessment of academic skills (TAAS) is used to monitor the progress of students in grades 3 to 8. Language-proficiency assessment committees at each school (a site administrator, bilingual educator, English as a second language educator, and a parent of a child currently enrolled) determine which assessment each child will take. On the basis of six criteria—literacy in English and/or Spanish; oral language proficiency in English and/or Spanish; academic program participation, language of instruction and planned language of assessments; number of years continuously enrolled in school; previous testing history; and level of academic achievement—the committee decides whether English-language learners are tested on the English TAAS, tested on the Spanish TAAS, or exempted and given an alternative assessment. The committee also makes program entry and exit decisions and monitors students' progress after special services are ended. Those entering U.S. schools in the 3rd grade or later are required to take the English TAAS after three years.

The TAAS scores, whether for the English or the Spanish TAAS, are used as base indicators in the accountability rating system. In the near future, scores on the reading proficiency test in English for students taking the Spanish TAAS or for those delayed in taking the English TAAS will be publicly reported. Schools are designated "exemplary," "recognized," "acceptable," and "low performing" based on aggregated student scores, and rewards and sanctions are meted out on this basis.

or more before being required to take the test. The superintendent prevailed in the district court. It is unclear whether or how these requirements and disputes will be affected by a June 1998 California referendum that sharply limits bilingual education in the state's public schools.

Accommodations

A recent survey of state assessment programs for 1996-1997 (Council of Chief State School Officers, 1998) reported that only seven states do not permit accommodations in the administration of at least one assessment for English-language learners. The most common accommodations were giving tests to small groups (29 states), repeating of directions (28 states), allowing extra time (same day) (25 states), taking the test in a separate room (25 states) or alone in a study carrel (25 states), having a person familiar with the child's language and culture give the test (23 states), giving more time breaks (22 states), reading questions aloud in English (21 states), translating directions (19 states), extending the session over multiple days (15 states), simplifying directions (14 states), and using word lists or dictionaries (14 states). Ten states reported that they test students in a language other than English. Other accommodations included allowing student to respond in the native language to English questions, explaining directions, and oral reading of questions in the native language.

Other alternative assessment methodologies that have been suggested include using portfolios to collect a child's best work over time, developing computer-assisted assessments tailored to respond to language needs and content knowledge of students, extending scaffolding and sheltered instruction to assessments, dynamic assessment, and allowing English-language learners to display their knowledge using alternative forms of representation (e.g., showing math operations in numbers and knowledge of graphing in problem solving).

The survey indicated that 11 states currently have an alternative assessment in place for English-language learners in at least one assessment program. These range from a Spanish-language version of the Stanford 9 for students literate in Spanish, used in Arizona, to an option to local districts to determine their own alternative methods of assessment.

TRACKING, RETENTION, AND
HIGH SCHOOL GRADUATION

No systematic information is available about whether or how English-language learners are accommodated in tests used for tracking or retention. In addition, we know very little about current assessment practices used to place English-language learners in Title I targeted assistance programs or other remedial programs, gifted and talented classes or advanced academic course work, or special education programs; there is an urgent need for research on these important questions.

A survey conducted in 1993-1994 (Rivera and Vincent, 1997) found that 17 states require students to pass one or more content-area tests to receive a standard high school diploma. States approach the testing of English-language learners in various ways (see Box 9-2). Eight states exempt them from the first administration of the test for a set period of time. For example, if the state first gives a graduation test in 10th grade, a newly arrived student who is judged to have insufficient English proficiency may be temporarily excused from taking the test. According to the survey, such deferrals are usually for six months to a year.

Eleven states permit accommodations, the most frequent being extra time, small-group administration, clarifying directions, flexible scheduling, and the use of dictionaries. Only two states, New York and New Mexico, give the test in students' native languages. Four states permit or require alternative assessments.

A major task in deciding how to assess English-language learners for purposes of high school graduation is to determine what level of English proficiency (if any) should be prerequisite to receiving a diploma. This decision will dictate whether graduation requirements in some domains can or should be assessed in the student's native language.

Deciding whether English proficiency should be a requirement for graduation—and, if so, what type and what level of English proficiency—could be considered a moral and policy decision about how society defines "basically educated." A more pragmatic view might see it as an economic decision about basic workplace requirements and improving students' employability. In other words, it is not essentially a psychometric decision. But it has enormous consequences for other psychometric activity, because any state or district that requires little or no English, or only conversational English, thus commits itself to developing bilingual and/or other language versions of all content tests. In most states, all children who do not graduate on time, including English-language learn-

BOX 9-2
Examples of Graduation Testing Policies for English-Language Learners

Florida: Students who have been classified as limited-English-proficient and have been in an approved program for English-language learners for fewer than two years may be temporarily exempted from taking the high school competency test at the discretion of local school personnel, but such students cannot be awarded a standard high school diploma until the test is passed. English-language learners not receiving English-language learner services or former English-language learners may not be exempted. English-language learners who do not pass the competency test can return for a 13th year to study for sections of the test that were not passed; students may also opt for a certificate of completion in lieu of a high school diploma. According to state personnel, English-language learners generally pass the exit exam because most enter school in Florida in the early grades and are proficient in English by high school.

New York: In November 1997 the State Board of Regents approved revised high school graduation requirements, to be put in place for the class entering 9th grade in 2001. In four core subjects (English, mathematics, social studies, and science), students will be required to pass state Regents exams or approved alternative examinations (for special education), in addition to courses, to demonstrate achievement of the state standards.

English-language learners entering school in this country in 9th grade or later can take all required Regents examinations, except for the English examination, in their native language if available (Spanish, Haitian-Creole, Russian, Chinese, and Korean) if it is within three years of entering the United States.

ers and students with disabilities, may remain in school until age 21 or 22; thus English-language learners can retake the graduation test as their English-language proficiency increases. Box 9-3 explores important issues in this area using two hypothetical school systems.

Although graduation decisions are essentially different from promotion and tracking decisions, some of the considerations concerning relations between instructional methods and testing and concerning test presentation apply equally. As summarized in *Improving Schooling for Language-Minority Children* (National Research Council and Institute of Medicine, 1997), research on second-language learners suggests that:

However, all English-language learners must pass the English Regents exam, in English, to receive a diploma. New York state officials are concerned about the ability of two groups of English-language learners to pass the English Regents exam—students entering U.S. schools in the middle and secondary grades and those with limited or interrupted formal schooling at all grade levels. Thus the state is putting into place a comprehensive strategy to help ensure that they pass. This fourfold strategy includes: (1) a national and state search for effective program models and the dissemination of these models through a bilingual/English as a second language web site and funds to schools to help them prepare students to pass the Regents exams; (2) professional development for all teachers of English-language learners to help them integrate the English language arts standards into English as a second language and native-language arts instruction; (3) review of programs for English-language learners to ensure they are aligned with state standards, along with monitoring of school districts to ensure compliance with all regulations pertinent to English-language learners; and (4) other activities, including publications in the area of technology applications for bilingual and English-language learners, bilingual math glossaries, invitational statewide symposia on the education of adult English-language learners, and the identification and distribution of resources to provide increased after-school, weekend, and summer language arts academies for English-language learners.

Texas: Students must pass a high school exit test in reading, writing, and math (in English), taken in the 10th grade, to graduate. Governor George Bush is exploring the possibility of using the Texas assessment of academic skills (TAAS) at crucial grade levels to ensure that students have the requisite skills to proceed to the next grade level.

• Second-language learners can display a higher level of comprehension of texts that are read in a second language when discussing or when questioned about those texts in their first language than if all the discussion or testing activity occurs in the second language.

• Even at relatively low levels of proficiency in a second language, tasks that have been taught and practiced in that language may be performed better in the second than the first, stronger, language. This is particularly likely to be true for tasks that have relatively restricted formats, such as giving definitions, solving syllogisms, and making analogies.

• Transfer of knowledge and of skills from a first to a second language occurs, and it accounts for the relatively stronger academic perfor-

BOX 9-3
Graduation Requirements:
Two Hypothetical Cases

NEW COLOMBIA

The large city school district of New Colombia decides that it will require as a prerequisite to high school graduation that students (a) display sufficient control of English to function adequately in a job interview for an unskilled position in the restaurant or retail sector and (b) perform adequately on knowledge assessments in the domains of mathematics, U.S. government, and American literature. It also includes among its educational goals raising the high school graduation rates and decreasing disparity among language groups in rates of high school completion.

New Colombia adopts a language proficiency assessment designed to reflect conversational skill that requires one-on-one testing, using a scripted interaction protocol such as that developed for application of the guidelines developed by the American Council on the Teaching of Foreign Languages. Education officials recognize that test formats such as those used for the Test of English as a Foreign Language (TOEFL) reflect knowledge of vocabulary, formally taught grammar, and listening comprehension but do not relate to conversational/interactive proficiency, and furthermore recognize that TOEFL-style tests are more appropriate for those who have been explicitly taught a language than for those who have acquired it in a second-language setting. Teacher judgments are used to determine which students must take the conversation proficiency assessment, although New Colombia officials suspect that perhaps teacher judgment concerning conversational proficiency would be as good an indicator as teacher judgment concerning whose conversational fluency needs to be tested.

The American literature knowledge test presupposes having read works by Washington Irving, Mark Twain, Nathaniel Hawthorne, Willa Cather, F. Scott Fitzgerald, and Toni Morrison and being able to answer multiple-choice questions and provide short written answers to questions. New Colombia educators had a long debate about what form of access to these works of literature they considered essential, and what form of display of knowledge about them they considered appropriate for high school graduates. They eventually decided that English-language learners could choose to study these texts in English, or in translation, or in English with extensive footnotes providing interpretations and translations. They also decided that tests should be provided in booklets that included English and a translated version of all questions, and that students could respond to short-answer questions in any language or language mix. Provision of dual-language test versions is unlimited, upon student request.

In seven of the eight secondary schools in New Colombia, U.S. government courses are provided in languages other than English, with one focus of these courses in some schools being to ensure knowledge of translation equivalents for key terms/concepts (e.g., "representation," "Senate," "bill," "gerrymander," "appeal," "reconciliation," "appropriation," "entitlement"). The graduation test requires knowledge of these terms in English, on the basis that such knowledge is essential to effective functioning in the domain of citizenship; thus, test booklets prepared for English-language learners that included translations of other test questions do not translate these key concepts, even in the other-language questions. Again, any student who requests a dual-language version of the test may get it.

The math test includes both straightforward calculation problems and problems involving analysis, and it requests that students display their work for both kinds of problems. Test scoring is sometimes difficult because the work displayed sometimes conforms to conventions or uses heuristics unfamiliar to the U.S. test monitors. Assuming that performance on the analysis problems would be heavily confounded by the level of comprehension of the text presenting the problem, New Colombia test writers decided that text should be provided in the native language as well as English. Bilingual presentation was considered important, since the student had been studying such problems in U.S. classrooms, thus some aspects of their formulation might be more familiar in English than in the native language. Students could opt for a dual-language version.

New Colombia encountered considerable support from the large language-minority groups for its approach to high-stakes testing for graduation, as well as many problems of ensuring comparability and fairness in its test materials. Since practical considerations limited the production of bilingual test materials to 17 languages, inevitably parents from the other 54 language groups represented in New Colombia objected, but as these groups aggregated to only 0.65 percent of the population, it was decided to ignore their demands. Protests from monolingual English-speaking parents started when it emerged that a higher percentage of students taking the bilingual versions of the test were passing compared to those taking the English-only version; English speakers pointed out that the bilingual tests gave students more information and more support than the equivalent English-only version.

NORTH BRICKLEY

North Brickley, a city with a somewhat smaller population of nonnative speakers of English than New Colombia, also considers English proficiency an important component of the skills needed for high school graduation. But North Brickley decides that English proficiency means the full array of English language skills—reading, writing, speaking and listening, and the capacity to carry out academic work in English. North Brickley also prioritizes the educational goal of high standards and ensuring high levels of competence of its high school graduates, over the goal of increasing high school graduation rates. Thus, North Brickley rejects the New Colombia solution of allowing students to study and be tested on literature, government, and math with native-language support. Instead, a single, English-language test for each of these areas is developed, and students are told that answers provided in any language other than English will not be scored.

In consequence, North Brickley decides not to assess oral proficiency in English of nonnative speakers, reasoning that the written tests are more rigorous and demanding and that high academic performance depends more on literacy skills in English than on oral skills in any case. North Brickley's organization of its graduation requirement has the immediate consequence that graduation rates decline for nonnative speakers of English and that parents request transfer of their children out of bilingual classrooms and into English as a second language and English-only classrooms. Remediation efforts, introduced for English-language learners who fail the test on the first administration in response to parental and student demands, focuses on teaching English skills rather than on teaching subject matter, with the result that graduation rates on subsequent administrations rise only slightly.

Despite the insistence by the test administrators that performance in English is prerequisite to performance on the test, the results for the math subtest deviate strongly from the other subtests, in that nonnative speakers perform quite well. Some qualitative analysis of test-taking behavior indicates that these students are solving all the calculation problems in their native languages—Pascal, after all, did arithmetic in French and algebra in English—with considerably higher success rates than native English speakers. Because there are relatively few analytical problems on the test, this excellent performance on the calculations masks somewhat more mixed performance by the nonnative speakers on the problems requiring reading and analyzing a problem.

mance in the second language of students who start the process of second-language learning with stronger language and literacy skills in the native language. But such transfer is not automatic; it occurs only when conditions for the emergence of the analogous second-language skills exist, and it can be aided by explicit support for the process of transfer.

• Bilinguals do not typically replicate their capacities across their two languages, unless the array of task demands in the two languages are similar. Thus, estimating total vocabulary of a bilingual requires, in effect, adding across independent vocabulary assessments in the two languages; and allowing a bilingual full opportunity to display knowledge may require allowing code-switching (the use of either or both languages during the same speech event). Similarly, assessing the full extent of the knowledge of a bilingual in any domain, which may or may not be a reasonable goal, may well necessitate some procedure for compiling knowledge across two languages.

If promotion and tracking decisions are meant to determine which available placement or treatment is most likely to benefit individual students, then it seems clear, given the relation between first-language accomplishments and likely performance in second-language settings, that first-language testing must play a role in these decisions for English-language learners. To predict whether a Spanish-speaking high school junior who has just arrived in the United States will be able to function in an advanced algebra/trigonometry class, it is much more important to know how much algebra she has mastered than to know how much English she speaks. And to predict whether a Haitian Creole 12-year-old will be able to move into secondary school after a year of elementary schooling in the United States, it is much more important to have available information about his literacy skills in Creole and/or French than to know how much English he speaks right now.

PSYCHOMETRIC AND MEASUREMENT ISSUES

As we have stated throughout this report, the use of any assessment should meet the basic professional standards of validity and reliability (American Educational Research Association et al., 1985). But if a student is not proficient in the language of the test, her performance is likely to be affected by construct-irrelevant variance—that is, her test score is likely to underestimate her knowledge of the subject being tested. How can a student's content knowledge be validly assessed by someone who speaks only English if that student cannot readily express what she knows in English?

Some validity problems come from the "mainstream bias" of formal testing, including a norming bias (small numbers of English-language learners in the sample, making it potentially unrepresentative); from content bias (the test reflects the dominant-culture standards of language, knowledge, and behavior); and from linguistic and cultural biases affecting students' formal test performance (timed testing, difficulty with English vocabulary, and the great difficulty of determining what bilingual students know in their two languages) (National Research Council and Institute of Medicine, 1997:115).

When non-English versions of a test are used, other problems arise, including translation and score equivalence: Is the translated test comparable in content to the original? Can scores from the two different language versions be accurately compared? For example, would a score of 50 in one language be interpreted the same way as a score of 50 in another language? (American Educational Research Association et al., 1998:9-4).

"Every assessment is an assessment of language," the committee wrote in *Improving Schooling for Language-Minority Children*. "This is even more so given the advent of performance assessments requiring extensive comprehension and production of language."[5] Research indicates that lack of proficiency in the language of the test can result in significant underestimation of the test taker's knowledge. A further problem is errors in the scoring of open-ended or performance-based measures. There is evidence that scorers may be influenced by linguistic features of students' answers unrelated to the content of the assessment. Thus, scorers may downgrade the performance of English-language learners unfairly, confounding the accuracy of the score (National Research Council and Institute of Medicine, 1997:120-122).

Research that can inform policy and guidelines for making decisions about exemptions, modifications, and accommodations in assessment procedures is urgently needed. A number of such research efforts are under way, including efforts to include more English-language learners in the National Assessment of Educational Progress (NAEP).[6] A recent report of the National Center for Educational Statistics (NCES) describes many of these current research efforts (Olson and Goldstein, 1997); these are summarized in the appendix to this chapter.

The research base regarding various strategies that can be used to enhance the participation of English-language learners in large-scale as-

---

[5]For example, the performance description for "mathematical communication," one of seven mathematical performance areas for elementary schoolchildren, requires the student to "use appropriate mathematical terms, vocabulary, and language based on prior conceptual work; show ideas in a variety of ways including words, numbers, symbols, pictures, charts, graphs, tables, diagrams, and models; explain clearly and logically solutions to problems, and support solutions with evidence, in both oral and written form; consider purpose and audience when communicating; and comprehend mathematics from reading assignments and from other sources" (New Standards, 1995). Quite clearly, this assessment of mathematical skills is also an assessment of language proficiency.

[6]More complete discussion of the issues of including English-language learners in NAEP can be found in *Grading the Nation's Report Card: Evaluating NAEP and Transforming the Assessment of Educational Progress* (National Research Council, 1999).

sessments (National Research Council and Institute of Medicine, 1997; Olson and Goldstein, 1997) covers several areas:

Use of native-language assessments. Assessments can be developed in languages other than English, a strategy under active investigation. New York state, for example, will offer three of its four core subject Regents examinations in five languages in addition to English (Spanish, Haitian-Creole, Russian, Chinese, and Korean); the English exam must be taken in English.

A number of technical difficulties arise in attempting to create a comparable test in another language. Difficulties include "problems of regional and dialect difference, nonequivalence of vocabulary difficulty between the two languages, problems of incomplete language development and lack of literacy development in students' primary languages, and the extreme difficulty of defining a 'bilingual' equating sample (each new definition of a bilingual sample will demand a new statistical equating). Minimally, back-translation should be done to determine equivalent meaning, and ideally, psychometric validation should be undertaken as well" (National Research Council and Institute of Medicine, 1997:121).

Results of a recent NAEP field test of mathematics items illustrates the challenge of using native-language assessments (Anderson et al., 1996). "Spanish-language items were translations of English-version items. This research found substantial psychometric discrepancies in students' performance on the same test items across both languages, leading to the conclusion that the Spanish and English versions of many test items were not measuring the same underlying mathematical knowledge. This result may be attributable to a lack of equivalence between original and translated versions of test items and needs further investigation" (National Research Council and Institute of Medicine, 1997:122).

Implementation of non-English-language achievement tests as part of assessment systems needs to be accompanied by research establishing the validity and reliability of such assessments and their comparability to scores on related assessments in English.

Decreasing the English-language load through modification of items or instructions. This is difficult to do and research thus far is limited. "While some experts recommend reducing nonessential details and simplifying grammatical structures (Short, 1991), others claim that simplifying the surface linguistic features will not necessarily make the text easier to understand (Saville-Troike, 1991). When Abedi et al. (1995) reduced the linguistic complexity of the NAEP mathematics test items in English, they reported only a modest and statistically unreliable effect in favor of the modified items for students at lower levels of English proficiency" (National Research Council and Institute of Medicine, 1997:122). Although this approach simplified sentence structure, semantic simplification might also be beneficial. One would need to decide, however, whether to simplify vocabulary directly related to the content being assessed, less related to the content, or both. Also, one would have to determine whether it is possible to simplify vocabulary without compromising conceptual complexity. Another approach to modifying text is to make the instructions more explicit.

Accommodations. The 1996 NAEP mathematics assessment included field trials of new criteria for including English-language learners in the assessment and the provision of accommodations. Results suggest that providing more accommodation options increased participation rates for English-language learners.

The diversity of the population of English-language learners is an important factor to consider in researching and designing accommodations. Researchers at the National Center for Research on Evaluation, Standards, and Student Testing have suggested a number of important background variables to examine with respect to their impact on test performance, including English-language proficiency, prior formal schooling, and length of time in the United States (Butler and Stevens, 1997). These researchers point out that two major obstacles to conducting research and to systematizing the procedures for including English-language learners are (1) inconsistencies in the definitions of English-language learners and (2) lack of agreement on common methods for measuring academic proficiency in a language. They argue that "any research on accommodations must begin by addressing these two issues" (p. 22).

A 1994 NCES conference on including English-language learners in assessments (National Center for Education Statistics, 1996) highlighted the need for a definition of English proficiency that could be consistently applied across states, districts, and schools (Olson and Goldstein, 1997). Related issues included the following:

- The best criterion to determine readiness to meaningfully participate in an English-language assessment is level of English literacy, rather
than years in English-only instruction (or native-language instruction) or
other background characteristics. This is because years in English-only
instruction may not accurately predict English literacy, given variation in
language acquisition due to individual factors and home, school, and
community linguistic contexts.
- A measure of proficiency should not be limited to oral language
proficiency, because such a measure is not sufficient to determine whether
an English-language learner can meaningfully participate in a written
assessment.
- Implementation of an approach that tailors testing to a student's
English literacy level would require the development, validation, and
adoption of a standard procedure to determine levels of English literacy.
An empirically determined threshold level would indicate that the student could take the standard English assessment. Similar thresholds
could be established for modified versions of the standard English assessment. An alternative would be to use current scores, including literacy
subtests of language proficiency tests or reading/language arts scores on
standardized achievement tests or other assessments.
- When a test is available in multiple languages, and when testing a
student proficient in two or more languages for which the test is available, the student's relative language proficiencies should be determined,
and the test generally should be administered in the test taker's most
proficient language—unless the test is designed to determine proficiency
in a certain language (American Educational Research Association et al.,
1998).
- Generally, decisions about the language of assessment should take
into account how much instruction in the native language students have
received in the specific content to be assessed, i.e., reading or math (National Center for Education Statistics, 1996). However, because of the
complexity of deciding which English-language learners are most appropriately assessed in their native language,[7] this decision might be left up

---

[7]For example, most native speakers of other languages (even Spanish) are not instructed in their native language. Even students instructed in bilingual programs receive
more instruction in English. Thus an assessment in the native language may not be
appropriate for these students. For students who have recently arrived in the United
States and have received most of their instruction in a language other than English, it
would be more accurate to assess their subject-matter knowledge (e.g., math, science) in
their native language.

to states or local school committees who have deliberated and developed clear policy and assessment guidelines (as in Texas) for such decisions.

The NRC and IOM committee that wrote *Improving Schooling for Language-Minority Children* called for more research that would inform decision making about how to get valid test scores for English-language learners in large-scale assessments, particularly in developing guidelines for determining when they are ready to take the same tests as their English-proficient peers (1997:130).

The committee's findings and recommendations about English-language learners are reported in Chapter 12.

APPENDIX
Including Students with Limited English Proficiency in Large-Scale Assessments: Summary of Current and Ongoing Research Activities

This appendix is a catalogue of the projects summarized and described in more detail in Olson and Goldstein (1997:44-58).

National Center for Education Statistics (NCES)

This research program proposes to examine issues around the participation of English-language learners in large-scale assessments, including the National Assessment of Educational Progress (NAEP). The following is a list of these activities.

- *NCES Conference on Inclusion Guidelines and Accommodations for Limited English Proficient Students in NAEP.* This report summarizes the results from a conference on the inclusion of English-language learners in assessments. Many issues are raised including possible modifications in NAEP administration procedures and the need to develop a set of guidelines and accommodations to promote increased participation of English-language learners in NAEP (National Center for Education Statistics, 1996).
- *Working Paper on Assessing Students with Disabilities and Limited English Proficiency.* This NCES working paper describes the current state of NCES policies that resulted in the exclusion of some students from NCES assessments, as well as concerns about data validity, assessment modifications, and the inclusion of English-language learners (Houser, 1995).

Office of Bilingual Education and Minority Languages Affairs (OBEMLA)

The Office of Bilingual Education and Minority Languages Affairs provides funding for research on the education of language minority students. Some of its activities include grants to various agencies and services, including the National Clearinghouse for Bilingual Education, which collects, analyzes, synthesizes, and disseminates information on studies of assessment and performance of English-language learners.

National Academy of Education (NAE)

Studies on the inclusion and accommodation of English-language learners have been carried out along with the NAE evaluation of NAEP. They focus on assessment development, exclusion decisions, and appropriate adaptations and accommodations for English-language learners. Several reports contain the results of these studies.

The Prospects Study

Previously mandated by Congress to evaluate Chapter 1 (now Title I), this study has been funded to examine English-language learners in the Title I program. It provides data collected from students, parents, and educators, on samples of students who were in 1st, 3rd, or 7th grade during the academic year 1991-1992 and were in schools with high concentrations of English-language learners (U.S. Department of Education, 1993, 1996).

Stanford Working Group

• This group makes recommendations regarding state-level assessments and Goals 2000. Some examples of recommendations include state development of assessments appropriate for English-language learners and the use of native-language and other alternative assessments (August et al., 1994).

• A working paper was prepared in 1994 both to help develop strategies for making appropriate and consistent decisions about assessment of English-language learners and to maximize their participation, particularly in NAEP (see National Center for Education Statistics, 1996).

Council of Chief State School Officers State Collaboration of Assessment and Student Standards (SCASS)

The purpose of the SCASS project is to develop guidelines for effective language learning and the assessment of English-language learners on statewide content standards for language and core content areas. SCASS has developed plans to improve assessments of language proficiency for selection and placement purposes; develop appropriate content assessments; conduct research on learning English; and work on the development of accommodations for English-language learners. A pilot study of the guidelines was planned for academic year 1996-1997 on accurate scoring for content knowledge.

National Center for Research on Evaluation, Standards and Student Testing (CRESST)

CRESST studies focus on the assessment of quality education. Its current studies of language issues look specifically at the linguistic features of NAEP items and how they may affect the performance of students with background in languages other than English (e.g., see Abedi et al., 1995; Shepard, 1996).

George Washington University Center for Equity and Excellence in Education (GWU/CEEE)

The goal of these research activities is to provide tools for policymakers, educators, and community members looking to develop strategies for designing and evaluating services for English-language learners. One report summarizes findings from a national survey of state assessment directors on the prevalence and use of assessments, modifications in assessments, and exemption of English-language learners from assessment programs (Rivera et al., 1997). Another report documents data from the GWU/CEEE and SSAP Council of Chief State School Officers/NCREL surveys on assessment policies for English-language learners in states requiring a test for high school graduation (Rivera and Vincent, 1997).

National Research Council/Institute of Medicine

A 1997 report of the National Research Council and the Institute of Medicine contributes to the understanding of the education of English-language learners, reviews methodologies used, discusses assessment issues, and makes recommendations regarding future research in order to inform policy and practice (National Research Council and Institute of Medicine, 1997). See also National Research Council (1999).

REFERENCES

Abedi, J., C. Lord, and J. Plummer
　　1995　　*Language Background as a Variable in NAEP Mathematics Performance.* National Center for Research on Evaluation, Standards, and Student Testing. Los Angeles: University of California at Los Angeles.
American Educational Research Association, American Psychological Association, and National Council on Measurement in Education
　　1985　　*Standards for Educational and Psychological Testing.* Washington, DC: American Psychological Association.
　　1998　　*Draft Standards for Educational and Psychological Testing.* Washington, DC: American Psychological Association.

Anderson, N.E., F.F. Jenkins, and K.E. Miller
   1996   NAEP Inclusion Criteria and Testing Accommodations. Findings from the
           NAEP 1995 Field Test in Mathematics. Washington, DC: Educational Test-
           ing Service.
August, D., K. Hakuta, and D. Pompa
   1994   For all students: Limited English proficient students and Goals 2000. Occa-
           sional Papers in Bilingual Education 10(1994):4.
Berman, P., J. Chambers, P. Gandara, B. McLaughlin, C. Minicucci, B. Nelson, L. Olsen,
and T. Parrish
   1992   Meeting the Challenge of Language Diversity: An Evaluation of Programs for
           Pupils with Limited Proficiency in English. Vol. 1 [R-119/1: Executive Sum-
           mary; Vol. 2 [R-119/2]: Findings and Conclusions; Vol. 3 [R-119/3]: Case
           Study Appendix. Berkeley, CA: BW Associates.
Butler, F.A., and R. Stevens
   1997   Accommodation Strategies for English Language Learners on Large-Scale Assess-
           ments: Student Characteristics and Other Considerations. CSE Technical Re-
           port 448. National Center for Research on Evaluation, Standards, and Stu-
           dent Testing, University of California, Los Angeles.
Council of Chief State School Officers
   1998   Survey of State Student Assessment Programs. Washington, DC: Council of
           Chief State School Officers.
Durán, Richard P.
   1989   Assessment and instruction of at-risk Hispanic students. Exceptional Children
           56(2):154-158.
Education Week
   1998   S.F. files suit over testing of LEP students. Education Week April 8.
Fleishman, Howard L., and Paul J. Hopstock
   1993   Descriptive Study of Services to Limited English Proficient Students, Volume 1,
           Summary of Findings and Conclusions. Prepared for U.S. Department of Edu-
           cation. Arlington, VA: Development Associates, Inc.
Florida Department of Education
   1993   November 1, 1993, Memorandum from Walter McCarroll to District Superinten-
           dents. Testing Limited English Proficieny Students. Tallahassee, Florida:
           The Florida Education Center
   1996   December 4, 1996, Memorandum from David Mosrie to District Superintendents.
           Accomodations for Limited English Proficient Students in the Administra-
           tion of Statewide Assessments. Tallahassee, Florida: The Florida Education
           Center.
Garcia, G.E.
   1991   Factors influencing the English reading test performance of Spanish-speaking
           Hispanic children. Research Reading Quarterly 26(4):371-392.
Garcia, G.E., and P.D. Pearson
   1994   Assessment and diversity. Review of Research in Education (20):337-391.
Houser, J.
   1995   Assessing Students with Disabilities and Limited English Proficiency. Working
           Paper Number 95-13. Washington, DC: National Center for Education
           Statistics, Policy and Review Branch, Data Development Division.

Meisels, S.
  1994   Designing meaningful measurements for early childhood. Pp. 202-222 in
          *Diversity and Developmentally Appropriate Practices: Challenges for Early Child-
          hood Education*, B. Mallory and R. New, eds.. New York: Teachers College
          Press.
National Academy of Education
  1993   *Third Report to Congress on the evaluation of the NAEP Trial State Assessment.*
          National Academy of Education.
  1994   *The Trial State Assessment: Prospects and Realities: Background Studies*, George
          Bohrnstedt, ed. American Institutes for Research Palo Alto, CA: Armadillo
          Press.
  1996   *Quality and Utility: The 1994 Trial State Assessment in Reading, Background
          Studies.* Stanford, CA: National Academy of Education.
National Center for Education Statistics
  1994   A Study Design to Evaluate Strategies for the Inclusion of LEP Students in
          the NAEP State Trial Assessment. K. Hakuta and G. Valdes, eds. Office of
          Educational Research and Improvement, U.S. Department of Education,
          Washington, DC.
  1996   Proceedings of the Conference on Inclusion Guidelines and Accommoda-
          tions for Limited English Proficient Students in the National Assessment of
          Educational Progress (December 5-6, 1994), D. August and E. McArthur,
          eds. National Center for Education Statistics, Office of Educational Research
          and Improvement, U.S. Department of Education, Washington, DC.
National Research Council
  1999   *Grading the Nation's Report Card: Evaluating NAEP and Transforming the As-
          sessment of Educational Progress*, J. Pellegrino, L. Jones, and K. Mitchell, eds.
          Committee on the Evaluation of National and State Assessments of Educa-
          tional Progress, Board on Testing and Assessment. Washington, DC: Na-
          tional Academy Press.
National Research Council and Institute of Medicine
  1997   *Improving Schooling for Language-Minority Children*, D. August and K. Hakuta,
          eds. Board on Children, Youth, and Families. Washington, DC: National
          Academy Press.
New Standards
  1995   *Performance Standards. English Language Arts, Mathematics, Science, and Ap-
          plied Learning.* Volumes 1, 2, and 3. Consultation Drafts. Washington, DC:
          National Center for Education and the Economy.
New York State Education Department
  1997   Proposal for Revising Graduation Requirements. November 14, 1997 Memo-
          randum from Richard Mills to the Members of the Board of Regents.
  1998   Regents Strategy for Intensive Instruction in the English Language for Lim-
          ited English Proficient Students at the Secondary Level. January 6, 1998
          Memorandum from James A. Kadamus to the Board of Regents.

Olson, J.F., and A.A. Goldstein
1997 *The Inclusion of Students with Disabilities and Limited English Proficient Students in Large-Scale Assessments: A Summary of Recent Progress.* NCES 97-482. Washington, DC: U.S. Department of Education, Office of Educational Research and Improvement.

Philadelphia School District
1998 *Reaching Higher.* Consultation Draft. Philadelphia, Penn: School District of Philadelphia.

Rivera, C., and Carolyn Vincent
1997 High school graduation testing: Policies and practices in the assessment of English language learners. *Educational Asssessment* 4(4):335-355.

Rivera, C., C. Vincent, A. Hafner, and M. LaCelle-Peterson
1997 *Statewide Assessment Programs: Policies and Practices for the Inclusion of Limited English Proficient Students—Findings from a National Survey of State Assessment Directors.* TM #026831. Washington, DC: ERIC Clearinghouse on Assessment and Evaluation. The Catholic University of America.

Saville-Troike, Muriel
1991 *Teaching and Testing for Academic Achievement: The Role of Language Development.* Focus, Occasional Papers in Bilingual Education, No. 4. Washington, DC: National Clearinghouse for Bilingual Education.

Shepard, L.A.
1996 *Research Framework for Investigating Accommodations for Language Minority Students.* Presentation made at CRESST Assessment Conference, UCLA.

Shepard, L., S.L. Kagan, and E. Wurtz
1998 *Principles and Recommendations for Early Childhood Assessments.* The National Education Goals Panel. Washington, D.C.: National Education Goals Panel.

Short, D.
1991 *How to Integrate Language and Content Instruction: A Training Manual.* Washington, DC: Center for Applied Linguistics.

Texas Education Agency
1996 *Assessment System for Limited English Proficient Students Exempted from the Texas Assessment Program at Grades 3-8.* Austin, Texas: Texas Education Agency.
1998 *Assessment Requirements for Students of Limited English Proficiency in the 1997-98 State Testing Program.* Memorandum to Texas Education Agency Administrators. Austin, Texas: Texas Education Agency.

Thurlow, M., K. Liu, S. Weiser, and Hamdy El Sawaf
1997 *High School Graduation Requirements in the U.S. for Students with Limited English Proficiency.* State Assessment Series Minnesota Report 13. Minneapolis, MN: National Center on Educational Outcomes.

U.S. Department of Education
1993 PROSPECTS: *The Congressionally Mandated Study of Educational Growth and Opportunity, Interim Report: Language Minority and Limited English Proficient Students.* Washington, DC: U.S. Department of Education.
1996 PROSPECTS: *The Congressionally Mandated Study of Educational Growth and Opportunity, First Annual Report.* Washington, DC: U.S. Department of Education.

LEGAL REFERENCES

Goals 2000, Educate America Act, 20 U.S.C. sections 5801 *et seq.*

Lau v. Nichols, 414 U.S. 563 (1974).

Title I, Elementary and Secondary Education Act, 20 U.S.C. sections 6301 *et seq.*

Title VI, Civil Rights Act of 1964, 42 U.S.C. sections 2000(e) *et seq.*

Title VII (Bilingual Education Programs), Improving America's Schools Act of 1994, P.L. 103-382.

10
Use of Voluntary National Test Scores for Tracking, Promotion, or Graduation Decisions

The purpose of the proposed voluntary national tests (VNTs) is to inform students, parents, and teachers about the students' performance in 4th grade reading and 8th grade mathematics relative to high national and international standards. The committee takes no position on whether the VNTs are practical or appropriate for this purpose.

The VNT proposal has evolved in many ways since its birth in January 1997, but here we focus on major features of the initial plan. Achievement tests in English reading at the 4th grade level and in mathematics at the 8th grade level would be offered to states, school districts, and localities for administration each spring. The tests would be voluntary, because the federal government would prepare but not require them, nor would data on any individual or school be reported to the federal government. The tests would be distributed and scored through licensed commercial firms. A major effort would be made to include and accommodate students with disabilities and English-language learners in the testing program. The tests would not be long or detailed enough to provide diagnostic information about individual learning problems. They would, however, provide sufficiently reliable information that all students (and their parents and teachers) would know where they stand in relation to high national standards and, in mathematics, in comparison with levels of achievement in other countries. For the 4th grade reading test, the standards would be set by the achievement levels of the corresponding

238

tests in the National Assessment of Educational Progress (NAEP): basic, proficient, and advanced. For the 8th grade mathematics test, corresponding standards would be set by the 8th grade mathematics tests of NAEP, and student performance would be compared with that in other nations in the Third International Mathematics and Science Study (TIMSS).

In order to provide maximum preparation and feedback to students, parents, and teachers, sample tests would be circulated in advance, and a copy of the original test would be returned with the student's original and the correct answers noted. A major effort would be made to communicate test results clearly to students, parents, and teachers, and all test items would be published on the Internet just after the national administration of each test.

The proposal does not suggest any direct use of VNT scores to make decisions about the tracking, promotion, or graduation of individual students. Representatives of the U.S. Department of Education have stated that the VNTs are not intended for use in making such decisions, and the tests are not being developed to support such uses. Nonetheless, some civil rights organizations and other groups have expressed concern that test users would inappropriately use VNT scores for such purposes. Indeed, under the voluntary testing plan, test users (states, school districts, and schools) would be free to use the tests as they wish, just as test users are now free to use commercial tests for purposes other than those recommended by their developers and publishers. The freedom of test users has been reinforced by the action of the Congress in placing control of the VNT project with the National Assessment Governing Board, the same independent commission that oversees NAEP.

Accordingly, and because this study was mandated in the context of the discussion of the VNTs, the committee has considered whether it would be appropriate to make tracking, promotion, or graduation decisions about individual students based on their VNT scores. The committee recommends that the VNT not be used for decisions about the tracking, promotion, or graduation of individual students. The evidence for this recommendation is elaborated in the following sections.

USE OF VNT SCORES IN TRACKING DECISIONS

The committee foresees several basic problems with using VNT scores to track individual students.

First, to the extent that VNTs could be used for tracking decisions at all, their use would be limited to placement decisions for 5th grade reading and 9th grade mathematics. They would be inappropriate for placement decisions in other subjects or grade levels.

Second, using VNT scores to make future class placements would be valid only to the extent that the VNT assessments were predictive of success in future placements in a particular school. There is no guarantee, however—and little reason to expect, at least initially—that there would be a sufficiently close relationship between VNT scores and available future placements in any particular class or school to justify the use of the scores in making tracking decisions.

Third, VNT proficiency levels, which are expected to be the same as those of NAEP, do not correspond well to other common definitions of proficiency: those embodied in current state content and performance standards (Linn, 1998a), those found in such widely used tests as advanced placement exams and the Scholastic Assessment Test (SAT),[1] and those used in tracking decisions. Indeed, the large proportion of students who score below the "basic" level on NAEP has led to justifiable concerns that reports of achievement on the VNTs will provide little information about lower levels of academic performance.

For example, of all 8th graders who took the 1996 NAEP grade 8 mathematics assessment, roughly 39 percent scored below "basic," and the figures for Mississippi and the District of Columbia were roughly 62 percent and 80 percent, respectively (Linn, 1998a: Figure 14, citing Reese et al., 1997). It is hard to imagine placing that high a proportion of students in low-track 9th grade math classes, particularly in view of the negative consequences that are associated with such placements. The high standards of NAEP, to which the VNT would conform, do not correspond well, if at all, to traditional high, middle, and low tracks. For these reasons, the committee concludes that VNT scores should not be used in making tracking decisions about individual students.

---

[1] Shepard and her colleagues used comparisons of the percentage of students achieving scores of 3 or higher on advanced placement examinations (the score level frequently used to award college credit) and the percentage of students obtaining scores of 600 or higher on the SAT mathematics test or 550 or higher on the SAT verbal test (levels on the 1992 SAT scales that correspond to the 86th percentile of test takers on the verbal test and the 82nd percentile on the mathematics test) to argue that a higher percentage of 12th graders actually perform at the level defined as advanced than are so classified on NAEP (Shepard et al., 1993).

USE OF VNT SCORES IN PROMOTION AND RETENTION DECISIONS

Despite efforts to discourage possible high-stakes uses of the VNTs for individual students, the possibility of using them to determine promotion or retention is implicit in President Clinton's proposal: "Good tests will show us who needs help, what changes in teaching to make, and which schools need to improve. They can help us to end social promotion."[2] The committee has therefore considered the possible use of voluntary national tests for decisions about promotion.

The committee sees clear incompatibilities between features of the VNTs that would facilitate their use for informing students, parents, and teachers about student achievement and their use to make promotion and retention decisions about individual students.

First, the plan is to report student achievement relative to the high standards of NAEP and to international achievement levels in TIMSS. Use of these national and international standards is an appropriate way to set and communicate higher educational goals. But there is no guarantee that the framework or content of the tests will be aligned with the curriculum that students study. That is, students may have had insufficient opportunity to learn the materials on which they are being tested, and this could render the test inappropriate as a criterion for promotion. Standards used to lead the curriculum may not be compatible with those appropriate for these high-stakes decisions.

Second, the VNT plan focuses on reporting in terms of the proficiency levels of the NAEP tests—basic, proficient, and advanced. The tests must be able to distinguish reliably these levels of performance. Some testing experts have expressed concern about the reasonableness of reporting and interpreting NAEP results in terms of the NAEP proficiency levels.[3] The new VNT results, also to be reported by NAEP

---

[2]President Clinton's (1998) call for an end to social promotion referred specifically to retention at grades 4 and 8.

[3]The issue of cutscore validation is particularly relevant in light of the criticism that has accompanied the 1990 and 1992 NAEP standard-setting efforts (e.g., Linn, 1998b; Linn et al., 1991; Shepard, 1995). The proposed voluntary national tests may substantially increase the importance of the evaluative function of the NAEP achievement levels because it is planned that the national tests would be linked to NAEP and have results reported in terms of the achievement levels. If the previously mentioned math test used to assign students to beginning or advanced math classes were the 8th grade voluntary national test in math, then cutscores on the test might be used to justify the

proficiency levels, are subject to similar concerns; they are unlikely to be sufficiently trustworthy for making high-stakes decisions about individual students (National Research Council, 1999b). Moreover, decisions about promotion are likely to require high accuracy in distinguishing levels of proficiency other than those identified in NAEP. Indeed, as noted above, the large share of students who score below the basic level in NAEP has led to justifiable concerns that the VNTs might provide little or no information to distinguish different levels of academic performance among these students. This problem is compounded by the likelihood that states and school districts will adopt varying standards and varying cutscores for their high-stakes decisions about students.

Third, it is proposed that all test items be made public through the Internet and returned to students with the correct answers indicated. In high-stakes testing situations, demands for fairness, as well as the committee's criteria of validity and reliability in measurement, require that students who fail be permitted to take the test again. Public release of the items, however, would mean that a test could not be used more than once. This technical problem could be overcome by developing multiple forms of the test, so a student who failed could take an equivalent form of the test later. In fact, the plan is for several equivalent forms of each test to be developed in each year in order to provide comparable test results in the next year. But no extra forms are planned for release or use in "second-chance" administrations. If such extra forms were developed, this would add to problems of test security.

Fourth, there are other ways in which the VNTs could be misused in high-stakes decisions—for example, if performance on a single test administration were the only criterion for promotion. In this respect, however, the VNTs would not differ from any other new or existing test.

The committee finds it most unlikely that the VNTs could serve both the objectives of communicating higher academic standards across the country and of providing a fair and accurate measurement tool for high-stakes decisions about promotion or retention of individual students.

---

placement of students in one or another of the math classes. Thus, the need to validate cutscores on this test would take on an added importance in light of such a high-stakes use of the test. The consequences of using the NAEP cutscores to make such decisions has been demonstrated by Shepard et al. (1993). See also the forthcoming National Research Council report (1999a) *Grading the Nation's Report Card: Evaluating NAEP and Transforming the Assessment of Educational Progress.*

The VNTs should therefore not be used in making decisions about the promotion of individual students.

USE OF VNT SCORES IN GRADUATION DECISIONS

The committee sees several basic problems in using VNT scores to make graduation decisions about individual students.

First, as noted previously, there is no guarantee—and little reason to expect, at least initially—that the framework or content of these tests would be aligned with the curriculum and instruction that students experience. If VNT content is not representative of what students have been taught, this would render the test inappropriate as a criterion for graduation. In addition, although some states have deemed achievement at the 8th grade level sufficient to meet their graduation standard in mathematics, it is doubtful that there would be any potential use for the results of a 4th grade reading test in determining an individual's fitness to receive a high school diploma.

Second, the VNT plan has focused on reporting in terms of the basic, proficient, and advanced proficiency levels of the NAEP. The questions noted above about the accuracy of these proficiency levels and their usefulness for making high-stakes decisions about individual students apply here as well. Moreover, decisions about graduation are quite likely to require high accuracy at levels of proficiency other than those already identified in NAEP. This could cause problems. To make reliable distinctions between levels of performance that separate proficiency levels, the tests would have to include many items near the levels of difficulty that separate these new proficiency levels. This may not always be feasible. The difficulties involved would be further compounded if states and school districts were to set different proficiency levels for their graduation decisions.

Third, the problems of fairness, validity, and reliability created by making VNT items public through the Internet and returning them to students with correct answers apply here as well. Students should be permitted to retake a graduation test if they have failed on the first administration. Public release of the items implies, however, that the same test could not be used more than once. As noted above, however, no extra forms are planned for release and use in "second-chance" administrations. The lack of alternative forms would make the VNTs inappropriate for use as a graduation test.

REFERENCES

Clinton, W.J.
  1998   Public Papers of the Presidents of the United States. Washington, DC: Government Printing Office.

Linn, R.
  1998a   Assessments and Accountability. Paper presented at the annual meeting, American Educational Research Association, San Diego, CA.
  1998b   Validating inferences from National Assessment of Educational Progress Achievement-Level Reporting. Applied Measurement in Education 11(1):23-47.

Linn, R.L., D. Koretz, E.L. Baker, and L. Burstein
  1991   The Validity and Credibility of the Achievement Levels for the 1990 National Assessment of Educational Progress in Mathematics. Los Angeles: University of California, Center for the Study of Evaluation.

National Research Council
  1998a   Grading the Nation's Report Card: Evaluating NAEP and Transforming the Assessment of Educational Progress. J.W. Pellegrino, L.R. Jones, and K.J. Mitchell, eds. Committee on the Evaluation of National and State Assessments of Educational Progress, Board on Testing and Assessment. Washington, DC: National Academy Press.
  1998b   Uncommon Measures: Equivalence and Linkage Among Educational Tests, M.J. Feuer, P.W. Holland, B.F. Green, M.W. Bertenthal, and F.C. Hemphill, eds. Committee on Equivalency and Linkage of Educational Tests, Board on Testing and Assessment. Washington, DC: National Academy Press.

Reese, C.M., K.E. Miller, J. Mazzeo, and J.A. Dossey
  1997   NAEP 1996 Mathematics Report Card for the Nation and the States. Washington, DC: National Center for Education Statistics.

Shepard, L.A.
  1995   Implications for standard setting of the National Academy of Education evaluation of the National Assessment of Educational Progress achievement levels. In Proceedings of the Joint Conference on Standard Setting for Large-Scale Assessments of the National Assessment Governing Board and the National Center for Education Statistics (Vol. II, p. 143-160). Washington, DC: National Assessment Governing Board and the National Center for Education Statistics.

Shepard, L., R.G. Glaser, and R. Linn
  1993   Setting Performance Standards for Student Achievement: A Report of the National Academy of Education of the NAEP Trial State Assessment: An Evaluation of the 1992 Achievement Levels. Stanford, CA: The National Academy of Education.

Part III

Ensuring Appropriate Uses of Tests

11

Potential Strategies for Promoting Appropriate Test Use

Throughout this report, the committee has articulated principles of appropriate, nondiscriminatory use of tests for student tracking, promotion, and graduation. We have adopted a three-part framework (National Research Council, 1982) for determining whether a planned or actual test use is appropriate (see Chapter 1). We have also considered issues related to the participation of students with disabilities and English-language learners in large-scale assessments. More generally, we have recognized that high-stakes test use can produce both intended benefits and unintended negative consequences; policymakers need to be sensitive to both individual and collective benefits and costs of the different uses of tests, and they need to explore policy strategies that balance those benefits and costs.

But defining appropriate test uses and a means of identifying them is only a necessary condition: it is not sufficient to ensure that producers and users of tests will understand and follow these guidelines. The Congress recognized this fact when it asked the National Research Council, as part of this report, to consider "appropriate methods, practices and safeguards to ensure that . . . existing and new tests . . . are not used in a discriminatory manner or inappropriately . . . ."

This chapter considers such potential methods, practices, and safeguards. The first section deals with the two *existing* monitoring and enforcement mechanisms: professional standards and legal action. These approaches are important but inadequate. The second section, drawing in part on research and practice in fields other than testing, explores several other approaches that, coupled with existing mechanisms, may help ensure that tests with high stakes for students are used properly. These include deliberative forums, a test-monitoring body, better information about the content and purposes of particular tests, and increased government regulation. We also consider the criteria one might use in evaluating alternative approaches. In this discussion, we again maintain our focus on the uses of tests for high-stakes decisions about individual students, recognizing that other uses of tests can also have important indirect consequences on student learning.

The committee does not recommend any specific course of action or combination of strategies. Public officials have long recognized that achieving a policy goal often requires reliance on a variety of complementary strategies. Over the past decade, policy analysts have tried to make the logic of that conventional wisdom explicit and to help policymakers think more systematically about the range of strategies and tools they have available to address any given problem.

Policy design theory posits that public policies consist of goals or problems to be solved; target populations; agents and implementation structures; rules that specify responsibilities, resource levels, and time frames; tools that provide the motivation for targets and agents; and rationales that legitimate and explain the policy logic (Schneider, 1998; Schneider and Ingram, 1997). Once goals are set, tools are chosen to change people's behavior. The motivation for change may come from the allocation of resources, the threat of sanctions, or an appeal to deeply held values.

Rarely does a policy rely on a single strategy. Most embody multiple tools that reinforce each other. Although analysts can categorize generic policy tools (e.g., Schneider and Ingram, 1990, 1993; McDonnell and Elmore, 1987), the choice of an appropriate strategy depends on a given locale's needs, resources, and political culture, as well as its past experience with similar policies. Therefore, we offer no prescription except to argue that ensuring appropriate test use requires multiple strategies. Further research should yield more detailed evidence of their relative strengths and weaknesses in different settings.

EXISTING METHODS, PRACTICES, AND SAFEGUARDS

The professional standards that govern testing are embodied in the Standards for Educational and Psychological Testing and the Code of Fair Testing Practices in Education. Joint committees of the American Psychological Association (APA), the American Educational Research Association (AERA), and the National Council on Measurement in Education (NCME) initiated work on the Code; other associations joined the effort later.

Although professional concerns and attempts to improve test quality date back to 1895, the first formal guidelines for test development were the 1954 Technical Recommendations for Psychological Tests and Diagnostic Techniques (American Psychological Association et al., 1954; Novick, 1982). A specific set of guidelines for achievement tests, Technical Recommendations for Achievement Tests, quickly followed and served to reinforce the 1954 guidelines (National Education Association, 1955). The major aim of both documents was to define standards for informing test users in judging the utility of a given test.

The 1954 standards focused on six critical areas: dissemination of information, interpretation, validity, reliability, administration, and scales and norms. The various standards were differentiated into three categories: essential, very desirable, and desirable. The document struck a balance in defining the uses and misuses of tests and called for self-regulation in the testing community: "Almost any test can be useful for some functions and in some situations. But even the best test can have damaging consequences if used inappropriately. Therefore, ultimate responsibility for improvement of testing rests on the shoulders of test users" (American Psychological Association et al., 1954:7). The 1954 standards were well received by both professional test developers and test users, and they exerted a significant influence on textbooks, test manuals, and research (Novick, 1982).

The 1954 standards were revised and superseded by the 1966 Standards for Educational and Psychological Tests and Manuals (American Psychological Association et al., 1966), which were revised again in 1974 and in 1985. Each revision reflected the expansion of testing and a growing concern among professionals about the effects of the uses of tests. The 1985 Joint Standards reflected the influence of testing on educational policy and included chapters on the uses of tests for minorities, students with disabilities, and others. In 1998, as this report is written, the Standards are being revised again.

In an attempt to make the Standards for Educational and Psychological Tests and Manuals accessible to a broader audience of test users, the APA, the AERA, and the NCME jointly developed the Code of Fair Testing Practices in Education. The principles outlined in the code are widely held by professionals as crucial to promoting fair use of tests (Office of Technology Assessment, 1992). All testing companies that were approached explicity endorsed the Code.

Ethical Codes

At each stage of their evolution, the Joint Standards and the Code have been written in intentionally broad terms to reflect the array of acceptable professional practices that can be used to accomplish a single goal. But their effectiveness depends on professional judgment and good will. The Office of Technology Assessment (OTA) put it this way: "the test-taker's fate rests on the assumption that good testing practice has been upheld by both the test developer when it constructed the test and the test user (such as the school) when it selected, interpreted, and made a decision on the basis of the test" (1992:68).

Compliance with the Joint Standards is voluntary for members of the AERA and the NCME, who are mainly academics and researchers. These organizations encourage compliance, in accordance with their ethical guidelines, but they lack monitoring or enforcement procedures (American Educational Research Association, 1992; National Council on Measurement in Education, 1995). The APA does have standing policies for monitoring and enforcing its ethical principles. At most, however, violations appear to result in expulsion from the organization (American Psychological Association, 1981).

Perhaps because of the reliance on self-regulation for enforcing the Joint Standards, many critics have questioned whether these documents have in fact improved test use (Haney and Madaus, 1991; Kohn, 1977; Madaus et al., 1993; National Commission on Testing and Public Policy, 1990; Office of Technology Assessment, 1992). One of the problems with professional self-regulation is its inability to inform or influence people outside the testing profession. Many of the principal users of educational test results—school administrators, teachers, and policy-makers—are unaware of the Standards and are "untrained in appropriate test use" (Office of Technology Assessment, 1992). Despite the best efforts of numerous professional associations, inappropriate test use continues to be a serious problem. As a result, individuals and groups aggrieved by inappropriate practices have turned to the courts. Some people have questioned whether the Standards have any real enforcement capacity.

Legal Challenges

The National Commission on Testing and Public Policy found that "the most common way to challenge important tests is through the courts" (1990:21).

This is no accident. Federal constitutional provisions (see Chapter 3), federal legislation, and, in some instances, state laws and regulations provide some norms regarding proper use of educational tests. These norms can be enforced judicially and in, some cases, administratively. For several reasons, however, legal challenges are a highly imperfect mechanism for ensuring proper test use.

First, almost all the provisions of federal law that concern educational testing were designed to protect particular groups of students rather than the entire population. The Individuals with Disabilities Education Act (IDEA), for example, contains rules on testing students with disabilities. Title VI and Title IX regulations include provisions on tests that have disproportionate impact by race, national origin, or sex, but neither they nor the constitution's equal protection clause covers inappropriate test uses that affect all children equally. Moreover, federal civil rights protections are far less extensive or specific with respect to educational tests (under Titles VI and IX) than they are under Title VII, which covers employment testing. The Buckley Amendment is perhaps the only federal statute that covers the test scores of all students, and it protects only the confidentiality of student records. In short, federal law is a patchwork of rules rather than a coherent set of norms governing proper test use for tracking, promotion, or graduation.

Enforcement is similarly patchy, for several reasons. First, the law is not self-enforcing; students or parents generally must file complaints, either with administrative agencies or with courts, if they believe that school officials have violated legal norms governing test use. This can happen only if students and parents know their rights and how to enforce them. If the complaints lead to lawsuits, the students and parents must have the means to obtain legal representation. These are big if's.

Second, most court decisions are not binding everywhere. For example, in a leading constitutional case on competency testing, *Debra P.*

v. Turlington (1981), a federal appeals court ruled that "[s]tudents should have opportunities to learn the material on the tests in school [and that] [s]tudents should receive adequate notice to prepare for the tests" (Office of Technology Assessment, 1992:74). Although this decision has influenced test policy in many states and continues to do so, it is legally binding in only one region of the country. In some instances, courts in different jurisdictions face identical legal questions but reach opposite results (compare *Larry P. v. Riles*, 1984, with *Parents in Action on Special Education v. Hannon*, 1980, both of which are discussed in Chapter 3).

Third, courts vary in the degree of deference they give to the educators who are responsible for test policy and practice. Some courts pay careful attention to the testing standards: "The body of case law reveals some broad themes about how courts view tests, and some general principles about acceptable and unacceptable uses of tests. In general, courts have a great respect for well-constructed, standardized tests that are clearly tied to the curriculum" (Office of Technology Assessment, 1992:73-74).

On other occasions, however, courts have approved test uses inconsistent with the Joint Standards or the policies of the test maker. This was the case when a court sustained the use of fixed cutoff scores on the National Teacher Examination as the basis for certifying new teachers, even though the test developer, the Educational Testing Service, in an amicus brief, claimed that such use was improper (*United States v. South Carolina*, 1977). In such cases, courts may defer too readily to the judgments of educators who do not know about the Joint Standards or choose to ignore them.

Fourth, when a legal challenge is mounted, "the test questions often can be seen only by expert witnesses, and testimony about their quality is given in secret. Many problems associated with such publicly funded tests thus may not become public, particularly if the court challenge is unsuccessful" (National Commission on Testing and Public Policy, 1990:21).

Last but not least, court challenges are expensive, divisive, and time-consuming for plaintiffs and defendants alike. "[E]ven when court challenges succeed and compensatory damages are awarded, the cases often drag on so long that opportunities for work and learning may be denied claimants for years" (National Commission on Testing and Public Policy, 1990:22).

For all these reasons, it is important to explore alternative mechanisms for regulating test use.

ALTERNATIVE POLICY MECHANISMS

The two existing enforcement methods outlined above—professional standards and legal action—represent two ends of a continuum of institutional mechanisms for promoting appropriate test use. In this section, the committee explores possible alternatives that might represent intermediate points on that scale, in order of increasing degree of coerciveness. These options stem from the committee's review of literature from policy sciences and draw from analogies to other policy realms. As noted above, the committee does not recommend any one option or combination of options, but we offer these as possible alternatives that could be included in a mix of strategies. These options are worthy of consideration, in the committee's view, for two main reasons: (1) they are variants of mechanisms that have been applied to other policy problems that share some characteristics with the problem of test use (e.g., information asymmetry between producers and users of tests) and (2) there is an empirical literature on the theoretical and practical implications of these options.

Deliberative Forums

Noting a decline in public trust in government and growing evidence that Americans are becoming disengaged from civic life (Putnam, 1995), some theorists have proposed a politics of deliberation as an alternative to the current interest-based politics (Gutmann and Thompson, 1996; Fishkin, 1991; Bickford, 1996). Deliberative politics assumes the primacy of talk—that is, reasoned argumentation, persuasion, and consensus building—in place of power and bargaining. In a deliberative model, access to the decision-making process is open and relatively cost-free; sufficient information is available so that participants can understand how proposals affect their interests and values. All participants have equal standing in the process, regardless of their resources or social status, and issues are considered on their merits, rather than on the balance of resources available to advocates and how they are bargained.

In a deliberative model, participants' preferences are not fixed, and they are expected to change over the course of the deliberations. Deliberation need not result in consensus or agreement on a particular decision. Rather, participants can reach a mutual understanding about their commonalties and differences. When decisions are reached, however, participants are more likely to accept even outcomes with which they disagree because they feel that they have influenced the outcome.

This approach sounds attractive, but it has obvious problems. First, there are few actual examples of such an approach. The jury system is perhaps the most common deliberative forum in a public institution; New England town meetings are another example. Recently, those advocating deliberative approaches have begun to create forums in which serious public deliberation can occur. For example, as a result of a mandate by the Texas Public Utilities Commission that power companies must consult their customers, the utilities in that state have begun to use a form of deliberative polling, in which random samples of Texans meet for a weekend, learn about the issues related to energy production and conservation, and then discuss a range of options and trade-offs. The result has been that, after the process, participants expressed a greater willingness to pay more for energy efficiency and for renewable sources (*The Economist*, 1998). Similarly, Oregon used a series of citizen discussion sessions when the state was attempting to expand access to health insurance and had to make difficult decisions about how to balance cost, quality, and access (Marmor, 1998).

A second problem is that a deliberative process can lock in existing political, economic, and social inequalities unless extraordinary efforts are made to ensure that access is open, information is easily available, all participants with a stake in the outcome are represented, and their views are heard respectfully and considered seriously. Meeting these conditions is not impossible, but it is a tall order in a system that assumes political equality but is characterized by enduring inequalities in resources and skills.

Finally, deliberation requires time, patience, and skill. Yet many people are reluctant to invest them and lack the inclination to cultivate deliberative skills. Consequently, a deliberative model would be more likely to be effective if it were used only for those decisions that embody significant values over which there is substantial disagreement. These are contested rather than settled issues, which cannot easily be resolved by bureaucratic or expert authority. In addition, deliberation is unlikely to be successful unless there are institutional supports for maintaining and supporting the process and its outcomes. Deliberation will not be effective if it is conceived as a short-term, one-shot strategy.

Policymakers also need to recognize that deliberation is open-ended, and they may have little control over its direction or its results once the process begins. The advantage for public officials, however, is that, if they take the results of a deliberative process seriously in policy decisions, the public will be more likely to accept the outcome, thus giving policy-makers added legitimacy.

How Deliberative Forums Might Work in Testing

Decisions about what constitutes appropriate test use are typically made by test developers and policymakers. But they rarely talk to each other or explain their decisions to parents and the public. One strategy for bridging the gap among technical, policy, and public perspectives on test use would be to create deliberative forums in which all the various parties with a stake in assessments would be represented.[1] The purpose would be to consider key questions related to test use from a variety of perspectives. For example, what constitutes "educational quality" and "achievement to high standards"? What is the appropriate role of testing in shaping and measuring progress toward those goals? Under what conditions should test scores be used in making decisions about individual students? How much error is acceptable if test scores are used in those decisions?

Such forums might be convened at the state or local levels; they could be held under governmental auspices or more informally by such organizations as the League of Women Voters or parent and community groups. These forums could be standing groups that are advisory to official policymaking bodies, such as state or local boards of education, or they might be special-purpose groups established when a state or district is considering a major change in its testing program or in how it intends to use test results. Use of a deliberative forum would need to be combined with other strategies that embody the authority to sanction test misuse. Nevertheless, deliberative forums could enhance the design of these other policy tools by ensuring that they reflect thoughtfully constructed, public preferences and by giving greater legitimacy to the policies that result. Establishing a deliberative forum acknowledges that testing is a process of political communication (Kettl, 1998), and, as such, debates over its use cannot be settled on technical criteria alone. Widespread interest in testing issues make this an auspicious time to consider the development of such forums.

---

[1]See also *Educating One and All* (National Research Council, 1997:66-67).

Independent Oversight Body

The complexity of consumer products and the demands for information by consumers have led to the creation of independent organizations that provide reputable, sound information about the quality and limitations of consumer options. Most notable among these organizations are Consumers Union, which publishes the widely respected *Consumer Reports*, and *Good Housekeeping Magazine*, whose seal of approval buyers look for and manufacturers covet.

George Madaus and his colleagues have proposed the creation of an independent organization to monitor and audit high-stakes testing programs (Madaus et al., 1993, 1997):

> Evaluating and monitoring testing programs does mean, however, that the public which pays for such programs and those that use and are directly affected by such tests should have assurances that the programs are technically sound, that the benefits outweigh harms for all groups in society, that negative side effects are minimized, and that misuses are curtailed (Madaus et al., 1993:3).

This proposal, which would reconstitute the National Commission on Testing and Public Policy (1990), is not intended to establish a regulatory body per se, nor is it aimed at awarding a seal of approval to particular programs. Rather, it is intended to improve test use by monitoring test programs.

The proposed commission would include experts from a variety of fields and representatives of test user groups. It would establish a standing technical panel, creating other panels as needed. The commission would conduct public forums, sponsor research, hold workshops for educators and policymakers, and disseminate information through a variety of media. The commission's evaluative judgments would be based on the Joint Standards as well as other criteria, applying them in the context of their use. The goal would be to offer formative assistance, encouraging test makers and users to improve their design and implementation as part of their professional practice.

The proposed commission could supplement the labeling approach described below by providing a forum for educating the profession and the public about testing practice. It could also serve as a deterrent to inappropriate practices by creating the prospect of adverse publicity (House, 1998).

Even in conjunction with other approaches, however, this proposal should be evaluated in terms of both its potential benefits and its potential shortcomings. First, although an oversight body can certainly identify tests and test uses that are seriously flawed, there are other issues on which even testing experts disagree. Studies in which multiple expert panels independently evaluated the appropriateness of certain test practices would help to identify—and possibly to narrow—such differences. Second, there is no way to ensure that test publishers or school administrators would submit their programs for the commission's review. Last but not least, there is no guarantee that test users would abide by the commission's judgments. In many cases, political pressures to adopt high-stakes testing programs could outweigh concerns about improper test use.

These problems could diminish over time, however. If the commission proved itself trustworthy, credible, and impartial, then publishers and administrators might find that the costs of ignoring its judgement were too high. Prospective users might question why a program had not been reviewed, and critics—and potential litigants—could hold up the commission's judgments as a tool in challenging inappropriate programs. We should reiterate that the concept of such an oversight body is not universally accepted or viewed as flawless; nonetheless, it is worthy of consideration in conjunction with other policy tools.

Labeling

In a number of other domains, information has been used as a policy strategy. A variety of "right-to-know" policies provide information to the public about the health risks and benefits associated with various drugs, food products, and toxins. In the case of food labels, the overwhelming majority of consumers are not in a position to ascertain the nutritional value of the foods they buy. In contrast to other attributes, such as taste and freshness, nutritional content is an area in which sellers have considerably more information than buyers, thus violating the ideal of a perfect market (Caswell and Mojduszka, 1995). Similarly, consumers often lack sufficient information to make informed decisions about complex but infrequent purchases, such as refrigerators and air conditioners (Magat and Viscusi, 1992). In these instances, giving consumers information makes the market work more efficiently. In other cases, there is evidence that provision of information can reduce hazardous behavior and/or mitigate the harmful effects of such behavior, even without sanctions that are tied to the information. For example, in a recent study of workplace safety inspections, researchers found that inspections initiated by workers reduce injuries regardless of penalty, suggesting that information can be a critical factor in effecting changes in behavior (Scholz and Gray, 1997).

The assumption behind these policies is that disclosure will correct the information imbalance between producers and consumers, enabling people to make informed purchases and to participate on a more equitable basis in public decisions. This approach is viewed as a way to give individuals the resources to choose the risks and benefits they will accept, rather than leaving the decision to government regulators (Stenzel, 1991). Labeling is often accepted across the political spectrum because it involves considerably less governmental intervention than a solely regulatory strategy. For this policy model to operate as intended, however, individuals must seek and be able to understand information about potential risks and benefits, and they must have opportunities for choice of action in response to that information (Pease, 1991).

Even though information is the primary mechanism to motivate action, a mandate is often involved in these policies as well. The information required under a particular policy may not be voluntarily offered, because its dissemination runs counter to the interests of those who must produce the information. For example, some manufacturers might not voluntarily release nutritional information, because consumers might be less likely to buy prepared foods knowing they contain a lot of additives or fats. So policies that use information as their primary strategy typically mandate its production and dissemination. Prime examples are food labeling and community right-to-know statutes requiring that the presence of hazardous materials be publicly reported.[2]

Data on the effectiveness of these policies are limited, and their track record is mixed. Perhaps the most visible use of this strategy has been the warning labels that cigarette manufacturers are required to place on their products and advertising. These messages have contributed to a reduction in smoking among Americans, although other factors have also

---

[2]In the case of food labeling, federal law requires that food manufacturers report standardized information on the nutrients found in prepared food. The health claims that manufacturers can make about food products (e.g., low sodium, high fiber) are also circumscribed under the same law, and the Food and Drug Administration has the authority to enforce compliance. In the toxic waste area, a variety of federal and state laws require public disclosure about potential exposure to toxic substances. For example, California's Proposition 65 requires businesses to warn citizens if they might be exposed to significant levels of a chemical known to cause either cancer or reproductive harm; failure to comply with the law carries both civil and criminal penalties. Although information is the primary tool used to prompt action for these policies, they are part of a regulatory framework.

played a role. Other strategies, like an outright ban on cigarette sales to minors and prohibitions against smoking in public places, may in the long term be more effective, but labeling has been the most politically feasible and easiest approach to implement.

Some policies, such as nutritional labeling, target both producers and consumers. There is evidence, for example, that in response to labeling requirements, food manufacturers have reformulated their products to enhance nutritional value, and that better information leads consumers to change their buying habits (Caswell, 1992; Ippolito and Mathios, 1990).

Despite its potential as a relatively inexpensive, minimally intrusive policy strategy, labeling also has some significant disadvantages. Users can easily be inundated with data, with little context for interpreting it. Or the data can be presented in a confusing or inaccessible format.[3]

Other analysts have suggested a potentially more serious problem. In requiring the reporting of something as straightforward as a warning that a substance has been known to cause cancer, a disclosure policy may mislead the public into believing that there are simple answers to complex questions about assessing risk. In fact, most risk assessments are tentative; researchers do not fully understand, for example, the causal relationship between exposure to a substance and the incidence of cancer (Stenzel, 1991).

This same dilemma arises in the case of testing. In reducing student achievement to a single test score, there is always the danger that the public and parents will assume that this score encompasses the full measure of a student's or a school's performance. In essence, there is a trade-off between making information understandable and accessible and ensuring that it can be validly interpreted.

A labeling strategy may also create incentives for selective disclosure and other attempts at "gaming" the system by those required to report information. Such problems could very well be exacerbated if there is no neutral, expert body to evaluate the accuracy of the information on labels.

---

[3]For example, the data reported under California's Proposition 65 have been described by one analyst as "unwieldy and confusing"; industry reports typically run from 100 to more than 1,000 pages, but the format of the reports means that important contextual data, such as the environmental conditions under which released chemicals pose a hazard, are omitted (Black, 1989:1049). Consequently, the information presented cannot be accurately interpreted.

Research on policies that rely on information and persuasive communication has focused on whether targets have a sufficient incentive to act. But there is also the question of whether they have the capacity to do what is expected of them. At one level, building the public's capacity to understand and act on the information provided can be accomplished with careful attention to the quality of that information. Using experimental and survey data, Magat and Viscusi (1992) examined various approaches to informing people about hazardous materials. They concluded that, to succeed, such policies need to take into account the specific context in which they are operating, because people are likely either to under- or overreact to information that does not also communicate the size and nature of the risk. As more information about risk is provided, they found, people tend to process and recall less information about other important aspects of a product, such as its proper use. They also found that consumers are more likely to understand and act upon information that is provided in a standardized format so they can make comparative judgments across products.

Consumers may require more information than is provided directly by the labeling policy. Consumers cannot use nutritional profiles to advantage, for example, if they are unfamiliar with the building blocks of a healthy diet or do not know how to prepare nutritious meals. Similarly, parents cannot participate effectively in educational decisions based on their children's test scores if they lack information about the available alternatives and how they fit with their children's abilities, needs, and interests. Building people's capacity and willingness to act depends on more than just disseminating information; it requires a long-term investment in learning and support.

How Labeling Might Work in Testing

It is important to clarify both the party or parties responsible for providing the information (label) and the targets of the labeling strategy. There would be two main targets of a labeling strategy. First, test developers and producers might be required to report to test users, such as public officials and educational administrators at the state and local levels, on the appropriate uses of their tests. Currently, most major test publishers (e.g., Harcourt Brace, Riverside, CTB/McGraw Hill) and nonprofit testing organizations voluntarily publish guides that describe the appropriate uses and limits of their products. But these guides, as well as technical manuals commonly provided by test publishers, are not widely available to the public, and the manuals are quite costly if purchased independently of the full testing package.

For example, the Iowa Test of Basic Skills (ITBS) guide for administrators lists the following uses of test results as inappropriate when decisions are based solely on a test score: screening children for school enrollment, retaining students at a grade level, and selecting students for special instructional programs. As we have seen with Chicago's promotion policy, however, those with responsibility for test policy may choose to ignore the warnings of test publishers. Not only do the publishers have little recourse in such instances, but they also know that if they refuse to sell their products to those using them inappropriately, test users will simply take their business elsewhere.

As with professional standards, labeling aimed at test users would be designed to appeal to their sense of appropriate teaching and learning for the students in their care. But professional values are not always a clear guide to practice and must often be applied in light of conflicting values—such as the tension between the collective goals of public accountability and individual student needs.

One of the reasons that test users can ignore publishers' warnings is that little information about what constitutes appropriate test use ever gets to their constituents—parents, the public, and the media. Therefore, a second target of a labeling strategy might be test consumers. In such a strategy, policymakers and education officials would be required to report to parents, the public, and the media on whatever tests they chose to administer. The following kinds of information might be required about all high-stakes tests:

- the purpose of the test;
- how individual test results will be used;
- whether they will be the sole basis for a particular decision or if other indicators will be used;
- the immediate consequences of this test use for individual students, such as whether poor performance on a test will automatically result in a particular placement or treatment;
- whether the test has been validated for the purpose(s) for which it is being used and by whom;
- some indication of the degree of consistency between what is being tested and what is taught;

• a brief description of the options available to parents who want more information or who question decisions based on a test score. A toll-free telephone number could also be included.

Because the primary targets of this information would be parents, it would need to be concise, jargon-free, written in the languages that parents read, and easily understandable to noneducators. This information would be provided in a variety of formats, both well before a test is administered and when scores were reported to parents. Other direct users might include the news media, which could include such information when they reported test results.

A requirement that information be reported to parents could be based on federal (as part of the Title I and IDEA testing requirements) and state legislation. Policymakers would probably have a variety of incentives for requiring that this information be reported. It would be a minimally intrusive way to address concerns about appropriate test use and should therefore appeal to those who eschew a strong regulatory role for government. Yet a strategy of informing the public would not preclude—and in fact could trigger—the use of other kinds of enforcement mechanisms, so it would probably also appeal to those who want stronger policy levers but who see the advantages of having a range of options. In addition, this strategy would be relatively inexpensive, although not without administrative and other kinds of transaction costs (e.g., in responding to public and parental concerns).

This kind of strategy could also affect other targets besides parents and the media. For example, local schools would be likely to be more attentive to opportunity-to-learn issues if they knew that information about the consistency between testing and teaching would be publicly disseminated. Similarly, test developers and publishers would be likely to be more responsible in promoting their tests, because an information reporting policy would solve a major collective action problem for them: everyone would have to report the same information and be subject to public scrutiny about the veracity of that information, so there would be little incentive to make exaggerated claims about a particular test.

The Joint Standards and the Code of Fair Testing Practices would be used to frame a test labeling policy. Responsibility for implementing such a policy would rest with a publicly accountable institution. That requirement would not, however, preclude an agency operating under governmental authority from delegating responsibility to others. Some tasks, such as designing the reporting form and the measures used and then verifying the information provided by testing agencies and contractors, could be performed by third parties, such as the proposed National Commission on Testing and Public Policy; the National Center for Evaluation, Standards, and Student Testing; the Center for Research on the Education of Students Placed at Risk; the Center for Research on Education, Diversity and Excellence; universities; and nonprofit organizations.

There are certainly differences between the labeling of tests and labeling in other spheres, such as nutrition. For example, some people might argue that information on food ingredients is more factual than information about tests. The committee notes, however, that competing claims surrounding nutrition and its relation to health status are quite numerous. Nutritional labeling has not resolved those competing claims, but it has raised public awareness, pushed advocates toward more evidence-based arguments, and led to more research.

There are at least two major shortcomings that could impede the effectiveness of the labeling strategy in testing. First, it could be an insufficient resource for those who most need it (poor parents with few political resources), and it would be unlikely to curb the most serious cases of inappropriate test use. Moreover, labeling tests and test results may miss the mark entirely if tests are merely reflecting accurately the fact that students have not acquired skills and knowledge because they have not received an adequate education (Schneider, 1998; Levin, 1998). For these reasons, this strategy would probably not be useful except in combination with others. Aggrieved parties would still have recourse to the courts, and efforts to equalize financial and political resources (e.g., school finance equalization, enforcement of parental rights in special education) would need to continue. Nevertheless, this strategy could significantly redress the information imbalance that now exists in testing, and it could serve as a critical mobilizing resource for those concerned about just treatment for all students.

Federal Regulation

Perhaps the most powerful tool for promoting and ensuring appropriate test use is federal regulation. Although the federal government provides a small fraction of the $300 billion the United States spends annually for precollege education, and states are constitutionally responsible to provide public education, the federal government, particularly in the past 30 years, has played a significant role in educational practice nationwide. By making federal aid contingent on the adoption of particular practices, the federal government can exert a substantial influence on practice in virtually every school district in the United States.

The use of federal regulation as a means of promoting appropriate practice in other realms is widespread. Consider traffic safety. Like education, highways are primarily a state responsibility, with the federal government providing financial support for interstate roads. That leverage, however, allows the federal government to set rules for practice—such as the national speed limit of 55 miles per hour—on all highways. (The limit was repealed in 1996.) The federal government used similar methods to raise the drinking age in all states to 21.

One possible source of regulation of test practice is Title I, the largest federal effort in K-12 education. Created in 1965, when the federal government first agreed to provide aid to elementary and secondary schools, the program was designed to "level the playing field" for disadvantaged students by providing financial assistance that would compensate such students for the advantages their peers from more affluent families enjoyed. With a current annual budget of approximately $8 billion—one-fourth of the U.S. Department of Education's total budget—the program reaches more than 6 million students in three-fourths of all elementary schools and half of all secondary schools.

Despite its relatively modest share of the education budgets in the 50 states, Title I has exerted a powerful influence on schools and school districts throughout the country. This is particularly true in the area of testing. From its inception, Title I required the use of "appropriate objective measures of educational achievement" to ensure that the program was meeting its goal of reducing the gap between low-income and higher-income students. In carrying out this requirement, states and school districts typically used standardized, norm-referenced tests both to determine eligibility and to measure gains. As a result, Title I increased dramatically the number of tests that states and districts administered (Office of Technology Assessment, 1992).

The Congress revamped Title I substantially in 1994, and perhaps the most far-reaching changes concerned assessment. The 1994 law eliminated the requirement for a separate testing program for Title I students. Instead, Title I testing was integrated into state systems aimed at holding all students—including those eligible for the federal aid program—to high standards of performance. To that end, the law required states to develop both challenging standards for student performance and assessments that measure student performance against those standards. Significantly, the current law states that the standards and assessments should be the same for all students, regardless of whether they are eligible for Title I.

Other possible sources of regulation are federal civil rights statutes such as Title VI and Title IX.

How Regulation Might Work in Testing

Can regulations under Title I or other federal statutes serve as regulatory monitors to help ensure appropriate test use? In some respects, the 1994 Title I statute and regulations already serve that objective. For one thing, the law now makes schools and school districts, rather than students, the unit of accountability. As a result, current law removes any incentives that previous versions of Title I may have provided for states to administer tests that have high stakes for individual students.

In addition, the law helps ensure appropriate test use by requiring multiple measures of performance. U.S. Department of Education guidelines recommend that "different approaches and formats be used in the assessment system. Examples include criterion-referenced tests, multiple choice tests, writing samples, completion of graphic representations, standardized tests, observation checklists, performance of exemplary tasks, performance events, and portfolios of student work" (U.S. Department of Education, 1997:25). This provision helps ensure that a single measure is not used to make decisions about individual students, schools, or school districts.

The statute also includes provisions that promote fair test use. The law requires "reasonable adaptations and accommodations for students with diverse learning needs," and the inclusion of English-language learners "to the extent practical, in the language and form most likely to yield accurate and reliable information on what they know and can do, to determine their mastery of skills in subjects other than English." Thus Title I, properly implemented, helps ensure that students with disabilities and English-language learners participate in large-scale assessment programs, and that such students are assessed in ways that are valid.

Despite these important safeguards, Title I is silent with respect to many tests that states and school districts use. They could therefore use those tests inappropriately even while complying with the federal law.

For example, to comply with Title I a state could submit a plan under which students in 4th, 8th, and 10th grades would take standardized tests and a writing assessment and would submit portfolios, to determine school and district progress in enabling students to reach state standards. At the same time, however, a school district in that state could administer a test on the basis of which students would automatically be retained in grade—an inappropriate practice under current standards of the testing profession.

The objective of assessment under Title I—holding all students to challenging standards for performance—can be undermined by improper use of tests for student tracking, promotion, or graduation. To guard against such a situation, Title I regulations could be revised to ensure that all large-scale assessments administered within a state complied with the Standards for Educational and Psychological Testing (American Educational Research Association et al., 1985) and the Code of Fair Testing Practices in Educational Tests (Joint Committee on Testing Practices, 1988). State Title I plans could address the extent to which state and local assessment systems met these professional norms.

There are other federal statutes whose regulations could be amended to include—or to reference—standards of appropriate test use. These include federal civil rights statutes, such as Title VI of the Civil Rights Act of 1964 and Title IX of the Education Amendments of 1972.

Title VI and Title IX prohibit recipients of federal funds from discriminating on the basis of race, national origin, or sex, and most disputes about testing have involved tests that carry high stakes for students. Under existing regulations, when an educational test has disproportionate adverse impact by race, national origin, or sex, the federal aid recipient responsible for the test and its use must demonstrate that the test and its use are an educational necessity (see Chapter 3). Federal regulations do not, however, define what an educational necessity is. As a result, there has been uncertainty about how to apply these rules, whether administratively or judicially.

Thus, a possible use of federal regulation to promote proper test use would involve defining educational necessity in terms of compliance with the Joint Standards and the Code of Fair Testing Practices. A high-stakes test use inconsistent with relevant provisions of the Joint Standards and the Code would not be considered educationally necessary.

Using federal regulations in this way would offer certain advantages. Most important, the regulations apply to all 50 states and nearly all school districts, because they receive federal funds. Policymakers and administrators are understandably reluctant to jeopardize this funding. Historically, Title I, Title VI, and Title IX have had an important influence on test policy and practice in the country.

In addition, federal regulations could provide a powerful tool for educating policymakers and the public about appropriate test use. Through conferences, technical assistance centers, and handbooks and newsletters, the U.S. Department of Education provides a wealth of information and support to states and districts about federal law and its requirements. Including the principles of appropriate test use in federal regulations would result in their wide dissemination and would make educators and the public much more aware of the potential risks of inappropriate practices. In conjunction with the labeling and deliberative functions described above, the regulatory approach could significantly enhance the information available to educators and the public about appropriate test use.

Relying on federal regulation—under Title I, Title VI, Title IX, or other statutes—would also make use of existing mechanisms, administrative and judicial, to enforce standards of the testing profession that, for reasons discussed above, often go unenforced. Combining professionally developed norms with existing enforcement mechanisms could help address some of the principal weaknesses of each approach: professional norms would become more enforceable, and federal authorities (administrative agencies and judges) would not need to create their own definitions of appropriate test use.

The regulatory approach also entails significant risks, however. It is a blunt instrument, and the sanctions available for failure to comply—the cutoff of federal aid—often make it unwieldy. This is because the federal government loses its leverage when it applies the penalty. The Office of Juvenile Justice and Delinquency Prevention (OJJDP) discovered this problem when it attempted to develop state mandates regarding the deinstitutionalization of status offenders (minors who commit acts that are not crimes for adults, such as underage drinking). The mandates applied to states that accepted grant funds, but if states rejected the funds, they did not have to comply with the mandates. States then put pressure on the Congress to provide the funds without requiring them to comply with the mandates, and the OJJDP did not object strongly, because it wanted the states to continue to participate in the program (Schneider, 1998).

Moreover, using federal regulation to promote proper test use would be subject to many of the usual disadvantages of administrative and judicial enforcement, as well as to disadvantages stemming from any ambiguities in the Joint Standards and the Code. These issues are likely to become formidable barriers to increased regulation, especially in today's climate that favors "devolution" and a reduced federal role.

Perhaps the most serious risk involved in the regulatory approach is the possibility of a backlash against all federal regulation, which would make it more difficult for the the U.S. Department of Education to guide local practice. Disenchantment with regulation generally, as well as specific instances in which test regulation has produced unintended consequences, would need to be considered in developing effective regulatory strategies. Despite the goal of the Congress and the Department of Education to permit maximum local flexibility under federal rules, some members of Congress already consider federal law too prescriptive and want to lighten the hand of Washington over local education policy. Proposals to convert federal education aid to block grants, which states could use as they see fit rather than following federal guidelines, reflect such concerns. A regulatory approach that was seen as infringing on local prerogatives could strengthen support for such plans, and it could ultimately restrict the federal government's capacity to influence state and local practice on testing and many other issues.

CONCLUSION

Deliberative forums, an independent oversight body, labeling, and federal regulation represent a range of possible options that could supplement professional standards and litigation as means of promoting and enforcing appropriate test use. The committee is not recommending adoption of any particular strategy or combination of strategies, nor does it suggest that these four approaches are the only possibilities. We do think, however, that ensuring appropriate test use will require multiple strategies.

Given the inadequacy of current methods, practices, and safeguards, there should be further research on these and other policy options to illuminate their possible effects on test use. In particular, we encourage empirical research on the effects of these strategies, individually and in combination, on products and practice and an examination of the associated potential benefits and risks.

REFERENCES

American Educational Research Association
  1992   Ethical standards of the American Educational Research Association. *Educational Researcher* 21(7):23-26.
American Educational Research Association, American Psychological Association, and National Council on Measurement in Education
  1985   *Standards for Educational and Psychological Testing.* Washington, DC: American Psychological Association.
  1998   *Draft Standards for Educational and Psychological Testing.* Washington, DC: American Psychological Association.
American Psychological Association
  1981   Ethical principles of psychologists. *American Psychologist* 36:633-638.
American Psychological Association, American Educational Research Association, and National Council on Measurement in Education
  1954   *Technical Recommendations for Psychological Tests and Diagnostic Techniques.* Washington, DC: American Psychological Association.
  1966   *Standards for Educational and Psychological Tests and Manuals.* Washington, DC: American Psychological Association.
  1974   *Standards for Educational and Psychological Tests and Manuals.* Washington, DC: American Psychological Association.
  1985   *Standards for Educational and Psychological Tests and Manuals.* Washington, DC: American Psychological Association.
Bickford, S.
  1996   *The Dissonance of Democracy.* Ithaca, NY: Cornell University Press.
Black, E.G.
  1989   California's community right-to-know. *Ecology Law Quarterly* 16:1021-1064.
Caswell, J.A.
  1992   Current information levels on food labels. *American Journal of Agricultural Economics* 74(5):1196-1201.
Caswell, J.A., and E.M. Mojduszka
  1995   Using informational labeling to influence the market for quality in food products. *American Journal of Agricultural Economics* 78:1248-1253.
Fishkin, J.S.
  1991   *Democracy and Deliberation: New Directions for Democratic Reform.* New Haven, CT: Yale University Press.
Gutmann, A., and D. Thompson
  1996   *Democracy and Disagreement.* Cambridge, MA: Belknap Press of Harvard University Press.
Haney, W., and G. Madaus
  1991   The evolution of ethical and technical standards for testing. In *Advances in Educational and Psychological Testing: Theory and Applications*, R.K. Hambleton, and J.N. Zaal, eds. Boston: Kluwer.
House, E.R.
  1998   Preventing Test Abuse. Memorandum to the Committee on Appropriate Test Use.

Ippolito, P.M., and A.D. Mathios
   1990   Information, advertising and health choices: A study of the cereal market. *RAND Journal of Economics* 21(3):459-480.
Joint Committee on Testing Practices
   1988   *Code of Fair Testing Practices in Education.* Washington, DC: National Council on Measurement in Education.
Kettl, D.F.
   1998   Uses of Educational Tests. Memorandum to the Committee on Appropriate Test Use.
Kohn, S.D.
   1977   The numbers game: How the testing industry operates. Pp. 158-182 in *The Myth of Measurability*, P.L. Houts, ed. New York: Hart.
Levin, H.M.
   1998   Design and Use of Educational Tests. Memorandum to the Committee on Appropriate Test Use.
Madaus, G.F.
   1992   An independent auditing mechanism for testing. *Educational Measurement: Issues and Practices* 11(1):26-31.
Madaus, G.F., W. Haney, K.B. Newton, and A.E. Kreitzer
   1993   *A Proposal for a Monitoring Body for Tests Used in Public Policy.* Boston: Center for the Study of Testing, Evaluation, and Public Policy.
   1997   *A Proposal to Reconstitute the National Commission on Testing and Public Policy as An Independent, Monitoring Agency for Educational Testing.* Boston: Center for the Study of Testing Evaluation and Educational Policy.
Magat, W.A., and W.K. Viscusi
   1992   *Informational Approaches to Regulation.* Cambridge, MA: MIT Press.
Marmor, T.
   1998   Policy Instruments for Testing in Schools. Memorandum to the Committee on Appropriate Test Use.
McDonnell, L.M., and R. Elmore
   1987   Getting the job done: Alternative policy instruments. *Educational Evaluation and Policy Analysis* 9(2):133-152.
National Commission on Testing and Public Policy
   1990   *From GATEKEEPER to GATEWAY: Transforming Testing in America.* Boston National Commission on Testing and Public Policy.
National Council on Measurement in Education
   1995   *Code of Professional Responsibilities in Educational Measurement.* Washington, DC: National Council on Measurement in Education.
National Education Association
   1955   *Technical Recommendations for Achievement Tests.* Washington, DC: National Education Association.
National Research Council
   1982   *Placing Children in Special Education: A Strategy for Equity*, K.A. Heller, W.H. Holtzman, and S. Messick, eds. Committee on Child Development Research and Public Policy. Washington, DC: National Academy Press.

1997   *Educating One and All: Students with Disabilities and Standards-Based Reform*, L.M. McDonnell, M.J. McLaughlin, and Patricia Morison, eds. Committee on Goals 2000 and the Inclusion of Students with Disabilities, Board on Testing and Assessment. Washington, DC: National Academy Press.

Novick, M.
1982   Ability testing: Federal guidelines and professional standards. In *Ability Testing: Uses, Consequences, and Controversies. Part II: Documentation Section*, A.K. Wigdor, and W.R. Garner, eds. National Research Council. Washington, DC: National Academy Press.

Office of Technology Assessment
1992   *Testing in American Schools: Asking the Right Questions.* Washington, DC: U.S. Government Printing Office.

Pease, W.S.
1991   Chemical hazards and the public's right to know: How effective is California's Proposition 65. *Environment* 33(10):12-20.

Putnam, R.D.
1995   Bowling alone: America's declining social capital. *Journal of Democracy* 6(1):65-78.

Schneider, A.L.
1990   The behavioral assumptions of policy tools. *Journal of Politics* 52(2):511-529.
1993   Social construction and target populations: Implications for politics and policy. *American Political Science Review* 87(2):334-347.
1997   *Policy Design for Democracy.* Lawrence, KS: University Press of Kansas.
1998   Policy Tools for Addressing the (Mis)use of Standardized Tests. Memorandum to the Committee on Appropriate Test Use.

Schneider, A.L., and H. Ingram
1990   The behavioral assumptions of policy tools. *Journal of Politics* 52(2):511-529.
1993   Social constructions and target populations: Implications for politics and policy. *American Political Science Review* 87:334-347.
1997   *Policy Design for Democracy.* Lawrence, KS: University Press of Kansas.

Scholz, J.T., and W.B. Gray
1997   Can government facilitate cooperation? An informational model of OSHA enforcement. *American Journal of Political Science* 41(3):693-717.

Stenzel, P.L.
1991   Right-to-know provisions of California's Proposition 65: The naivete of the Delaney Clause revisited. *Harvard Environmental Law Review* 15:493-527.

The Economist
1998   Democracy in Texas: The frontier spirit. 31(May 16).

U.S. Department of Education
1997   *Guidance on Standards, Assessments, and Accountability.* Washington, DC: U.S. Department of Education.

LEGAL REFERENCES

Debra P. v. Turlington, 474 F. Supp. 244 (M.D. Fla. 1979); *aff'd in part and rev'd in part*, 644 F.2d 397 (5th Cir. 1981); *rem'd*, 564 F. Supp. 177 (M.D. Fla. 1983); *aff'd*, 730 F.2d 1405 (11th Cir. 1984).

Individuals with Disabilities Education Act, 20 U.S.C. section 1401 *et seq.*

Larry P. v. Riles, 495 F. Supp. 926 (N.D. Cal. 1979); *aff'd*, 793 F.2d 969 (9th Cir. 1984).

Parents in Action on Special Education v. Hannon, 506 F. Supp. 831 (N.D. Ill. 1980).

Title I, Elementary and Secondary Education Act, 20 U.S.C. sections 6301 *et seq.*

Title VI, Civil Rights Act of 1964, 42 U.S.C. sections 2000d *et seq.*

Title VII, Civil Rights Act of 1964, 42 U.S.C. sections 2000e *et seq.*

Title IX, Education Amendments of 1972, 20 U.S.C. sections 1681 *et seq.*

United States v. South Carolina, 445 F. Supp. 1094 (D.S.C. 1977); *aff'd per curiam sub nom. National Education Ass'n v. South Carolina*, 434 U.S. 1026 (1978).

12

Findings and Recommendations

The Congress asked the National Academy of Sciences to "conduct a study and make written recommendations on appropriate methods, practices and safeguards to ensure that—

A. existing and new tests that are used to assess student performance are not used in a discriminatory manner or inappropriately for student promotion, tracking or graduation; and

B. existing and new tests adequately assess student reading and mathematics comprehension in the form most likely to yield accurate information regarding student achievement of reading and mathematics skills."

Congressional interest in this subject stems from the widespread movement in the United States for standards-based school reform, from the consideration of voluntary national tests, and from the increased reliance on achievement tests for various forms of accountability: for school systems, individual schools, administrators, teachers, and students. Moreover, there are sustained high levels of public support for high-stakes testing of individual students, even if it would lead to lower rates of promotion and high school graduation (Johnson and Immerwahr, 1994; Hochschild and Scott, 1998). Because large-scale testing is increasingly used for high-stakes purposes to make decisions that significantly affect the life chances of individual students, the Congress has asked the National Academy of Sciences, through its National Research Council, for guidance in the appropriate and nondiscriminatory use of such tests.

This study focuses on tests that, by virtue of their use for promotion, tracking, or graduation, have high stakes for individual students. The committee recognizes that accountability for students is related in important ways to accountability for educators, schools, and school districts. This report does not address accountability at those other levels, apart from the issue of participation of all students in large-scale assessments. The report is intended to apply to all schools and school systems in which tests are used for student promotion, tracking, or graduation.

Test form (as mentioned in part B of the congressional mandate) could refer to a wide range of issues, including, for example, the balance of multiple-choice and constructed-response items, the use of student portfolios, the length and timing of the test, the availability of calculators or manipulatives, and the language of administration. However, in considering test form, the committee has chosen to focus on the needs of English-language learners and students with disabilities, in part because these students may be particularly vulnerable to the negative consequences of large-scale assessments. We consider, for these students, in what form and manner a test is most likely to measure accurately a student's achievement of reading and mathematics skills.

Two policy objectives are key for these special populations. One is to increase their participation in large-scale assessments, so that school systems can be held accountable for their educational progress. The other is to test each such student in a manner that accommodates for a disability or limited English proficiency to the extent that either is unrelated to the subject matter being tested, while still maintaining the validity and comparability of test results among all students. These objectives are in tension, and thus present serious technical and operational challenges to test developers and users.

ASSESSING THE USES OF TESTS

In its deliberations the committee has assumed that the use of tests in decisions about student promotion, tracking, or graduation is intended to serve educational policy goals, such as setting high standards for student learning, raising student achievement levels, ensuring equal educational opportunity, fostering parental involvement in student learning, and increasing public support for the schools.

Determining whether the use of tests for student promotion, tracking, or graduation produces better overall educational outcomes requires that the various intended benefits of high-stakes test use be weighed against unintended negative consequences for individual students and groups of students. The costs and benefits of testing should also be balanced against those of making high-stakes decisions about students in other ways, using criteria other than test scores; decisions about tracking, promotion, and graduation will be made with or without information from standardized tests. The committee recognizes that test use may have negative consequences for individual students even while serving important social or educational policy purposes. We believe that the development of a comprehensive testing policy should be sensitive to the balance among individual and collective benefits and costs.

The committee follows an earlier work by the National Research Council (1982) in adopting a three-part framework for determining whether a planned or actual test use is appropriate. The three principal criteria are (1) *measurement validity*—whether a test is valid for a particular purpose and the constructs measured have been correctly chosen; (2) *attribution of cause*—whether a student's performance on a test reflects knowledge and skill based on appropriate instruction or is attributable to poor instruction or to such factors as language barriers or construct-irrelevant disabilities; and (3) *effectiveness of treatment*—whether test scores lead to placements and other consequences that are educationally beneficial. This framework leads us to emphasize several basic principles of appropriate test use.

First, the important thing about a test is not its validity in general, but its validity when used for a specific purpose. Thus, tests that are useful in leading the curriculum or in school accountability are not appropriate for use in making high-stakes decisions about individual student mastery unless the curriculum, the teaching, and the tests are aligned.

Second, tests are not perfect. Test questions are a sample of possible questions that could be asked in a given area. Moreover, a test score is not an exact measure of a student's knowledge or skills. A student's score can be expected to vary across different versions of a test—within a margin of error determined by the reliability of the test—as a function of the particular sample of questions asked and/or transitory factors, such as the health of the student on the day of the test.

Third, an educational decision that will have a major impact on a test taker should not solely or automatically be made on the basis of a single test score. Other relevant information about the student's knowledge and skills should also be taken into account.

Finally, neither a test score nor any other kind of information can justify a bad decision. For example, research shows that tracking, as typically practiced, harms students placed in low-track classes. In the absence of better treatments, better tests will not lead to better educational outcomes. Throughout the report, the committee has considered how these principles apply to the appropriate use of tests in decisions about tracking, promotion, and graduation and to possible uses of the proposed voluntary national tests.

Blanket criticisms of testing and assessment are not justified. When tests are used in ways that meet relevant psychometric, legal, and educational standards, students' scores provide important information that, combined with information from other sources, can lead to decisions that promote student learning and equality of opportunity (Office of Technology Assessment, 1992). For example, tests can identify learning differences among students that the education system needs to address. Because decisions about tracking, promotion, and graduation will be made with or without testing, proposed alternatives to testing should be at least equally accurate, efficient, and fair.

It is also a mistake to accept observed test scores as either infallible or immutable. When test use is inappropriate, especially in the case of high-stakes decisions about individuals, it can undermine the quality of education and equality of opportunity. For example, it is wrong to suggest that the lower achievement test scores of racial and ethnic minorities and students from low-income families reflect inalterable realities of American society.[1] Such scores reflect persistent inequalities in American society and its schools, and the inappropriate use of test scores can legitimate and reinforce these inequalities. This lends a special urgency to the requirement that test use in connection with tracking, promotion, and graduation should be appropriate and fair. With respect to the use of tests in making high-stakes decisions about students, the committee concludes that statements about the benefits and harms of testing often go beyond what the evidence will support.

---

[1]For recent evidence of major changes in group differences in test scores, see Hauser (1998), Grissmer et al. (1998), Huang and Hauser (1998), and Ceci et al. (1998).

CROSS-CUTTING THEMES

In important ways, educational decisions about tracking, promotion, and graduation are different from one another. They differ most importantly in the role that mastery of past material and readiness for new material play as decision-making criteria and in the importance of beneficial educational placement relative to certification as consequences of the decision. Thus, we have considered the role of large-scale, high-stakes testing separately in relation to each type of decision. However, tracking, promotion, and graduation also share common features that pertain to appropriate test use and to their educational and social consequences. These include the alignment between testing and the curriculum, the social and economic sorting that follows from the decisions, the range of educational options potentially linked to the decisions, the use of multiple sources of evidence, the use of tests among young children, and improper manipulation of test score outcomes for groups or individuals. Even though we also raise some of these issues in connection with specific decisions, each of them cuts across two or more types of decisions. We therefore discuss them jointly in this section before turning separately to the use of tests in tracking, promotion, and graduation decisions.

It is a mistake to begin educational reform by introducing tests with high stakes for individual students. If tests are to be used for high-stakes decisions about individual mastery, such use should follow implementation of changes in teaching and curriculum that ensure that students have been taught the knowledge and skills on which they will be tested. Some school systems are already doing this by planning a gap of several years between the introduction of new tests and the attachment of high stakes to individual student performance, during which schools may achieve the necessary alignment among tests, curriculum, and instruction. Others may see high-stakes student testing as a way of leading curricular reform, not recognizing the danger that a test may lack the "instructional validity" required by law (*Debra P. v. Turlington*, 1981)— that is, a close correspondence between test content and instructional content.

To the extent that all students are expected to meet "world-class" standards, there is a need to provide world-class curricula and instruction to all students. However, in most of the nation, much needs to be done before a world-class curriculum and world-class instruction will be in place (National Academy of Education, 1996). At present, curriculum does not usually place sufficient emphasis on student understanding and application of concepts, as opposed to memorization and skill mastery. In addition, instruction in core subjects typically has been and remains highly stratified. What teachers teach and what students learn vary widely by track, with those in lower tracks receiving far less than a world-class curriculum. If world-class standards were suddenly adopted, student failure would be unacceptably high (Linn, 1998a).

> **Recommendation:** Accountability for educational outcomes should be a shared responsibility of states, school districts, public officials, educators, parents, and students. High standards cannot be established and maintained merely by imposing them on students.

> **Recommendation:** If parents, educators, public officials, and others who share responsibility for educational outcomes are to discharge their responsibility effectively, they should have access to information about the nature and interpretation of tests and test scores. Such information should be made available to the public and should be incorporated into teacher education and into educational programs for principals, administrators, public officials, and others.

> **Recommendation:** A test may appropriately be used to lead curricular reform, but it should not also be used to make high-stakes decisions about individual students until test users can show that the test measures what they have been taught.

The consequences of high-stakes testing for individual students are often posed as a either-or propositions, but this need not be the case. For example, social promotion and simple retention in grade are really only two of many educational strategies available to educators when test scores and other information indicate that students are experiencing serious academic difficulty. Neither social promotion nor retention alone is an effective treatment, and schools can use a number of possible strategies to reduce the need for these either-or choices—for example, by coupling early identification of such students with effective remedial education. Similar observations hold for decisions about tracking and about high school graduation.

> **Recommendation:** Test users should avoid simple either-or options when high-stakes tests and other indicators show that

students are doing poorly in school, in favor of strategies combining early intervention and effective remediation of learning problems.

Large-scale assessments are used widely to make high-stakes decisions about students, but they are most often used in combination with other information, as recommended by the major professional and scientific organizations in testing (American Educational Research Association et al., 1985, 1998; Joint Committee on Testing Practices, 1988). For example, according to a recent survey, teacher-assigned grades, standardized tests, developmental factors, attendance, and teacher recommendations form the evidence on which most school districts say that they base promotion decisions (American Federation of Teachers, 1997). A test score, like any other source of information about a student, is not exact. It is an estimate of the student's understanding or mastery of the content that a test was intended to measure.

Recommendation: High-stakes decisions such as tracking, promotion, and graduation should not automatically be made on the basis of a single test score but should be buttressed by other relevant information about the student's knowledge and skills, such as grades, teacher recommendations, and extenuating circumstances.

Problems of test validity are greatest among young children, and there is a greater risk of error when such tests are employed to make significant educational decisions about children who are less than 8 years old or below grade 3—or about their schools. However, well-designed assessments may be useful in monitoring trends in the educational development of populations of students who have reached age 5 (Shepard et al., 1998).

Recommendation: In general, large-scale assessments should not be used to make high-stakes decisions about students who are less than 8 years old or enrolled below grade 3.

All students are entitled to sufficient test preparation, but it is not proper to expose them ahead of time to items that will actually be used on their test or to give them the answers to those questions. Test results may also be invalidated by teaching so narrowly to the objectives of a particular test that scores are raised without actually improving the broader set of academic skills that the test is intended to measure (Koretz et al.,

1991). The committee also recognizes that the desirability of "teaching to the test" is affected by test design. For example, it is entirely appropriate to prepare students by covering all the objectives of a test that represents the full range of the intended curriculum. Thus, it is important that test users respect the distinction between genuine remedial education and teaching narrowly to the specific content of a test.

> **Recommendation: All students are entitled to sufficient test preparation so their performance will not be adversely affected by unfamiliarity with item format or by ignorance of appropriate test-taking strategies. Test users should balance efforts to prepare students for a particular test format against the possibility that excessively narrow preparation will invalidate test outcomes.**

There is an inherent conflict of interest when teachers administer high-stakes tests to their own students or score their own students' exams. On one hand, teachers want valid information about how well their students are performing. On the other hand, there is often substantial external pressure on teachers (as well as principals and other school personnel) for their students to earn high scores. This external pressure may lead some teachers to provide inappropriate assistance to their students before and during the test administration or to mis-score exams. The prevalence of such inappropriate practices varies among and within states and schools. Consequently, when there is evidence of a problem, such as from observations or other data, formal steps should be taken to ensure the validity of the scores obtained. This could include having an external monitoring system with sanctions, or having someone external to the school administer the tests and ensure their security, or both. Only in this way can the scores obtained from high-stakes tests be trusted as providing reasonably accurate results regarding student performance.

Members of some minority groups, English-language learners, and low-socioeconomic (SES) students are overrepresented in lower-track classes and among those denied promotion or graduation on the basis of test scores. Moreover, these same groups of students are underrepresented in high-track classes, "exam" schools, and "gifted and talented" programs (Oakes et al., 1992). In some cases, such as courses for English-language learners, such disproportions are not problematic. We would not expect to find native English speakers in classes designed to teach English to English-language learners.

In other circumstances, such disproportions raise serious questions.

For example, although the grade placement of 6-year-olds is similar among boys and girls and among racial and ethnic groups, grade retardation among children cumulates rapidly after age 6, and it occurs disproportionately among males and minority group members. Among children 6 to 8 years old in 1987, 17 percent of white females and 22 percent of black males were enrolled below the modal grade for their age. By ages 9 to 11, 22 percent of white females and 37 percent of black males were enrolled below the modal grade for their age. In 1996, when the same children were 15 to 17 years old, 29 percent of white females and 48 percent of black males were either enrolled below the modal grade level for their age or had dropped out of school (U.S. Bureau of the Census, *Current Population Reports*, Series P-20). These disproportions are especially disturbing in view of other evidence that grade retention and assignment to low tracks have little educational value.

The concentrations of minority students, English-language learners, and low-SES students among those retained in grade, denied high school diplomas, and placed in less demanding classes raise significant questions about the efficacy of schooling and the fairness of major educational decisions, including those made using information from high-stakes tests.

The committee sees a strong need for better evidence on the benefits and costs of high-stakes testing. This evidence should tell us whether the educational consequences of particular decisions are educationally beneficial for students, e.g., by increasing academic achievement or reducing school dropout. It is also important to develop statistical reporting systems of key indicators that will track both intended effects (e.g., higher test scores) and other effects (e.g., changes in dropout or special education referral rates). For example, some parents or educators may improperly seek to classify their students as disabled in order to take advantage of accommodation in high-stakes tests. Indicator systems could include measures such as retention rates, special education identification rates, rates of exclusion from assessment programs, number and type of accommodations, high school completion credentials, dropout rates, and indicators of access to high-quality curriculum and instruction.

> **Recommendation: High-stakes testing programs should routinely include a well-designed evaluation component. Policymakers should monitor both the intended and unintended consequences of high-stakes assessments on all students and on significant subgroups of students, including minorities, English-language learners, and students with disabilities.**

APPROPRIATE USES OF TESTS IN TRACKING, PROMOTION, AND GRADUATION

Tracking

The intended purpose of tracking is to place each student in an educational setting that is optimal given his or her knowledge, skills, and interests. Support for tracking stems from a widespread belief that students will perform optimally if they receive instruction in homogeneous classes and schools, in which the pace and nature of instructions are tailored to their achievement levels (Oakes et al., 1992; Gamoran and Weinstein, 1998). The research evidence on this point, however, is unclear (Mosteller et al., 1996).

"Tracking" takes many different forms, including: (1) grouping between classes within a grade level based on perceived achievement or skill level; (2) selection for exam schools or gifted and talented programs; (3) identification for remedial education programs, such as "intervention" schools; and (4) referral for possible placement in special education (Oakes et al., 1992; Mosteller et al., 1996). Tracking is common in American schools, but tracking policies and practices vary, not only from state to state and district to district, but also from school to school. Because tracking policies and procedures are both diverse and decentralized, it is difficult to generalize about the use of tests in tracking.

Research suggests that (1) as a result of tracking, the difference in average achievement of students in different classes in the same school is far greater in the United States than in most other countries (Linn, 1998a); (2) instruction in low-track classes is far less demanding than in high-track classes (Welner and Oakes, 1996; McKnight et al., 1987); (3) students in low-track classes do not have the opportunity to acquire knowledge and skills strongly associated with future success; and (4) many students in low-track classes would acquire such knowledge and skills if placed in more demanding educational settings (Slavin et al., 1996; Levin, 1988; Title I of the Elementary and Secondary Education Act).

Recommendation: As tracking is currently practiced, low-track classes are typically characterized by an exclusive focus on basic skills, low expectations, and the least-qualified teachers. Students assigned to low-track classes are worse off than they would be in other placements. This form of tracking should be eliminated. Neither test scores nor other information should be used to place students in such classes.

Some forms of tracking, such as proficiency-based placement in foreign language classes and other classes for which there is a demonstrated need for prerequisites, may be beneficial. We make no attempt here to enumerate all forms of beneficial tracking. The general criterion of what constitutes beneficial tracking is that a student's placement, in comparison with other available placements, yields the greatest chance that the student will acquire the knowledge and skills strongly associated with future success.

The role that tests play in tracking decisions is an important and subtle issue. Educators consistently report that, whereas test scores are routinely used in making tracking decisions, most within-grade tracking decisions are based not solely on test scores but also on students' prior achievement, teacher judgment, and other factors (White et al., 1996; Delany, 1991; Selvin et al., 1990). Research also suggests that "middle class parents intervene to obtain advantageous positions for their children" regardless of test scores or of teacher recommendations (Lucas, in press:206). Nonetheless, even when test scores are just one factor among several that influence tracking decisions, they may carry undue weight by appearing to provide scientific justification and legitimacy for tracking decisions that such decisions would not otherwise have. Some scholars believe that reliance on test scores increases the disproportionate representation of poor and minority students in low-track classes. However, test use can also play a positive role, as when a relatively high test score serves to overcome a negative stereotype (Lucas, in press). Tests may play an important, even dominant, role in selecting children for exam schools and gifted and talented programs (Kornhaber, 1997), and they also play an important part in the special education evaluation process (Individuals with Disabilities Education Act, 1997).

Although standardized tests are often used in tracking decisions, there is considerable variation in what tests are used. Research suggests that some tests commonly employed for tracking are not valid for this purpose (Darling-Hammond, 1991; Glaser and Silver, 1994; Meisels, 1989; Shepard, 1991) but that other standardized tests are.

Although test use varies with regard to tracking, certain test uses are inconsistent with sound psychometric practice and with sound educational policy. These include: using tests not valid for tracking purposes; relying exclusively on test scores in making placement decisions; relying on a test in one subject for placement in other subjects—which in secondary schools may occur indirectly when placement in one class, combined with scheduling considerations, dictates track placements in other subjects (Oakes et al., 1992; Gamoran, 1988); relying on subject-matter tests in English, without appropriate accommodation, in placing English-language learners in certain classes; and failing to reevaluate students periodically to determine whether existing placements remain suitable. It is also inappropriate to use test scores or any other information as a basis for placing children in settings in which their access to higher-order knowledge and skills is denied or limited.

> **Recommendation: Since tracking decisions are basically placement decisions, tests and other information used for this purpose should meet professional test standards regarding placement.**

> **Recommendation: Because a key assumption underlying placement decisions is that students will benefit more from certain educational experiences than from others, the standard for using a test or other information to make tracking decisions should be accuracy in predicting the likely educational effects of each of several alternative educational experiences.**

> **Recommendation: If a cutscore is to be employed on a test used in making a tracking or placement decision, the quality of the standard-setting process should be documented and evaluated.**

Promotion and Retention

The intended purposes of formal promotion and retention policies are (1) to ensure that students acquire the knowledge and skills they need for successful work in higher grades and (2) to increase student and teacher motivation to succeed. Many states and school districts rely on large-scale assessments, some heavily, in making decisions about student promotion and retention at specified grade levels. In the great majority of states and school districts, promotion and retention decisions are based on a combination of grades, test scores, developmental factors, attendance, and teacher recommendations (American Federation of Teachers, 1997). However, the trend is for more states and school districts to base promotion mainly on test scores.

Much of the current public discussion of high-stakes testing is motivated by calls for an end to social promotion. For example, in the Clinton administration's proposals for educational reform, an end to social promotion is strongly tied to early identification and remediation of learning problems. The proposal also calls for "appropriate use of tests and other indicators of academic performance in determining whether students should be promoted" (Clinton, 1998:3). The key question is whether testing will be used appropriately in such decisions.

Grade retention policies typically have positive intentions but negative consequences. The intended positive consequences are that students will be more motivated to learn and will consequently acquire the knowledge and skills they need at each grade level. The negative consequences, as grade retention is currently practiced, are that retained students persist in low achievement levels and are likely to drop out of school. Low-performing students who have been retained in kindergarten or primary grades lose ground both academically and socially relative to similar students who have been promoted (Holmes, 1989; Shepard and Smith, 1989). In secondary school, grade retention leads to reduced achievement and much higher rates of school dropout (Luppescu et al., 1995; Grissom and Shepard, 1989; Anderson, 1994). At present, the negative consequences of grade retention policies typically outweigh the intended positive effects. Simple retention in grade is an ineffective intervention.

Social promotion and simple retention in grade are only two of the educational interventions available to educators when students are experiencing serious academic difficulty. Schools can use a number of possible strategies to reduce the need for these either-or choices, for example, by coupling early identification of such students with effective remedial education. In this model, schools would identify early those students whose academic performance is weak and would then provide effective remedial education aimed at helping them to acquire the knowledge and skills needed to progress from grade to grade. The effectiveness of such alternative approaches would depend on the quality of the instruction that students received. It is neither simple nor inexpensive to provide high-quality remedial instruction. In the current political environment, the committee is concerned about the possibility that such remediation may be neglected once higher promotion standards have been imposed.

The committee did not attempt to synthesize research on the effectiveness of interventions that combine the threat of in-grade retention with other treatments, such as tutoring, reduced class size, enrichment classes, and remedial instruction after school, on weekends, or during the summer. Some states and localities are carrying out such research internally.

Pressure for test-based promotion decisions has resulted from the common but mistaken perception that social promotion is the norm. In fact, large numbers of students are retained in grade, and grade retention has increased over most of the past 25 years. For example, the percentage of 6- to 8-year-olds enrolled below the modal grade for their age rose from 11 percent in 1971 to a peak of 22 percent in 1990, and it was 18 percent in 1996. The rise reflects a combination of early grade retention and later school entry. At ages 15 to 17, the percentage enrolled below the modal grade for their age rose from 23 percent in 1971 to 31 percent in 1996 (U.S. Bureau of the Census, *Current Population Reports*, Series P-20). Thus, about 10 percent of students are held back in school between ages 6 to 8 and ages 15 to 17.

In some places, tests are being used inappropriately in making promotion and retention decisions. For example, achieving a certain test score has become a necessary condition of grade-to-grade promotion. This is inconsistent with current and draft revised psychometric standards, which recommend that such high-stakes decisions about individuals should not automatically be made on the basis of a single test score; other relevant information about the student's knowledge and skill should also be taken into account (American Educational Research Association et al., 1985: Standard 8.12; 1998). It is also inconsistent with the explicit recommendations of test publishers about using tests for retention decisions; for example, as noted by Hoover et al. (1994:12): "A test score from an achievement battery should not be used alone in making such a significant decision." Also, some tests used in making promotion decisions have not been validated for this purpose (Shepard, 1991); for example, tests are sometimes used for promotion decisions without having been aligned with the curriculum in either the current or the higher-level grade.

Recommendation: Scores from large-scale assessments should never be the only sources of information used to make a promotion or retention decision. No single source of information—whether test scores, course grades, or teacher judgments—should stand alone in making promotion decisions. Test scores should always be used in combination with other sources of information about student achievement.

Recommendation: Tests and other information used in promotion decisions should adhere, as appropriate, to psychometric standards for placement and to psychometric standards for certifying knowledge and skill.

Recommendation: Tests and other information used in promotion decisions may be interpreted either as evidence of mastery of material already taught or as evidence of student readiness for material at the next grade level. In the former case, test content should be representative of the curriculum at the current grade level. In the latter case, test scores should predict the likely educational effects of future placements— whether promotion, retention in grade, or some other intervention options.

Recommendation: If a cutscore is to be employed on a test used in making a promotion decision, the quality of the standard-setting process should be documented and evaluated— including the qualification of the judges employed, the method or methods employed, and the degree of consensus reached.

Recommendation: Students who fail should have the opportunity to retake any test used in making promotion decisions; this implies that tests used in making promotion decisions should have alternate forms.

Recommendation: Test users should avoid the simple either-or option to promote or retain in grade when high-stakes tests and other indicators show that students are doing poorly in school, in favor of strategies combining early identification and effective remediation of learning problems.

Awarding or Withholding High School Diplomas

The intended purposes of graduation test requirements are (1) to imbue the high school diploma with some generally recognized meaning, (2) to increase student and teacher motivation, (3) to ensure that students acquire the knowledge and skills they need for successful work or study after high school, and (4) to provide accurate information to parents, educators, and policymakers about student achievement levels. Graduation exams initially focused on basic skills and minimum competencies, but recently there has been a trend toward graduation tests that assess higher-order skills (American Federation of Teachers, 1997).

In most states, individuals earn high school diplomas based on Carnegie units, which are defined by the number of hours the student has attended class. Because this simply ensures that students have passed certain courses, an imprecise and nonuniform measure of what students know at the end of high school, 18 states require that students also pass a competency exam in order to graduate, usually in addition to satisfactorily completing other requirements for graduation (Council of Chief State School Officers, 1998).

Very little is known about the specific consequences of passing or failing a high school graduation examination, as distinct from earning or not earning a high school diploma for other reasons. We do know that earning a high school diploma is associated with better health and with improved opportunities for employment, earnings, family formation and stability, and civic participation (Hauser, 1997; Jaeger, 1989).

The consequences of using high-stakes tests to grant or withhold high school diplomas may be positive or negative. For example, if high-stakes graduation tests motivate students to work harder in school, the result may be increased learning for those who pass the test and, perhaps, even for those who fail. Similarly, if high-stakes tests give teachers and other local educators guidance on what knowledge and skills are most important for students to learn, that may improve curriculum and instruction. In fact, minimum competency tests do appear to have affected instruction, by increasing the amount of class time spent on basic skills (Darling-Hammond and Wise, 1985; Madaus and Kellaghan, 1991; O'Day and Smith, 1993), but available evidence about the possible effects of graduation tests on learning and on high school dropout is inconclusive (e.g., Kreitzer et al., 1989; Reardon, 1996; Catterall, 1990; Cawthorne, 1990; Bishop, 1997).

If students have not have been exposed to subject matter included on the test—which is more likely to be the case when tests "lead" curricular change or when tests are for some other reason not aligned with curriculum—this may be inconsistent with relevant legal precedents. If failing to achieve a certain score on a standardized test automatically leads to withholding a diploma, this may be inconsistent with current and draft revised psychometric standards, which recommend that other relevant information also be taken into account in such a high-stakes decision.

The current standards-based reform movement, which calls for high standards for all students, presents states with possible dilemmas when graduation testing is concerned (Bond and King, 1995). First, states must be able to show that students are being taught what the high-standards tests measure. At present, however, advanced skills are often not well defined and ways of assessing them are not well established. Second, there is evidence that graduation tests geared to high performance levels, such as those currently used in the National Assessment of Educational Progress, would result, at least in the short run, in denying diplomas to a large proportion of students (Linn, 1998b).

The committee recognizes that the passing rate on a test is dependent on the choice of a cutoff or cutscore. Moreover, we recognize that setting a relatively high cutscore will probably lead to large differences in passing rates among groups differing by race or ethnicity, socioeconomic status, gender, level of English proficiency, and disability status, unless ways are found to improve educational opportunities for all. This could include using tests to provide early identification of students who are at risk of failing a graduation test and offering them instruction that would be effective in increasing their chances of passing.

An alternate approach to a single, test-based graduation examination would be to require students to pass each of a series of end-of-course exams. Another policy would allow students to offset a low score in one area with a high score in another. A third approach would be to offer "endorsed" diplomas to students who have passed a test without denying a diploma to those who have failed a graduation test but completed all other requirements. The committee did not attempt to synthesize research on the effectiveness of interventions that combine the threat of diploma denial with other treatments, such as remedial instruction after school, on weekends, and during the summer. We do not know how best to combine advance notice of high-stakes test requirements, remedial intervention, and opportunity to retake graduation tests. Research is also needed to explore the effects of different kinds of high school credentials on employment and other post-school outcomes.

> **Recommendation: High school graduation decisions are inherently certification decisions; the diploma should certify that the student has achieved acceptable levels of learning. Tests and other information used for this purpose should afford each student a fair opportunity to demonstrate the required levels of knowledge and skill in accordance with psychometric standards for certification tests.**

Recommendation: Graduation tests should provide evidence of mastery of material taught. Thus, there is a need for evidence that the test content is representative of what students have been taught.

Recommendation: The quality of the process of setting a cutscore on a graduation test should be documented and evaluated—including the qualification of the judges employed, the method or methods employed, and the degree of consensus reached.

Recommendation: Students who are at risk of failing a graduation test should be advised of their situation well in advance and provided with appropriate instruction that would improve their chances of passing.

Recommendation: Research is needed on the effects of high-stakes graduation tests on teaching, learning, and high school completion. Research is also needed on alternatives to test-based denial of the high school diploma, such as endorsed diplomas, end-of-course tests, and combining graduation test scores with other indicators of knowledge and skill in making the graduation decision.

Using the Voluntary National Tests for Tracking, Promotion, or Graduation Decisions

The purpose of the proposed voluntary national tests (VNTs) is to inform students (and their parents and teachers) about the performance of the students in 4th grade reading and 8th grade mathematics relative to the standards of the National Assessment of Educational Progress (NAEP) and the Third International Mathematics and Science Study (TIMSS).

The VNT proposal does not suggest any direct use of the test scores to make decisions about the tracking, promotion, or graduation of individual students. Indeed, representatives of the U.S. Department of Education have stated that the VNT is not intended for use in making such decisions. Nonetheless, some civil rights organizations and other groups have expressed concern that test users would inappropriately use the scores for such purposes. Indeed, under the proposed plan, test users—including states, school districts, and schools—would be free to use the tests as they pleased, just as test users are now free to use commercial tests for purposes other than those recommended by test developers and publishers. Accordingly—and because this study was requested in the context of the discussion of the VNT—the committee has considered whether it would be appropriate to make tracking, promotion, or graduation decisions about individual students based on their VNT scores.

For tracking decisions, use of VNT scores would necessarily be limited to placement in 5th grade reading and 9th grade mathematics. Moreover, using the scores to make future class placements would be valid only to the extent that the VNT scores were predictive of success in future placements. VNT proficiency levels, which are expected to be the same as those of NAEP, do not correspond well with other common definitions of proficiency: those embodied in current state content and performance standards (Linn, 1998b), those found in such widely used tests as the SAT and advanced placement exams (Shepard et al., 1993), and those used in traditional tracking systems. Indeed, the large share of students who score below the basic level in NAEP has led to justifiable concerns that reports of achievement on the VNT will provide little information about lower levels of academic performance.

For promotion decisions, there is no guarantee that the framework or content of the VNT assessments would be aligned with the curriculum that students have experienced or would experience in the next-higher grade. Moreover, to make reliable distinctions based on the NAEP proficiency levels, the tests should include many items near the levels of difficulty that separate proficiency levels. Even with a focus on the NAEP proficiency levels, some testing experts have been concerned about the accuracy of VNT results, and if the tests are not accurate enough for descriptive purposes, they will surely not be accurate enough to use in making high-stakes decisions about individual students.

The need for multiple versions of a promotion test conflicts with the plan to release all VNT test items and their correct answers. In high-stakes testing situations, demands for fairness, as well as our criteria of validity and reliability in measurement, require that students who fail a promotion test be permitted to retake comparable versions of the test. However, there is no plan to develop or release extra forms of the VNT assessments for use in "second-chance" administrations, and, if such extra forms were developed, this would add to problems of test security.

Similar concerns apply to the use of VNT scores in making high school graduation decisions. It is doubtful that there would be any potential use for the results of a 4th grade reading test in determining an individual's fitness to receive a high school diploma. Although some states have deemed achievement at the 8th grade level sufficient to meet their graduation standard in mathematics, the lack of alternative test forms to allow students opportunities to retake the test makes the VNT inappropriate for this purpose.

There are clear incompatibilities between features of the VNT that would facilitate its use as a tool for informing students, parents, and teachers about student achievement, on one hand, and possible uses of the scores in making decisions about tracking, promotion, or graduation of individual students, on the other hand.

> **Recommendation:** The voluntary national tests should not be used for decisions about the tracking, promotion, or graduation of individual students.

> **Recommendation:** If the voluntary national tests are implemented, the federal government should issue regulations or guidance to ensure that VNT scores are not used for decisions about the tracking, promotion, or graduation of individual students.

The committee takes no position on whether the VNT is practical or appropriate for its primary stated purposes.

FORMS OF TESTING: PARTICIPATION AND ACCOMMODATIONS

Students with Disabilities

Recent legislative initiatives at both the federal and state levels mandate that all students be included in large-scale assessment programs, including those with special language and learning needs (Goals 2000, 1994; Improving America's School Act, 1994). For students with disabilities, the mandate is particularly strong due to the recently amended Individuals with Disabilities Education Act of 1997 (IDEA), which requires states and districts to provide for such participation as a condition of eligibility. However, in many cases, the demands that full participation of these students place on assessment systems are greater than current assessment knowledge and technology can support.

Participation of students with disabilities in large-scale assessments is important to ensure that schools are held accountable for the educational performance of these students and to obtain a fully representative, accurate picture of overall student performance. When these assessments are used to make high-stakes decisions about individual students, the potential negative consequences are likely to fall most heavily on groups with special learning needs, such as students with disabilities.

More than 5 million students with disabilities participate in special education programs under the IDEA. They vary widely in the severity of disability, educational goals, and degree of involvement in the general education curriculum. Although federal legislation defines 13 categories of disability, 90 percent of all special education students have one of four disabilities: speech or language impairment, serious emotional disturbance, mental retardation and/or specific learning disabilities. This diversity has important implications for how students with disabilities participate in large-scale assessments: for example, some participate fully in ways that are indistinguishable from their general education peers, some require modifications or accommodations in the testing procedure, and others are exempted from participation entirely (National Research Council, 1997).

For a number of reasons, many students with disabilities have previously not been included in the large-scale assessment programs conducted by their states and districts (National Research Council, 1997). In order for some students with disabilities to participate, accommodations—such as braille versions, alternate settings, extended time, and calculators—will need to be provided during testing. The purpose of accommodations is to correct for the impact of a disability that is unrelated to the subject matter being tested; in essence, the disability interferes with the student's capacity to demonstrate what he or she truly knows about the subject (Willingham, 1988).

Validity will be improved when testing accommodations are designed to correct for distortions in scores caused by specific disabilities. However, accommodations should be independent of the construct being measured (Phillips, 1993, 1994; American Educational Research Association et al., 1985). Determining whether an accommodation is independent of the construct is difficult for some types of disability, especially cognitive disabilities. Moreover, there is little research on how to design accommodations, a problem that is exacerbated by the lack of a reliable taxonomy for describing disabilities. Some strategies, such as computer adaptive testing for students who need extra time, may accommodate a large share of students with special needs without threatening the validity of test results. However, more research and development—along with access to the technology—are needed to bring this and other strategies into widespread use.

Accommodations should therefore be offered for two purposes: (1) to increase the participation of students with disabilities in large-scale assessments and (2) to increase the validity of the test score information. These two objectives—obtaining valid information while still testing all students—create a sizable policy tension for the design of assessment systems, particularly when they involve high stakes.

Recommendation: More research is needed to enable students with disabilities to participate in large-scale assessments in ways that provide valid information.   This goal significantly challenges current knowledge and technology about measurement and test design and the infrastructure needed to achieve broad-based participation.

In addition, students with disabilities are rarely included in adequate numbers in the pilot samples when new assessments are being developed; oversampling may be necessary to permit key statistical analyses, such as determining the impact of accommodations on test scores, norm development, and analyses of differential item functioning (Olson and Goldstein, 1997).

Recommendation: The needs of students with disabilities should be considered throughout the test development process.

As the stakes of testing become higher, there is a greater need to establish the validity of tests administered to students with disabilities. At present, policies on the kinds of testing accommodations offered and to whom they are offered vary widely from place to place (Thurlow et al., 1993). New federal regulations require that the individual education program (IEP) document the decisions made about each child's participation in assessments and the type and nature of the accommodations needed. The proportion of students that require accommodations will depend on the purpose, format, and content of the assessment.

Parents of students with disabilities play unique roles as advocates for their children's rights, important participants in the IEP process, and monitors of accountability and enforcement. If high stakes are to be attached to the assessment of students with disabilities, then parents and other members of the IEP team will need to be able to make informed choices about the nature and extent of a student's participation in the assessment and its possible implications for future education and post-school outcomes.

Recommendation: Decisions about how students with disabilities will participate in large-scale assessments should be guided by criteria that are as systematic and objective as possible. They should also be applied on a case-by-case basis as part of the child's individual education program and consistent with the instructional accommodations that the child receives.

Recommendation: If a student with disabilities is subject to an assessment used for promotion or graduation decisions, the IEP team should ensure that the curriculum and instruction received by the student through the individual education program is aligned with test content and that the student has had adequate opportunity to learn the material covered by the test.[2]

Although the basic principle should be to include all students with disabilities in the large-scale assessments, and to provide accommodations to enable them to do so, some number of students is likely to need to participate in a different or substantially modified assessment; the size of this group will depend on the nature of the assessment and the content being assessed. Obtaining meaningful information about the educational achievement and progress of these students is difficult. However, when the stakes are high, such as in deciding whether a student receives a diploma, it is critical for students who cannot take the test to have alternate ways of demonstrating proficiency. For students whose curriculum differs substantially from the general curriculum, there may also be a need to develop meaningful alternative credentials that can validly convey the nature of the student's accomplishments.

Recommendation: Students who cannot participate in a large-scale assessment should have alternate ways of demonstrating proficiency.

Recommendation: Because a test score may not be a valid representation of the skills and achievement of students with disabilities, high-stakes decisions about these students should consider other sources of evidence such as grades, teacher recommendations, and other examples of student work.

---

[2]To the extent that tracking decisions are based on readiness rather than mastery, there might not be any need to assume that the student has been exposed to particular curricular content. Thus, this recommendation does not pertain to tracking decisions.

English-Language Learners

Federal and state mandates increasingly require the inclusion of English-language learners in large-scale assessments of achievement (Goals 2000 [P.L. 103-227], Title I [Helping Disadvantaged Children Meet High Standards] and Title VII [Bilingual Education] of the Improving America's Schools Act of 1994 [P.L. 103-382]). In particular, high-stakes tests are used with English-language learners for decisions related to tracking, promotion, and graduation, as well as for system-wide accountability. The demands that full participation of English-language learners make on assessment systems are greater than current knowledge and technology can support. In addition, there are fewer procedural safeguards for English-language learners under federal law than for students with disabilities.

When English-language learners are not proficient in the language of the assessment, their scores will not accurately reflect their knowledge. Thus, requiring those who are not proficient in English to take an English-language version of a test without accommodations will produce invalid information about their true achievement (American Educational Research Association et al., 1985; National Research Council and Institute of Medicine, 1997). This can lead to poor decisions about individuals and about English-language learners as a group, as well as about school systems in which they are heavily represented.

Understanding the performance of English-language learners on achievement assessments requires satisfactory assessments of English-language proficiency, in order to determine whether poor performance is attributable to lack of knowledge of the test content or weak skills in English. Lack of a clear or consistent definition of language proficiency, and of indicators or measures of it, contributes to the difficulty of making these decisions more systematically (Olson and Goldstein, 1997).

Research evidence to date does not allow us to be certain about the meaning of test scores for students who are not yet proficient in English and who have received accommodations or modifications in test procedures. For any examination system employing accommodations or modifications, test developers or test users should conduct research to determine whether the constructs measured are the same for all children (Hambleton and Kanjee, 1994; Olson and Goldstein, 1997).

Accommodations and alternative tests should be provided (1) to increase the participation of English-language learners in large-scale assessments and (2) to increase the validity of test results. These two objectives—obtaining valid information while still testing all English-language learners—create a sizable policy tension for the design of assessment systems, particularly when they involve high stakes.

> **Recommendation:** Systematic research that investigates the impact of specific accommodations on the test performance of both English-language learners and other students is needed. Accommodations should be investigated to see whether they reduce construct-irrelevant sources of variance for English-language learners without disadvantaging other students who do not receive accommodations. The relationship of test accommodations to instructional accommodations should also be studied.

> **Recommendation:** Development and implementation of alternative measures, such as primary-language assessments, should be accompanied by information regarding the validity, reliability, and comparability of scores on primary-language and English assessments.

A sufficient number of English-language learners should be included when items are developed and pilot-tested and in the norming of assessments (Hambleton and Kanjee, 1994). Experts in the assessment of English-language learners might work with test developers to maintain the content difficulty of items while making the language of the instructions as well as actual test items more comprehensible. These modifications would have to be accomplished without making the assessment invalid for other students.

> **Recommendation:** The learning and language needs of English-language learners should be considered during test development.

Various strategies can be used to obtain valid information about the achievement of English-language learners in large-scale assessments. These include native-language assessments and modifications that decrease the English-language load. Such strategies, however, are often employed inconsistently from place to place and from student to student. Monitoring of educational outcomes for English-language learners as a group is needed to determine the intended and unintended consequences of their participation in large-scale assessments.

Recommendation: Policy decisions about how individual English-language learners will participate in large-scale assessments—such as the language and accommodations to be used—should balance the demands of political accountability with professional standards of good testing practice. These standards require evidence that such accommodations or alternate forms of assessment lead to valid inferences regarding performance.

Recommendation: States, school districts, and schools should report and interpret disaggregated assessment scores of English-language learners when psychometrically sound for the purpose of analyzing their educational outcomes.

In addition, the role of the test score in decision making needs careful consideration when its meaning is uncertain. For example, invalid low scores on the test may lead to inappropriate placement in treatments that have not been demonstrated to be effective. Multiple sources of information should be used to supplement test score data obtained from large-scale assessment of students who are not language proficient, particularly when decisions will be made about individual students on the basis of the test (American Educational Research Association et al., 1985).

Recommendation: Placement decisions based on tests should incorporate information about educational accomplishments, particularly literacy skills, in the primary language. Certification tests (e.g., for high school graduation) should be designed to reflect state or local deliberations and decisions about the role of English-language proficiency in the construct to be assessed. This allows for subject-matter assessment in English only, in the primary language, or using a test that accommodates English-language learners by providing English-language assistance, primary language support, or both.

Recommendation: As for all learners, interpretation of the test scores of English-language learners for promotion or graduation should be accompanied by information about opportunities to master the material tested. For English-language learners, this includes information about educational history, exposure to instruction in the primary language and in English, language resources in the home, and exposure to the mainstream curriculum.

POTENTIAL STRATEGIES FOR PROMOTING APPROPRIATE TEST USE

The two existing mechanisms for promoting and enforcing appropriate test use—professional standards and legal enforcement—are important but inadequate.

The Joint Standards, and the Code of Fair Testing Practices in Education, ethical codes of the testing profession, are written in broad terms and are not always easy to interpret in particular situations. In addition, enforcement of the Joint Standards and the Code depends chiefly on professional judgment and goodwill. Moreover, professional self-regulation does not cover the behavior of individuals outside the testing profession. Many users of educational test results—policymakers, school administrators, and teachers—are unaware of the Joint Standards and are untrained in appropriate test use (Office of Technology Assessment, 1992).

Litigation, the other existing mechanism, also has limitations. Most of the pertinent statutes and regulations protect only certain groups of students, and most court decisions are not binding everywhere. Court decisions in different jurisdictions sometimes contradict one another (*Larry P. v. Riles*, 1984; *Parents in Action on Special Education v. Hannon*, 1980). Some courts insist that educators observe the principles of test use in the Joint Standards (Office of Technology Assessment, 1992:73-74) and others do not (*United States v. South Carolina*, 1977). And court challenges are often expensive, divisive, and time-consuming. In sum, federal law is a patchwork of rules rather than a coherent set of norms governing proper test use, and enforcement is similarly uneven.

The committee has explored four possible alternative mechanisms that have been applied to problems similar to that of improper test use and about which empirical literature exists. It offers these as alternatives, some less coercive and others more so, that could supplement professional standards and litigation as means of promoting and enforcing appropriate test use.

• **Deliberative forums:** In these forums, citizens would meet with policymakers to discuss and make important decisions about testing. In this model, all participants have equal standing and are more likely to accept decisions, even those with which they disagree, because they feel that they have had an opportunity to influence the outcome. All parties with a stake in assessments would be represented. Such discussions could

300 HIGH STAKES: TESTING FOR TRACKING, PROMOTION, AND GRADUATION

help define what constitutes "educational quality" and "achievement to high standards," the role that tests should play in shaping and measuring progress toward those goals, and the level of measurement error that is acceptable where test scores are used in making high-stakes decisions about students.

Broad public interest in testing makes this a good time to consider the establishment of such forums. We note, however, the importance of considering potential limitations of this strategy, including: a scarcity of successful examples, the reluctance of those with authority to part with it, and the large amounts of time and patience it would require.

• **An independent oversight body:** George Madaus and colleagues have proposed creating an independent organization to monitor and audit high-stakes testing programs (Madaus, 1992; Madaus et al., 1997). It would not have regulatory powers but would provide information to the public about tests and their use, highlighting best practices in testing. It could supplement a labeling strategy (see below) by educating policymakers, practitioners, and the public about test practice. It could deter inappropriate test use by creating adverse publicity (Ernest House, personal communication 1998).

The shortcomings of this proposal include the monitoring body's lack of formal authority to require test publishers or school administrators to submit testing programs for review. Similarly, test users would be under no obligation to accept the body's judgments. It will be important for policymakers interested in the work of such a body to prevent unintended negative consequences.

• **Labeling:** Test producers could be required to report to test users about the appropriate uses and limitations of their tests. A second target of a labeling strategy would be test consumers: parents, students, the public, and the media. Relevant information could include the purpose of the test, intended uses of individuals' scores, consequences for individual students, steps taken to validate the test for its intended use, evidence that the test measures what students have been taught, other information used with test scores to make decisions about individual students, and options for questioning decisions based on test scores.

Limitations of this strategy include limited data on its effectiveness, the obstacles many parents face when they seek to challenge policies and actions with which they disagree, and the ineffectiveness of test labeling when the real problem is poor instruction rather than improper test use.

- **Federal regulation:** Federal statutes could be amended to include standards of appropriate test use. Title I regulations could be revised to ensure that large-scale assessments comply with established professional standards. State Title I plans could address the extent to which state and local assessment systems meet these professional norms. Title VI of the Civil Rights Act of 1964 and Title IX of the Education Amendment of 1972 prohibit federal fund recipients from discriminating on the basis of race, national origin, or sex; both have been cited in disputes about tests that carry high stakes for students. Under existing regulations, when a test has disproportionate adverse impact, the recipient of federal funds must demonstrate that the test and its use are an "educational necessity." Federal regulations do not, however, define this term. Thus, federal regulations could define educational necessity in terms of compliance with professional testing standards.

The advantages of this strategy would include its applying to all 50 states and virtually all school districts. Federal regulations could also be a powerful tool for educating policymakers and the public about appropriate test use. And relying on them would make use of existing administrative and judicial mechanisms to promote adherence to testing standards that are rarely enforced.

The risks of the regulatory approach are that the sanctions available for failure to comply—cutting off federal aid—make it unwieldy. Moreover, there is political resistance to federal regulation, creating the risk of a backlash that would make it more difficult for the U.S. Department of Education to guide local practice in testing and other areas. This strategy would also be subject to many of the usual disadvantages of administrative and judicial enforcement.

The committee is not recommending adoption of any particular strategy or combination of strategies, nor does it suggest that these four approaches are the only possibilities. We do think, however, that ensuring proper test use will require multiple strategies. Given the inadequacy of current methods, practices, and safeguards, further research is needed on these and other policy options to illuminate their possible effects on test use. In particular, we would suggest empirical research on the effects of these strategies, individually and in combination, on testing products and practice, and an examination of the associated potential benefits and risks.

REFERENCES

American Educational Research Association, American Psychological Association, and National Council on Measurement in Education
  1985   Standards for Educational and Psychological Testing. Washington, DC: American Psychological Association
  1998   Draft Standards for Educational and Psychological Testing. Washington, DC: American Psychological Association
American Federation of Teachers
  1997   Passing on Failure: District Promotion Policies and Practices. Washington, DC: American Federation of Teachers.
Anderson, D.K.
  1994   Paths Through Secondary Education: Race/Ethnic and Gender Differences. Unpublished doctoral thesis, University of Wisconsin-Madison.
Bishop, John H.
  1997   Do Curriculum-Based External Exit Exam Systems Enhance Student Achievment? New York: Consortium for Policy Research in Education and Center for Advanced Human Resource Studies, Cornell University.
Bond, Linda A., and Diane King
  1995   State High School Graduation Testing: Status and Recommendations. North Central Regional Educational Laboratory.
Catterall, James S.
  1990   A Reform Cooled-Out: Competency Tests Required for High School Graduation. CSE Technical Report 320. UCLA Center for Research on Evaluation, Standards, and Student Assessment.
Cawthorne, John E.
  1990   "Tough" Graduation Standards and "Good" Kids. Chestnut Hill, MA: Boston College, Center for the Study of Testing, Evaluation and Educational Policy.
Ceci, Stephen J., Tina B. Rosenblum, and Matthew Kumpf
  1998   The shrinking gap between high- and low-scoring groups: Current trends and possible causes. Pp. 287-302 in The Rising Curve, Ulric Neisser, ed. Washington, DC: APA Books.
Clinton, W.J.
  1998   Memorandum to the Secretary of Education. Press release. Washington, DC: The White House.
Council of Chief State School Officers
  1998   Survey of State Student Assessment Programs. Washington, DC: Council of Chief State School Officers.
Darling-Hammond, L.
  1991   The implications of testing policy for quality and equality. Phi Delta Kappan 73(3):220-225.
Darling-Hammond, L., and A. Wise
  1985   Beyond standardizaton: State standards and school improvement. Elementary School Journal 85(3).
Delany, B.
  1991   Allocation, choice, and stratification within high schools: How the sorting machine copes. American Journal of Education 99(2):181-207.

Gamoran, A.
 1988   A Multi-level Analysis of the Effects of Tracking. Paper presented at the annual meeting, American Sociological Association, Atlanta, GA.
Gamoran, A., and M. Weinstein
 1998   Differentiation and opportunity in restructured schools. *American Journal of Education* 106:385-415.
Glaser, R., and E. Silver
 1994   *Assessment, Testing, and Instruction: Retrospect and Prospect.* Los Angeles, CA: National Center for Research on Evaluation, Standards, and Student Testing.
Grissmer, David, Stephanie Williamson, Sheila N. Kirby, and Mark Berends
 1998   Exploring the rapid rise in black achievement scores in the United States (1970-1990). Pp. 251-285 in *The Rising Curve*, Ulric Neisser, ed. Washington, DC: APA Books.
Grissom, J.B., and L.A. Shepard
 1989   Repeating and dropping out of school. Pp. 34-63 in *Flunking Grades: Research and Policies on Retention*, L.A. Shepard and M.L. Smith, eds. London: Falmer Press.
Hambleton, R.K., and A. Kanjee
 1994   Enhancing the validity of cross-cultural studies: Improvements in instrument translation methods. In *International Encyclopedia of Education* (2nd Ed.), T. Husen and T.N. Postlewaite, eds. Oxford, UK: Pergamon Press.
Hauser, R.M.
 1997   Indicators of high school completion and dropout. Pp. 152-184 in *Indicators of Children's Well-Being*, R.M. Hauser, B.V. Brown, and W.R. Prosser, eds. New York: Russell Sage Foundation.
 1998   Trends in black-white test score differentials: 1. Uses and misuses of NAEP/SAT data. Pp. 219-249 in *The Rising Curve*, Ulric Neisser, ed. Washington, DC: APA Books.
Hochschild, J., and B. Scott
 1998   Trends: Governance and reform of public education in the United States. *Public Opinion Quarterly* 62(1):79-120.
Holmes, C.T.
 1989   Grade level retention effects: A meta-analysis of research studies. Pp. 16-33 in *Flunking Grades: Research and Policies on Retention*, L.A. Shepard and M.L. Smith, eds. London: Falmer Press.
Hoover, H.D., A.N. Hieronymus, D.A. Frisbie, et al.
 1994   *Interpretive Guide for School Administrators: Iowa Test of Basic Skills, Levels 5-14.* University of Iowa: Riverside Publishing Company.
Huang, Min-Hsiung, and Robert M. Hauser
 1998   Trends in black-white test-score differentials: 1. The WORDSUM Vocabulary Test. Pp. 303-332 in *The Rising Curve*, Ulric Neisser, ed. Washington, DC: APA Books.
Jaeger, Richard M.
 1989   Certification of student competence. In *Educational Measurement*, 3rd Ed. Robert L. Linn, ed. New York: Macmillan.

Johnson, J., and J. Immerwahr
  1994   *First Things First: What Americans Expect from the Public Schools*. New York: Public Agenda.
Joint Committee on Testing Practices
  1988   *Code of Fair Testing Practices*. Washington, DC: National Council on Measurement in Education.
Koretz, D.M., R.L. Linn, S.B. Dunbar, and L.A. Shepard
  1991   The Effects of High-Stakes Testing on Achievement: Preliminary Findings About Generalization Across Tests. Paper presented at the annual meeting of the American Educational Research Association and the National Council on Measurement in Education. Chicago, IL (April).
Kornhaber, M.
  1997   Seeking Strengths: Equitable Identification for Gifted Education and the Theory of Multiple Intelligences. Doctoral dissertation, Harvard Graduate School of Education.
Kreitzer, A.E., F. Madaus, and W. Haney
  1989   Competency testing and dropouts. Pp 129-152 in *Dropouts from School: Issues, Dilemmas and Solutions*, L. Weis, E. Farrar, and H. G. Petrie, eds. Albany: State University of New York Press.
Levin, H.
  1988   *Accelerated Schools for At-risk Students*. New Brunswick, NJ: Center for Policy Research in Education.
Linn, Robert
  1998a   Assessments and Accountability. Paper presented at the annual meeting of the American Educational Research Association, April, San Diego.
  1998b   Validating inferences from National Assessment of Educational Progress achievement-level setting. *Applied Measurement in Education* 11(1):23-47.
Lucas, S.
  in press *Stratification Stubborn and Submerged: Inequality in School After the Unremarked Revolution*. New York: Teachers College Press.
Luppescu, S., A.S. Bryk, P. Deabster, et al.
  1995   *School Reform, Retention Policy, and Student Achievement Gains*. Chicago, IL: Consortium on Chicago School Research.
Madaus, G.F., W. Haney, K.B. Newton, and A.E. Kreitzer
  1993   *A Proposal for a Monitoring Body for Tests Used in Public Policy*. Boston: Center for the Study of Testing, Evaluation, and Public Policy.
  1997   *A Proposal to Reconstitute the National Commission on Testing and Public Policy as An Independent, Monitoring Agency for Educational Testing*. Boston: Center for the Study of Testing Evaluation and Educational Policy.
Madaus, G.F., and T. Kellaghan
  1991   Examination Systems in the European Community: Implications for a National Examination System in the U.S. Paper prepared for the Science, Education and Transportation Program, Office of Technology Assessment, U.S. Congress, Washington, DC.

McKnight, C.C., and F.J. Crosswhite, J.A. Dossey, E. Kifer, S.O. Swafford, K. Travers, and T.J. Cooney
1987   The Underachieving Curriculum: Assessing U.S. School Mathematics from an International Perspective. Champaign, IL: Stipes Publishing.

Meisels, S.J.
1989   Testing, Tracking, and Retaining Young Children: An Analysis of Research and Social Policy. Commissioned paper for the National Center for Education Statistics.

Mosteller, F., R. Light, and J. Sachs
1996   Sustained inquiry in education: Lessons from skill grouping and class size. Harvard Educational Review 66(4):797-843.

National Academy of Education
1996   Quality and Utility: The 1994 Trial State Assessment in Reading, Robert Glaser, Robert Linn, and George Bohrnstedt, eds. Panel on the Evaluation of the NAEP Trial State Assessment. Stanford, CA: National Academy of Education.

National Research Council
1982   Placing Children in Special Education: A Strategy for Equity, K.A. Heller, W.H. Holtzman, and S. Messick, eds. Committee on Child Development Research and Public Policy, National Research Council. Washington, DC: National Academy Press.
1997   Educating One and All: Students with Disabilities and Standards-Based Reform, L.M. McDonnell, M.L. McLaughlin, and P. Morison, eds. Committee on Goals 2000 and the Inclusion of Students with Disabilities, Board on Testing and Assessment. Washington, DC: National Academy Press.

National Research Council and Institute of Medicine
1997   Improving Schooling for Language-Minority Children, Diane August and Kenji Hakuta, eds. Board on Children, Youth, and Families. Washington, DC: National Academy Press.

O'Day, Jennifer A., and Marshall S. Smith
1993   Systemic reform and educational opportunity. In Designing Coherent Educational Policy, Susan H. Fuhrman, ed. San Francisco: Jossey-Bass.

Oakes, J., A. Gamoran, and R. Page
1992   Curriculum differentiation: Opportunities, outcomes, and meanings. Handbook of Research on Curriculum, P. Jackson, ed. New York: MacMillan.

Office of Technology Assessment
1992   Testing in American Schools: Asking the Right Questions. OTA-SET-519. Washington, DC: U.S. Government Printing Office.

Olson, J.F., and A.A. Goldstein
1997   The Inclusion of Students with Disabilities and Limited English Proficient Students in Large-scale Assessments: A Summary of Recent Progress. NCES 97-482. Washington, DC: U.S. Department of Education, Office of Educational Research and Improvement.

Phillips, S.E.
1993   Testing accommodations for disabled students. Education Law Reporter 80:9-32.

1994   High-stakes testing accommodations. Validity versus disabled rights. *Applied Measurement in Education* 7(2):93-120.

Reardon, Sean F.
1996   Eighth Grade Minimum Competency Testing and Early High School Dropout Patterns. Paper presented at the annual meeting of the American Educational Research Assocation, New York, April.

Selvin, M.J., J. Oakes, S. Hare, K. Ramsey, and D. Schoeff
1990   *Who Gets What and Why: Curriculum Decisionmaking at 3 Comprehensive High Schools.* Santa Monica, CA: Rand.

Shepard, L.A.
1991   Negative policies for dealing with diversity: When does assessment and diagnosis turn into sorting and segregation? *Literacy for a Diverse Society: Perspectives, Practices and Policies*, E. Hiebert, ed. New York: Teachers College Press.

Shepard, L., et al.
1993   Evaluating test validity. *Review of Research in Education* 19:405-450.

Shepard, L., S. Kagan, and E. Wurtz, eds.
1998   *Principles and Recommendations for Early Childhood Assessments.* Washington DC: National Education Goals Panel.

Shepard, L.A., and M.L. Smith
1989   Academic and emotional effects of kindergarten retention in one school district. Pp. 79-107 in *Flunking Grades: Research and Policies on Retention*, L.A. Shepard and M.L. Smith, eds. London: Falmer Press.

Slavin, R.E., et al.
1996   *Every Child, Every School: Success for All.* Thousand Oaks, CA: Corwin Press.

Thurlow, M.L., J.E. Ysseldyke, and B. Silverstein
1993   *Testing Accommodations for Students with Disabilities: A Review of the Literature.* Synthesis Report 4. Minneapolis, MN: National Center on Educational Outcomes, University of Minnesota.

Welner, K.G., and J. Oakes
1996   (Li)Ability grouping: The new susceptibility of school tracking systems to legal challenges. *Harvard Educational Review* 66(3):451-70.

White, P., A. Gamoran, J. Smithson, and A. Porter
1996   Upgrading the high school math curriculum: Math course-taking patterns in seven high schools in California and New York. *Educational Evaluation and Policy Analysis* 18(4):285-307.

Willingham, W.W.
1988   Introduction. Pp. 1-16 in *Testing Handicapped People*, W.W. Willingham, M. Ragosta, R.E. Bennett, H. Braun, D.A. Rock, and D.E. Powers, eds. Boston, MA: Allyn and Bacon.

LEGAL REFERENCES

Debra P. v. Turlington, 474 F. Supp. 244 (M.D. Fla. 1979); *aff'd in part and rev'd in part*, 644 F.2d 397 (5th Cir. 1981); *rem'd*, 564 F. Supp. 177 (M.D. Fla. 1983); *aff'd*, 730 F.2d 1405 (11th Cir. 1984).

Goals 2000, Educate America Act, 20 U.S.C. sections 5801 *et seq.*

Improving America's Schools Act, 1994.

Individuals with Disabilities Education Act, 20 U.S.C. section 1401 *et seq.*

Larry P. v. Riles, 495 F. Supp. 926 (N.D. Cal. 1979); *aff'd,* 793 F.2d 969 (9th Cir. 1984).

Parents in Action on Special Education (PASE) v. Hannon, 506 F. Supp. 831 (N.D. Ill. 1980).

Title I, Elementary and Secondary Education Act, 20 U.S.C. sections 6301 *et seq.*

United States v. South Carolina

Biographical Sketches

Robert M. Hauser (*Chair*) is the Vilas research and Samuel A. Stouffer professor of sociology at the University of Wisconsin at Madison. His current research includes the Wisconsin Longitudinal Study, data from which are used for studies of aging and life course and social stratification, and the Study of Trends in the Schooling of Black Americans, an effort to trace trends in school enrollment, aspirations, and attainment of black Americans from the 1940s to the 1980s. He is a member of the National Academy of Sciences. Dr. Hauser received a B.A. degree in economics from the University of Chicago and M.A. and Ph.D. degrees in sociology from the University of Michigan.

Allison M. Black is a research associate with the Board on Testing and Assessment (BOTA). Previously, she worked with the NAACP Legal Defense and Education Fund and the District of Columbia Public Schools. Ms. Black has a J.D. from Howard University School of Law.

Naomi Chudowsky is a senior program officer with the Board on Testing and Assessment. Previously, she worked for the Connecticut State Department of Education as coordinator of the state's high school student assessment program and for the U.S. Department of Education on the President's voluntary national testing initiative. Dr. Chudowsky has a Ph.D. in educational psychology from Stanford University.

Marguerite Clarke, who served as a technical consultant to the committee, is a research associate with the National Commission on Testing and Public Policy, which is based in the Center for the Study of Testing, Evaluation and Educational Policy at Boston College. Ms. Clarke is a doctoral candidate in educational research, measurement, and evaluation at Boston College.

Lizanne DeStefano is an associate professor in educational psychology and director of the Bureau of Educational Research in the Department of Education at the University of Illinois, Urbana-Champaign. Her research interests and expertise include program evaluation and assessment of students with disabilities. Dr. DeStefano earned a PhD. degree in educational and school psychology from the University of Pittsburgh.

Pasquale J. DeVito is the director of the Office of Assessment and Information Services for the Rhode Island Department of Education. His research and expertise include educational research, measurement, and evaluation and related policy making. Dr. DeVito has a Ph.D. degree in educational research, measurement, and evaluation from Boston College.

Richard P. Durán is a professor in the Graduate School of Education at the University of California, Santa Barbara. His research interests and expertise include the learning, instruction, and assessment of language-minority students as well as the construction of culture through interaction. Dr. Durán has a Ph.D. degree in psychology from the University of California, Berkeley.

Michael J. Feuer is director of the Board on Testing and Assessment. His past positions include senior analyst and project director, U.S. Office of Technology Assessment, where he directed studies on testing and assessment, vocational education, and educational technology, and assistant professor, Department of Management and Organizational Sciences, at Drexel University. Dr. Feuer received M.A. and Ph.D. degrees from the University of Pennsylvania.

Jay P. Heubert, study director for the committee, is an associate professor of education at Teachers College, Columbia University, and an adjunct professor of law at Columbia Law School. From 1985 to 1998, he taught at Harvard University. His research and teaching focus on legal issues in schools and postsecondary institutions. Dr. Heubert holds J.D. and Ed.D. degrees in school administration, both from Harvard University.

Jennifer Hochschild is a professor of politics and public affairs in the Politics Department and the Woodrow Wilson School of Public and International Affairs at Princeton University. Her research interests and expertise include the intersection of racial, economic, and political conflicts in such areas as public education, political beliefs, and urban poverty. Dr. Hochschild has a Ph.D. degree from Yale University.

Viola C. Horek is administrative associate of the Board on Testing and Assessment. Before joining the board, she worked at the Board on Agriculture and the Committee on Education Finance at the National Research Council. Previously, she worked for the city of Stuttgart, Germany, as an urban planner and for the U.S. Department of Defense in Germany. Ms. Horek received an M.A. degree in architecture and urban planning from the University of Stuttgart.

Stephen P. Klein is a senior research scientist with the RAND Corporation, where he directs policy research studies in the fields of education, health, and criminal justice. He also serves as a consultant to several professional licensing and certification boards on matters relating to testing and assessment. Dr. Klein has a Ph.D. degree in industrial psychology from Purdue University.

Sharon Lewis is the director of research for the Council of the Great City Schools. As director of research, she is responsible for developing and maintaining a research program that articulates the status, needs, attributes, operation, and challenges of urban public schools and the children whom they serve. Ms. Lewis has a M.A. degree in educational research from Wayne State University.

Robert L. Linn is a distinguished professor in the School of Education at the University of Colorado at Boulder and the current chair of the Board on Testing and Assessment. His research and expertise include applied and theoretical problems in educational and psychological measurement. Dr. Linn has a Ph.D. degree in psychological measurement from the University of Illinois, Urbana-Champaign.

Lorraine M. McDonnell is a professor of political science and education at the University of California, Santa Barbara. Her research and expertise include the design and implementation of educational reform initiatives, the politics of student testing, and the development and use of educational accountability systems. Dr. McDonnell has a Ph.D. degree in political science from Stanford University.

Samuel Messick is a distinguished research scientist with the Educational Testing Service. His research and expertise include test use, validity, and the ethics of assessment. Dr. Messick has a Ph.D. degree in psychology from Princeton University.

Edward Miller, who served as consulting editor to the committee, is an education writer, editor, and policy analyst. As editor of the *Harvard Education Letter*, he twice won the distinguished achievement award of the Educational Press Association of America. He has taught writing at Harvard University, is the publisher of two small-town newspapers in Massachusetts, and is currently writing a book about the uses and misuses of technology in education.

Patricia Morison is director of the Board on International Comparative Studies in Education and senior progam officer with the Board on Testing and Assessment. She served as study director for *Educating One and All*, the NRC 1997 study of students with disabilities and standards-based reform. Previously, she was at the U.S. Office of Technology Assessment. Dr. Morison has an Ed.M. degree from Harvard and a Ph.D. degree in psychology from the University of Minnesota.

Ulric Neisser is a professor of psychology at Cornell University. His research and expertise include attention, memory, intelligence, and the self-concept. He is a member of the National Academy of Sciences. Dr. Neisser has a Ph.D. degree from Harvard University.

Andrew C. Porter is the director of the Wisconsin Center for Education Research, codirector of the National Institute for Science Education, and professor of educational psychology at the University of Wisconsin, Madison. His research and expertise include teaching, education policy analysis, student and teacher assessment, and psychometrics, especially the problem of measuring change. Dr. Porter has a Ph.D. degree in educational psychology from the University of Wisconsin at Madison.

Audrey L. Qualls is an associate professor of educational measurement and statistics at the University of Iowa. Her research and expertise include development of culturally relevant classroom assessments and the development of integrated assessments for large-scale use at the primary grades. Dr. Qualls has a Ph.D. degree in educational measurement and statistics from the University of Iowa.

Paul R. Sackett is a professor of psychology at the University of Minnesota, Minneapolis. He also serves as the cochair of the Joint Committee for the Revision of the *Standards for Educational and Psychological Testing* of the American Educational Research Association, the American Psychological Association, and the National Council on Measurement in Education. Dr. Sackett has a Ph.D. degree in industrial/organizational psychology from Ohio State University.

Kimberly D. Saldin is a senior project assistant with the Board on Testing and Assessment. She previously worked as a financial assistant for the Institute of Medicine. Ms. Saldin received a B.S. degree in business administration and English from Mary Washington College.

Catherine E. Snow is the Henry Lee Shattuck professor of education at the Harvard Graduate School of Education. Her research and expertise include language and literacy acquisition in children, including especially children from low-income families, non-mainstream cultural groups, and second-language learners. Dr. Snow has a Ph.D. degree in psychology from McGill University, Montreal, Quebec.

William T. Trent is an associate chancellor and a professor of educational policy studies and sociology at the University of Illinois, Urbana-Champaign. His principal area of research is the sociology of education, focusing on issues of inequality, race and ethnicity, and gender. Dr. Trent has a Ph.D. degree in sociology from the University of North Carolina, Chapel Hill.

Index

A

Department of Education, 65, 67-68, 265,
    267, 268, 290
  see also National Center for Education
    Statistics; *terms beginning
    "National Center…" and "Office
    of…"*
Developmental factors, promotion/
    retention in grade, 124, 279, 284
  see also Age factors; Learning
    disabilities; Retardation
Diana v. Board of Education, 54, 61
Diplomas, *see* Graduation requirements
Disabilities, *see* Learning disabilities;
    Students with disabilities
Discrimination, 1, 2, 9, 16, 17, 21, 23, 25,
    26, 45-46, 273
  African Americans, 20, 21, 53-54, 56,
    57
  gender-based, 51, 52
  historical perspectives, 20, 32
  legal issues, 18, 51-63, 67, 215, 218
    disparate impact, 57-62
    effects test, 52, 55-57
    intelligence tests, 53-55
    intentional discrimination, 52-55
    segregation/desegregation, 21, 32,
      53, 55-57
  retention in grade, 131-132
  students with disabilities, 191, 201
  voluntary national tests, 239, 290
Dropouts, 8
  employment, 177
  graduation tests, 172, 174-176
  indicator systems, 8, 281
  retention in grade and, 130, 131, 151,
    155-156, 181, 285
  students with disabilities, 189
  tracking and, 102, 104-105

E

Economic factors, *see* Cost-effectiveness
    factors; Funding; Poverty;
    Socioeconomic status
Educable mentally retarded, 21, 53-55,
    91, 93-94
  see also Special education

*Educating One and All: Students with
    Disabilities and Standards-Based
    Reform*, 188, 191-201 (passim)
Educational Testing Service, 205,
    252
Education Amendments of 1972, 58, 266,
    301
Education reform, 13-14, 34, 40
  Clinton Administration, v, 13, 14, 41,
    42, 114-115, 284-285
  curricular, 6, 278
  standards-based, general, 13-14, 15,
    36, 132, 199, 206, 273, 288-289
  students with disabilities, 195
  see also Accountability; Cost-
    effectiveness factors
Effectiveness of treatment, general, 3, 23,
    275
Elementary and Secondary Education Act
    of 1965, 15, 18, 25, 35, 40, 63
  see also Improving America's Schools
    Act
Elementary school, 37, 279
  English-language learners, 212,
    226(n.5)
  promotion/retention in grade, 120-
    121, 126-127, 129, 133, 137-146,
    149-153, 285, 286
  remediation, 133
  tracking, 91, 93, 103-104
  see also Kindergarten; Voluntary
    national tests
*Elston v. Talladega County Board of
    Education*, 58(n.12)
Emotional problems, 91, 190, 293
Employment factors
  diploma holders, 176-177
  see also Job qualifications and
    testing
English-language learners, 3, 4, 7, 16, 24,
    25, 40-41, 46, 81, 211-237, 274,
    280, 281, 296-298
  accountability, 7, 217, 296, 298
  accuracy of measurement, general, 7,
    66, 214, 226, 229-230, 232, 296
  age factors, 212, 216
  demographics, 212, 213

S

T

W